THE COMPUTER PRIVACY HANDBOOK

André Bacard

Peachpit Press
Berkeley, California

The Computer Privacy Handbook
André Bacard

Peachpit Press
2414 Sixth Street
Berkeley, CA 94710
510-548-4393
510-548-5991 (fax)

Peachpit Press is a division of Addison-Wesley Publishing Company.

Cover design: Adam Breivis

Interior illustration: Rose Cassano

Interior design and production: Sandra Taylor, The Graphic Page

ISBN 1-56609-171-3

9 8 7 6 5 4 3 2 1

Printed and bound in the United States of America

♻ Printed on recycled paper

Acknowledgments

❝ *Privacy is the freedom to be ourselves.* **❞**

~ Maritza Pick, author of How to Save Your Neighborhood,
City, or Town: The Sierra Club Guide to Community Organizing

❝ *Never doubt that a few committed individuals can change the world. Indeed, it is the only thing that ever has.* **❞**

~ Margaret Mead, anthropologist

~

The seed to write this book was planted on May 2-3, 1992, at the University of California at Berkeley. It was a beautiful, sunny weekend on a quiet part of the rolling campus — a setting where optimism is not only possible but probable. I was attending a symposium called DIAC-92 (Directions and Implications of Advanced Computing), which was sponsored by Computer Professionals for Social Responsibility (CPSR).

"The Genie is out of the bottle!" observed John Markoff, one of the speakers, who is the computer columnist for the *New York Times*. Markoff was referring to the magic of computer encryption — the ability of a computer to scramble data so that only intended readers can unscramble and read the data. Markoff noted that until recently, governments had a virtual monopoly on encryption: they owned both the Genie and the bottle. Markoff thought that the personal computer was giving birth to a new era of broad public access to encryption.

Encryption was a relatively new topic for me. Sure, I had made a few secret codes as a kid. But that was literally child's play. As for Genies, I have always wanted one. Encryption. Genie. The words stuck in the back of my mind as I walked across the campus to International House, a dormitory donated by the Rockefeller family to house foreign students.

The "I House" (as it's affectionately known to generations of students) was the setting for a cocktail party in honor of Evelyn Pine, the newly appointed executive director of CPSR. With wine in hand, I walked onto the balcony and looked out over Berkeley. So much history had been made in the buildings that lay before my eyes. J. Robert Oppenheimer, the physicist who led the Manhattan Project to build the first atomic bomb, had been in I House. Mario Savio, who started the Free Speech movement, had studied in the libraries below... . As my mind replayed history, I noticed an unusual fellow standing next to me.

His eyes first caught my attention. They were bold and direct. Then I surveyed his outfit. Dressed in a cowboy hat and a scarf, he looked more like West Texas than Berkeley. As we began talking, I was pleasantly surprised to have encountered an endangered species: an individual. This fellow actually had fresh thoughts, not just recycled media headlines. Furthermore, he valued experience much more than ideology or "political correctness."

John Perry Barlow, a rancher from Wyoming, was the mystery man at I House. We spoke of many topics. In particular, he told me how he had cofounded the Electronic Frontier Foundation (EFF) with Mitch Kapor, of Lotus 1-2-3 fame. In passing, Barlow recommended that if I wanted computer privacy, I should check out PGP. "But," he warned me, "be sure you use it correctly." It was the first time I had heard the initials PGP.

Encryption. Genie. Electronic Frontier Foundation. PGP. These were the new words that echoed in my mind after DIAC-92.

For many years, I had been intrigued by the ties between power and privacy. While writing an earlier book, *Hunger for Power: Who Rules the World and How*, I read how Hitler's Third Reich criminalized privacy. For instance, any Germans who tried to protect their money from Nazi confiscation faced execution. Nazi SS members escorted "suspicious" Germans into (politically neutral) Swiss banks. The German citizen, with a gun to his back, was forced to hand the bank teller a deposit. If the banker accepted the deposit, it meant the German had an (illegal) account. So next, the SS would force the German to withdraw his funds and would confiscate the money.

The Nazis also invaded routine privacy. For example, Nazis used telephone records to hunt, torture, and kill citizens who answered telephone calls from "suspicious" persons. To this day, European telephone companies do not record toll calls because of the former Nazi practice.

Outlawing and invading everyone's privacy in the name of pursuing "suspicious" persons is routine practice, to varying degrees, in many nations. DIAC-92 started me thinking about how to add computers to the power and privacy equation.

The next stage in this book's evolution occurred in March 1993, at the San Francisco Airport Marriott Hotel. The event was CFP '93 (the third

Conference on Computers, Freedom, and Privacy). This is the first time that I met, under one roof, the major players in the ongoing war to control our privacy. Three events had a direct impact on the book before you. First, I met Phil Zimmermann, the creator of PGP (Pretty Good Privacy) — which was the world's most controversial software. We only exchanged a few words, but I was impressed by his modesty and calmness. In my experience, many historically important figures radiate a similar internal peace. Second, I innocently asked a few people where I might get a copy of PGP. They looked at me as if I had just asked for a condom in a maternity ward. One fellow advised me, "You might find a PGP disk on the floor next to someone's foot, if you look closely." His meaning was clear. Practical computer privacy was a hot potato. Third, I ate dinner at a table shared with Mitch Kapor, co-founder of EFF; Jim Warren, founder of the Conferences on Computers, Freedom, and Privacy; and James B. Settle, an F.B.I. expert on computer security. I listened carefully to my fellow diners, and the pieces of my privacy puzzle started fitting together.

CFP '93 taught me that "nerds" ("technologically unimpaired persons," as a CalTech wit has defined them) are central to our efforts to regain our pre-Computer-Age privacy. This insight evokes a haunting historical parallel. Nuclear scientists, motivated in large degree by the fight to defeat Adolf Hitler, created nuclear weapons — which threaten all of our lives. Scientists, in turn, have led the global battle to control the proliferation of nuclear weapons. Computer engineers and entrepreneurs, inspired to build a positive "Information Age," have created an anti-privacy monster that threatens all of our lives. Now, computer experts are leading the struggle to oversee the electronic Frankenstein that they have let loose upon us.

When we get overly hyped by gadgetry, it is wise to remember that we, humanity, should always be the master, not the slave, of our technologies!

In Spring 1994, much research later, I called Jim Warren, founder of *InfoWorld*, and told him that I wanted to write the world's first book about PGP. Jim, never one to shy away from controversy, was excited by the idea. He recommended that I call Peachpit Press in Berkeley.

Ted Nace, Peachpit's publisher, was another remarkable person whom I encountered on the journey to write this book. Ted is a rare bird who has a clear vision, a social conscience, and a keen business sense. He encouraged me, to my delight, to go beyond PGP and to write about privacy with broad strokes. Ted has become a Genie.

One of the chic words in the computer world is "multimedia." This term is used by computer novices ("newbies") and by computer experts ("wizards"). In this multimedia spirit, I recommend that you go to your local video store and rent a movie to go along with this book. The film is called *Sneakers* and it stars Robert Redford and Sidney Poitier. *Sneakers* adds to the real-life suspense in every section of the book.

Many people have made this book possible. Here are a few of them; thank you one and all for helping us fight this difficult battle for freedom:

Special eternal gratitude goes to Nelson Bolyard, CPSR cryptologist, and Darrell Ticehurst, Silicon Valley entrepreneur. Both individuals read large portions of the book and gave me excellent comments. Nelson also taught me about the Clipper Chip and advised me about crypto. I incorporated Darrell's irreverent humor whenever possible.

Thank you also to (in alphebetical order): David Banisar, Policy Analyst at EPIC, for supplying me with fresh documents with a sense of humor; John Perry Barlow, Co-Founder of EFF, for introducing me to PGP; David Barnhart, Product Manager at ViaCrypt, for fixing a few glitches in my mind; Dr. David Chaum, creator of DigiCash, for conversing with me about financial privacy; Judi Clark, activist with CPSR, for persuading me to join CPSR; Simon Davies, at Privacy International, for advising me of British issues; Les Earnest, producer of the first word processor, for fighting for civil rights; Gary Edstrom, computer programmer, for his alt.security.pgp activism; Mike Godwin, of EFF, for writing "Privacy From Whom?" in *Playboy* and for his online legal advice; Dale Larson, author of *Connect Your Amiga!: A Guide to the Internet, LANs, BBSs, and Online Services*, for publishing my PGP FAQ; Dr. Martin Hellman, professor at Stanford University and eminent cryptologist, for granting me an interview; Chris Hibbert, activist at CPSR, for trying to control Social Security number usage; Michael Johnson, BBS operator, for his alt.security.pgp activism; Dr. Jeff Johnson, National Director of CPSR, for working against Caller ID; Ted Kaehler, at CPSR, for speculating about nanotechnology surveillance; Mitch Kapor, premier defender of computer privacy in America, for fighting for democracy and for writing the Introduction to this book; Patricia King, San Francisco bureau chief of *Newsweek*, for publishing my eclectic opinions; Bruce Koball, computer consultant, for organizing CFP '93; Romana Machado, computer programmer, for creating Stego; John Markoff, columnist for the *New York Times* and author of *Cyberpunk: Outlaws and Hackers on the Computer Frontier*, for helping let the Genie out of the bottle; Stanton McCandlish, online activist for EFF, for cheerfully aiding my research; Leonard Mikus, president of ViaCrypt, for encouraging words; Don Page, editor of *The Humanist*, for soliciting my "Technology and Society" column; Dr. David Redell, pillar of CPSR, for leading the Civil Liberties group; Ilene Rosenthal, general counsel for the Lightspan Partnership, Inc., for educating me about export laws; Marc Rotenberg, Project Director at EPIC, for winning important pro-privacy legal battles; Jeffrey Rothfeder, author of *Privacy for Sale*, for alarming me; Bruce Schneier, author of *Applied Cryptography*, for letting several cats out of the bag; Douglas Schuler, activist at CPSR, for organizing DIAC-92; Dr. Barbara Simons, at Association of Computing Machinery, for opposing the Clipper Chip; Bob Smart, a programmer, for advising me about PGP; Robert Smith, publisher of *Privacy Journal*, for educating a generation of privacy activists; David Sobel, legal counsel at EPIC, for chasing government documents with the patience of a saint; Rick Szykowny, editor of *The Humanist*, for publishing my columns without censorship; Jim Warren, columnist for *MicroTimes*, for generously sharing his expertise; Christopher Weber, research director at the Oxford Club, for publishing my work; Al Whaley, president of Sunnyside, Inc., for setting up the cpsr.org archives; and Philip Zimmermann, creator of PGP, for practicing grassroots democracy.

The opinions expressed in this book are my own. The people listed above may or may not agree with me. However, I thank all of them for their pioneering efforts to protect computer freedom.

See you in the future,

André Bacard

Stanford, California
email: abacard@well.com

TABLE OF CONTENTS

PART FOUR: USING PGP ON THE PC 151

" Every government degenerates when trusted to the rulers of the people alone. The people themselves therefore are its only safe depositories. "

~ Thomas Jefferson,
the "Father of American Cryptography"

Introduction

Issues of privacy are very much on the minds of those migrating to the wild new regions of the domain we call Cyberspace. What many of us seek, in picking up stakes and heading for the electronic frontier, is greater overall self-determination in life. This is impossible to achieve without being able to control information by and about us. This is the heart of privacy.

Privacy is both a matter of right and one of practice. It is a fundamental premise of this country's founding that rights of life, liberty, and the pursuit of happiness are inalienable. In Washington today, the Electronic Frontier Foundation, of which I am a founder, is deeply involved in the fight to make sure that rights such as privacy, as well as freedom of expression, are not abridged in Cyberspace. I am deeply troubled by the profound resistance of certain agencies of the U.S. government to see this matter through to its proper conclusion.

This resistance does not mean we give up the fight to make public policy that increases our privacy and our freedom. Far from it. It only makes us redouble our efforts.

At the same time, it does remind us that we have to look beyond Washington to solve our problems. Mere talk is not enough. When government is unable to respect the rights of individuals and stands in the way of those rights, direct action is required.

Fortunately, powerful and readily available new tools like PGP have been created to put control of privacy much more directly in the hands of Cyberspace citizens themselves. André Bacard's *The Computer Privacy Handbook* is an invaluable guide to the whole subject of privacy on the net, to the politics of privacy, and, most importantly, to the practical steps one can take right now to preserve one's privacy.

Mitchell Kapor

Co-Founder, Electronic Frontier Foundation,
Creator of Lotus 123

PART ONE

Guarding Our Privacy in the Information Age:

An Overview of Surveillance

I've Nothing to Hide. Why Do I Need Privacy?

We are frisking each other. Picture yourself going to work tomorrow, handing over blood and urine samples, taking a quick turn with the house polygraph, turning out your pockets and walking through some new fluoroscope. You object? Whatsamatter, you got something to hide?

~ William Safire, *New York Times* columnist

~

The question posed above would be a funny example of social naiveté, if the consequences of such innocence were not so serious.

Rebecca Schaffer, co-star of the television program *My Sister Sam*, heard the doorbell ring in her West Hollywood apartment one summer day in 1989. She opened the door. A man lunged forward, aimed a gun at her, and shot her dead. The killer (I refuse to give him notoriety by naming him), was a modern-day stalker who had hunted Schaffer down with his computer. By pushing computer keys, he found her address, her telephone number, her automobile information, and where she shopped. By using "private" computer databanks, the killer created a fictitious relationship between Rebecca Schaffer and himself in his mind — a relationship that ended in murder.

What did Rebecca Schaffer have to hide? This question insults Rebecca Schaffer and every other law-abiding citizen! If society had had the common decency to hide Schaffer's computer records from a psychotic, she would be alive today. If Schaffer had known more about America's irresponsible data proliferation, she might have taken steps to camouflage her computer records and to protect her life from crazed fans. Yet by taking these rational steps, Schaffer would have been ridiculed with the taunt, "Whatsamatter, you got something to hide?" — and would have been labeled "paranoid." So it is that many law-abiding citizens are damned for their innocence and damned for their knowledge. Meanwhile, the data sharks keeping feeding on the blood of more victims. Why do we keep hiding our heads in the sand and letting the data sharks terrorize innocent people? That is the real question society needs to answer.

Schaffer was part of a large crowd of victims. Actress Theresa Saldana was stabbed by a crazed fan. Talk-show host David Letterman was the prey of an obsessed fan who claimed to be his wife and who broke into his home several times. Actress Sharon Gless was targeted by a woman who said she was in love with her and who broke into Gless's house twice. Silicon Valley employee Laura Black was wounded, and seven of her co-workers were killed, by a relentless "romantic" pursuer. Some sociologists estimate that 100,000 Americans, mostly women, are being stalked at this moment. Our computer databases make it easy for certain stalkers to terrorize law-abiding citizens who have "nothing to hide." Suppose a potential victim takes all the trouble and money to quit her job and move out of state to save her life. The United States Postal Service will sell her new address to the stalker for $3.00, if he knows her old address!

Terry Dean Rogan is another law-abiding citizen who had more than his share of problems with data files. In 1981, an Alabama prison escapee (call him "Carl") secured a copy of Rogan's birth certificate. With this document, Carl applied for and received a California driver's license in Rogan's name. At a later date, Carl was arrested in Los Angeles as a murder suspect. After Carl was released from custody, the Los Angeles police entered a murder arrest warrant for Terry Dean Rogan into the Federal Bureau of Investigation's (FBI's) National Crime Information Center (NCIC) computer system. The warrant had no data about Carl's physical characteristics such as the fact that he had a tattoo. From 1982-83, the real Terry Dean Rogan (a man from Saginaw, Michigan) was arrested three times, and sometimes handcuffed and held at gunpoint, as a murder suspect. Each time, Terry Dean Rogan was set free when he was able to prove that his arrest was a case of mistaken identity. However, the Los Angeles police failed to change the false data in the NCIC files. Finally, Mr. Rogan's nightmare ended. With the help of a reporter for the *Saginaw News*, Rogan was able to erase the faulty data. In addition, a court ruled that the City of Los Angeles's error was "both grossly negligent and systemic in nature" because it deprived Rogan of his constitutional right to be free of faulty warrants. The Los Angeles police had received no training in how to delete incorrect data in criminal files!

Now suppose that a police officer *knowingly* enters false data about you into the NCIC computer. (Maybe the officer owes you money or holds a personal grudge. Possibly he wants to retaliate against your sister.) Or imagine that a secretary presses the wrong computer code after your name. How will you know about, much less repair, these database errors? How can you act as a responsible citizen to help your taxpayer-financed government act efficiently?

Visit your local police station, or FBI office, and ask the officer in charge to show you what, if anything, the NCIC computer says about you. It is a safe bet that he or she will judge you as a "crackpot." You risk getting harassed for doing so. Suppose you are a law-abiding, curious person who wants to push the matter a bit further. Ask the officer "Whatsamatter, you got something to hide?" and watch his face. His response will reveal the real meaning of "Whatsamatter, you got something to hide?" This question is a verbal club designed and used by authorities to intimidate common folk. The average, honest citizen is considered arrogant for asking the same question in return.

No doubt the NCIC system serves a useful purpose. It helps apprehend dangerous people who should be behind bars. But one problem with this database (and many others) is that people tend to believe computer entries are sacred and infallible. And by the way, the FBI wants to build a new, super database, called NCIC 2000, that would tie into airline-reservations computers, bank computers, car-rental computers, credit-bureau computers, Internal Revenue Service computers, and telephone-company computers — for a start.

Every computer user, and for that matter, every human being, has something to hide or someone to avoid. Show me any person who has no secrets from her family, her neighbors, or her colleagues, and I will show you someone who is an extraordinary exhibitionist or an incredible dullard.

Since this is a computer book and we are imaginative, let's have a little fun before leaving this topic. Suppose that Willy DoRight, at age 18, decides that he will become the super straight-arrow of his generation. He swears that he will never break a law or offend anyone for the rest of his life. This policy, Mr. DoRight trusts, will abolish any need for him to keep secrets, private thoughts, or discreet actions. Mr. DoRight becomes a computer programmer, learns golf, votes Republican, and joins the local church. How can Mr. DoRight avoid transgressing any laws? Each year, DoRight's legislators write and rewrite thousands of laws. One year it is illegal to gamble; the next year the state runs a lottery. One year capital gains are taxed; the next year they are not. The best and brightest attorneys grasp a tiny fraction of the existing laws — and these people get *paid* to disagree on what the laws mean! How can DoRight avoid irritating people? Whom does he obey when two bosses give him opposite orders? How can he voice any opinion about money, politics, sex, or sports without offending someone? It is logically impossible for Mr. DoRight to live a risk-free, controversy-free life. Many people will dislike him because he is a Republican, or because he belongs to a rival country club. Whomever knows DoRight's choices has power over him. If he wants to avoid constant trouble, Mr. DoRight has to learn to keep his mouth shut, and his thoughts to himself.

Robert Ellis Smith, Publisher of the *Privacy Journal*, responds admirably to Mr. DoRight's quixotic quest and to William Safire's "Whatsamatter, you got something to hide?" Smith quips: "An employee with nothing to hide may well be an employee with nothing to offer!"

What Price for Your Secrets?

❝ As every man goes through life he fills in a number of forms for the record [that become like invisible threads]. Every man, permanently aware of his own invisible threads, naturally develops a respect for the people who manipulate the threads. ❞

~ Alexander Solzhenitsyn

❝ A good many men and women want to get possession of secrets just as spendthrifts want to get money — for circulation. ❞

~ George Dennison Prentice, *Prenticeana*

Since you are reading this book, it is likely that you are concerned about your privacy in our computer-driven "Information Age." In a recent poll by Equifax, one of America's three biggest credit bureaus, 79 percent of Americans asserted that they would like to add "privacy" to the guarantees of "life, liberty, and the pursuit of happiness" in the Declaration of Independence. Perhaps you are one of these law-abiding supporters of democracy. Perhaps you have also heard rumors or read articles about PGP (Pretty Good Privacy) — the world's de facto software encryption standard for secure e-mail — and you are eager to learn practical steps to protect your computer files and e-mail from unauthorized people.

The good news first. . .My speculation about you is harmless for three reasons: 1) It consists of "soft" hunches rather than "hard" facts about you, 2) I am not in the business of selling demographic profiles to data dealers, and 3) Your name and address are unknown to me. Now the bad news. . .Any jealous spouse, spurned lover, business competitor, or enemy with a few dollars and the right contacts can uncover lots of revealing, personal data about you. The snoop, gossip, or criminal merely has to pay someone who knows which computer keys to press.

Are you sitting down? The news gets worse. Legislators, hospital clerks, bank tellers, and others devotedly tell us that the computer information they maintain about us is "private." This alleged privacy is a cruel hoax perpetuated by people and corporations who earn money by gathering and selling data about us. Some of these data collectors are honest folk who do not have a clue about what happens with the data they process. The grocery clerk who asks us to write our driver's license number on our check is an example. Other data dealers are sinister predators, who literally bank on our naiveté. Michael Thomas, author of the high-tech financial thriller *Black Money*, describes such a person: "a shark smoothly, dangerously cleaving the blue waters of human greed and gullibility in search of prey." People who use law-enforcement databases for personal profit are one variety of shark.

Politicians and lawyers are quick to assert that existing laws protect our privacy. However, in reality, your computer privacy does not exist when it is assailed by those who know how to play the privacy game.

Jeffrey Rothfeder, a former information management editor at *Business Week*, wrote an eye-opening book entitled *Privacy for Sale*. While researching this book, Rothfeder interviewed hundreds of information brokers, including members of the data "underground." Rothfeder acquaints us with John Branch (a composite character), who helps Rothfeder dig up monetary records about Dan Rather, the television reporter — even though Rather has consciously tried to hide his records. John Branch gives Rothfeder the following price list for Rather's — or our — secrets.

Bank Account: Given the person's name and current address, we will turn over the subject's bank account and balances. Cost: $200.

Credit Charges: Given a person's name and credit card number (obtainable from a credit report), we will provide the subject's most recent Visa, MasterCard, or American Express charges. Cost: $150.

Nonpublished Numbers: Given an address, we will show the telephone number or numbers at that location. Cost: $100.

Post Offices Boxes: Given a person's post-office box number, we will provide a street address. Cost: $100.

Social Security Earnings: Given a person's Social Security number, we will pull his Social Security report, with the historical records of the subject's earnings and employers. Cost: $150.

Safe Deposit Boxes: Given a person's name and address, we will provide the location of his safe-deposit box and what's in it. Cost: $200.

Telephone Calls: Given a person's telephone number, we will provide the numbers the subject has called for the last 60 days. Cost: $200.

IRS Records: Given a person's Social Security number, we will provide the subject's complete tax forms for the past three years. Cost: $550.

The only item in this list that makes me skeptical is the cheap price for revealing the contents of your safe-deposit box. Maybe I am still naive. In any case, John Branch's clients include business executives, law-enforcement agents, private investigators, and others who either cannot get the data elsewhere, or wish to purchase the data quickly without leaving a paper trail. These clients can use this data for blackmail, revenge, scams, theft, voyeurism, or worse.

Macworld magazine performed a notable experiment that confirms many of *Privacy for Sale*'s findings. For an article entitled "Shattering the Illusion of Privacy," *Macworld* investigated a group of prominent citizens, including:

Clint Eastwood, actor

William Hearst, III, publisher of the *San Francisco Examiner*

Frank Jordan, mayor of San Francisco

George Lucas, movie producer

Edwin Meese, former U.S. Attorney General

Joe Montana, football star

Leon Panetta, President Clinton's White House chief of staff

Janet Reno, U.S. Attorney General

Richard Rosenberg, CEO, Bank of America

Macworld sought all legally accessible data available about these people from four commercial and two governmental data suppliers. The magazine spent roughly $100 to research each person. Plus, *Macworld* looked through public records for criminal court filings, fictitious business names, bankruptcies, insider-trading transactions, trusts, deeds, powers of attorney, and other legal matters.

The computer magazine's staff was able to discover most, if not all, of the following data about these individuals:

Biography	Marriage record
Birth date	Neighbor's address/phone
Civil court filings	Real estate owned
Commercial loans/debts	Social Security number
Corporate ties	Tax liens
Driver record	Vehicles owned
Home phone	Voter registration
Home address	

At least one of *Macworld*'s subjects has received regular death threats over the years, and most of these people have bodyguards. With personal data so easy to find, it is natural that many law-abiding wealthy people feel compelled to hide their assets in dummy companies and to register their automobiles under corporate names. It is also clear that many qualified people refuse public service, knowing that a high public profile will attract the attention of dangerous persons. Our society would benefit if Janet Reno, George Lucas, and all of *Macworld*'s other subjects lobbied for stricter privacy rules — both for their own survival and for those of us who cannot pay bodyguards and lawyers to shield us from the data sharks.

The *Macworld* study suggests three disturbing ironies that deserve our keen attention. First, the U.S. Congress and our state legislatures regularly beat drums for us to pay more tax dollars to combat terrorists and criminals. At the same time, our legislators ignore the problem posed by weak privacy laws that hand confidential data to dangerous people, on a silver platter. Second, several people on this list work(ed) in professions (such as law enforcement and banking) that are pushing for greater proliferation of confidential data. The same data can be used by kidnappers, ex-cons, and psychotics against these very individuals. For rich and powerful people to encourage data proliferation is myopic thinking that is just short of suicidal. Third, social pundits from every political corner tell us that they support strong American families. Yet data proliferation is a direct attack against family privacy because anyone can buy a family's secrets.

The amassing and circulating of computer data about each of us has reached insane levels. In George Orwell's novel, *1984,* the British author imagined that "Big Brother" (that is, the government) would someday monopolize and store data about us in its computers. Orwell's form of tyranny has not befallen America — though it might, as we shall see in the Clipper Chip section. Our immediate problem is more subtle but just as deadly. Thousands of mom-and-pop businesses, and big companies, treat our personal data as a public commodity to be bought and sold in the marketplace like blocks of cheese. This marketplace reduces all human activity to the lowest common denominator of numbers — numbers to be crunched by computers.

This book is a wake-up call. *Paranoia* is a contagious emotional disease that immobilizes people. Life is too short for paranoia. The goal of this book is to coax *awareness.* Life is just the right length for awareness. Those of us who are computer literate have the electronic power and the social responsibility to fight for our freedom of privacy.

Who Is Leaking Our Secrets?

❝ *Nearly 370 employees of the Internal Revenue Service have been investigated or disciplined for using government computers to create fraudulent tax refunds or browse through tax records of friends, relatives, neighbors and celebrities...* **❞**

~ Stephen Barr, *Washington Post,* August 1993

~

In 1993, Senator John Glenn, the former astronaut, released a report that focused upon the Internal Revenue Service's (IRS's) Southeast Region, which is headquartered in Atlanta. Senator Glenn, Chairman of the Senate Governmental Affairs Committee, said that at least one employee "altered some 200 accounts and got kickbacks" from bogus refund checks that were issued to these taxpayers. Other IRS employees were caught selling businesses' tax records to competitors and altering tax records for personal gain. An IRS spokeswoman admitted that the incidents were "a serious concern to this agency." She went on to affirm that "a nationwide fix" is needed to enhance the IRS's computer security.

Some people are amazed when a few hundred IRS employees are caught red-handed in unethical or illegal activity. Walter Goldberg at the Price Waterhouse accounting firm was quoted in the *Washington Post* as saying, "At most, I think it would have been an isolated case, a rogue employee." Thomas Ochsenschlager at the Grant Thornton accounting firm added, "I find the number surprising...For the most part, I've always assumed that internally it was relatively hard to get at that information."

This particular IRS scandal is a drop in the bucket compared with the pool of potential other institutional leakers. Consider the following report from the August 3, 1993, *San Francisco Chronicle*:

> *The investigation in the agency's Southeast Region involved 369 employees suspected of misusing the agency's Integrated Data Retrieval System. The employees were described as rank-and-file workers who handle IRS mail and answer the tele-phone when taxpayers call.*
>
> *About 56,000 of the agency's 115,000 employees have access to this computer system, which is used to locate and adjust tax-payer accounts. The system provides employees with taxpayer data such as name, address, Social Security number, depen-dents claimed, adjusted gross income, taxable income and tax liability.*

Two alarming facts merit our special attention. Note that the IRS employees *caught* were the low-level "rank-and-file" employees, not the more urbane, polit-ically connected employees. Note also that 56,000 people have keyboard access to the computer system and, by extension, to your records! How many of these people will trade your data for a pizza? More ominously, how many IRS workers might be "dual employees," who are well-paid by divorce attorneys, Wall Street firms, or private detectives to systematically compromise our tax "privacy"?

Who is leaking our secrets? The IRS is only one bureaucracy. To compre-hend the magnitude of the problem, imagine how many men and women sit at computer terminals right now at banks, brokerage firms, credit companies, hospitals, insurance companies, and police agencies. On a recent Saturday morning, I dropped by the local hardware store and started chatting with a carpet salesman. Privacy came up, and I played dumb. This fellow bragged that his brother worked for the bank and his uncle was a cop. He boasted that he knew "everything going on in town" and convinced me that his relatives should be fired or jailed for what they told him. People all over America like the carpet salesman's relatives may well be leaking our secrets.

Privacy Defined

❝ *There is no such thing as a private individual in National Socialist Germany.* ❞

~ A Nazi admirer of Adolf Hitler

❝ *The human animal needs a freedom seldom mentioned, freedom from intrusion. He needs a little privacy quite as much as he wants understanding or vitamins or exercise or praise.* ❞

~ Phyllis McGinley, The Province of the Heart

~

The word *privacy* stems from the Latin word *privatus*, which literally means "apart from the public life." Every computer user has a private life. Jim Warren, the founder of *InfoWorld* and of the annual Conferences on Computers, Freedom and Privacy, is one of the most flamboyant, outspoken people in cyberspace. In 1993, Jim Warren led a victorious battle to force the State of California to make its legislative records available online, free of charge. This work earned Warren the 1994 Hugh M. Hefner First Amendment Award (named after the Hefner who founded *Playboy*). Now Warren is trying to make the executive branch's records available to all of us — plus he is fighting for online access to campaign-finance logs. Warren's activism is democracy at its best: these facts are part of the *public* record.

However, like all of us, even Jim Warren has a private life. Jim Warren likes architectural design and his Rottweiler dog. I could tell you more about Warren, but, being a privacy advocate, I will respect his privacy by not doing so.

Jim Warren embodies a theme that involves every computer user. To wit, he — and each of us — have the human right to judge how much to tell others about ourselves. Some people, like the French author Jean-Paul Sartre, publish serious autobiographies that turn their sexual, financial, and familial lives literally into an open book. Some of us crave what New York artist Andy

Warhol called our "15 minutes of fame" (or infamy). We go on the Oprah Winfrey, Sally Jessy Rafaël, or Phil Donohue show and take part in panels such as "Transvestite Dentists," "Mothers Who Pimp Their Daughters," or (weirder yet) "Nerds Who Read Computer Books." Still other people sell their perversion-of-the-day to the *National Enquirer* and other tabloids, which are by far America's most popular print publications. But most of us do not wish to be sensationalized or trivialized by the mass-media circus. We share our private lives only with a few friends — people who we trust have the experience and wisdom to empathize with us.

A healthy society has room for diverse personalities, and for disparate definitions of privacy. I know computer programmers who are so shy, it is literally painful for them to talk. Some people are very bright and see no need for "true confessions." They read between the lines and catch on quickly. As a rule, cautious people are distrustful of big-talkers, whom they see as "naive," "unreliable," and "flaky." Our personalities, our ambitions, and our IQs determine where we want to draw the line between our private and public lives. In a free society, we (not data peddlers) draw that line!

In 1890, Samuel D. Warren, a legal scholar, and Louis D. Brandeis, who became a U.S. Supreme Court justice, proposed a legal connection between privacy and personality. They published a visionary article in the *Harvard Law Review* entitled "The Right to Privacy." In that essay, the legal scholars asserted that United States Constitutional law, as well as common law, implicitly protects the right of each of us to exclude unwanted people from our private lives. Furthermore, they made the radical observation that our implicit right to privacy was being endangered by new technologies. (Note that Brandeis and Warren wrote this way before the first large general-purpose computer, Howard H. Aiken's Mark I, began computing in 1944!) Warren and Brandeis feared the beginning of mass audience journalism, which had little power then compared with today. They felt that if we lost control over private information about ourselves we would also lose a more general liberty. Warren and Brandeis called this broader freedom "the right to one's personality." Without control over one's personality, Warren and Brandeis dreaded the prospect that a conformist public scrutiny could erode the essence of "man's spiritual nature" and destroy him as a morally independent person and self-governing citizen. How can society protect this basic right? Warren and Brandeis argued that the law should be expanded to protect people against new technological hazards.

One century after Brandeis and Warren, we reside in an "Information Age" dominated by computers. Many of us store our intimate diaries in WordPerfect files, balance our checkbooks with Quicken software, and manage our businesses with Lotus spreadsheets. In addition, millions of us converse about personal, financial, and professional matters via electronic mail. These files and e-mail messages are extensions of our minds, of our personalities. Unless we are accused of a crime, nobody should have the power to see these files or messages without our permission. If every computer user must look over her shoulder, worrying that each keystroke might be intercepted by someone, free thought will be severely chilled. If every citizen must worry about who is scanning his tax forms and medical records, social spontaneity will be seriously harmed. Enemies of democracy, like those who cheered Hitler's Third Reich and those who detest private individuals, will gain a major victory over all of us.

Groups, not only individuals, need privacy to maintain their identity. *Wired* magazine must be able to shield anonymous journalistic sources in order to publish articles on very controversial topics; Texas Instruments must have control over trade secrets in order to survive; and American Express must possess secure data channels in order to curtail fraud. Some corporations, notably in the defense industry, are required by law to guarantee that nobody reads their customer lists. The organizations that demand the highest level of privacy — for themselves but not for others — are elite government agencies. These groups, such as the Central Intelligence Agency (CIA), use the most sophisticated technology that tax dollars can buy, in order to protect "national security." All of these groups realize — and justly so — that privacy, confidentiality, and discretion are often necessary for survival.

To summarize, privacy is one form of power that enables people and groups to survive. Privacy in the Computer Age exists to the degree that individuals and groups can determine how, what, and when information about them is communicated to other people.

Banking practices offer a prime model of how earnestly a society values privacy. Switzerland is a small country with a low population. Many Swiss reside in villages, where their families have known one another for centuries. The Swiss invented "numbered accounts" and true banking secrecy so that a law-abiding Swiss citizen could deposit and withdraw money without his bank teller, his cousin, his neighbor, and the village gossip chatting about his affairs. To this day, it is *illegal* for any Swiss bank employee to acknowledge the existence of, or to talk, about any client's account — much less to share banking data with any other bank or with the Swiss government. (They may do so under a court order, but these are rarely issued.) A cartoon shows two Swiss bankers at a cocktail party. The first banker asks the second, "How is business?" The second banker, appalled by such an indiscreet question, walks out of the room. This is privacy in the common-sense usage of the word. By comparison, American banks are data sieves that openly share information about our accounts with other people and with other institutions. This indiscretion by American banks is one reason that most large American companies, including banks, have bank accounts outside the United States.

The American right to privacy is rooted in part in the Fourth Amendment to the United States Constitution. This Amendment, which was ratified in 1791, states:

> *The right of the people to be secure in their persons, houses, papers, and effects, against unreasonable searches and seizures, shall not be violated, and no Warrants shall issue, but upon probable cause, supported by Oath or affirmation, and particularly describing the place to be searched, and the persons or things to be seized.*

Traditional common law goes beyond this amendment to ensure confidentiality in various professional roles. For example, the law says that priests who hear confessions, physicians who treat patients, and lawyers who advise clients do not have to disclose certain private facts about the people whom they serve. Privacy laws affect many other areas of activity — for instance, real-estate property and copyrights.

In the United States, the law generally recognizes a right to privacy — at least for those people who have sufficient money or political clout to fight for that right. In particular, we are protected in some cases from 1) the misappropriation of one's image or name for commercial purposes, 2) the public disclosure of private facts about us, 3) the reporting of our actions in a false though "nondefamatory" (i.e., non-harmful) light, and 4) intrusion (eavesdropping and bugging).

Computer law is constantly changing and is beyond the scope of this book. Here are two places to go if you want to learn more about these legal issues. First, Robert Ellis Smith, publisher of the *Privacy Journal*, is "the Paul Revere of the Information Age," in the words of journalist Bill Moyers. Smith's journal is full of fascinating legal details, written without jargon. Second, the Electronic Frontier Foundation, which we shall discuss later, employs attorneys who are experts in telecommunications law.

A Few Privacy Controversies

" Privacy. There seems to be no legal issue today that cuts so wide a swath through conflicts confronting American society. From AIDS tests to wiretaps, polygraph tests to computerized data bases, the common denominator has been whether the right to privacy outweighs other concerns of society. . . "

~ Robert Ellis Smith, the *Privacy Journal*

~

Here is a selection of topics that computer privacy, civil-liberties, and consumer-protection advocates are focusing on. In May 1994, a Washington state conference on "Individual Privacy on the Information Superhighway," dealt with some of these issues. Panelists at this event were Steve McAllister, from Planned Parenthood; Tim O'Connell, an attorney; Michael Woods, a surveillance expert; and Janeane Dubar, an activist with Computer Professionals for Social Responsibility.

◆ **Automatic Phone Calling Machines:** Machines exist that can be programmed to dial (for instance) all the telephone numbers in your neighborhood and to play recorded advertisements. People who use these machines say that they are exercising their right to freedom of speech. Opponents of these machines argue that advertisers do not have the right to barge into our homes and take up our time in order to give us their message.

◆ **Caller ID:** Caller ID permits the recipient of a telephone call to identify the caller's telephone number. Caller ID supporters argue that this system will reduce prank calls. Opponents contend the opposite — namely that Caller ID will enable telemarketers to record our telephone numbers when we call businesses asking for information, and then to bombard us with junk phone calls the way direct marketers fill our mailboxes with junk mail. Privacy advocates are also concerned that people who call government fraud hotlines, suicide prevention lines, and the like, will lose their anonymity.

◆ **Cellular Communications:**   Salespeople often tell us that our cellular telephone calls are private — that our neighbors cannot intercept them. This sales pitch is blatantly untrue. Anyone can eavesdrop on cellular calls (or cordless telephones) with inexpensive scanners that are sold over the counter.

◆ **Electronic Voting:**   Electronic vote-tallying is controversial in part because several elections have been rigged. Is a secure and reliable electronic-voting system feasible? Should electronic-voting systems be available for thorough examination? Can voting by phone be practical and confidential? Who has the technological expertise to monitor the validity of our local elections? These are a few questions that people are seeking answers to.

◆ **Intellectual Property Rights on the Internet:**   Millions of us post notices on computer networks. Who "owns" these messages? Can any reporter download our messages and publish them without our knowledge or permission? Without paying us a royalty? Suppose that we post messages in a high-tech conference, suggest product improvements. Can a computer company patent our ideas? Some of us believe that anything on the Internet becomes public property. Others believe that this "everything up for grabs" policy will drive away engineers, scientists, and scholars (the original users of the Internet), turning the Internet over to glib chatterers. In network jargon, the "noise to signal ratio will increase."

◆ **Free Speech on the Networks:**   We say anything we want on telephones. We can speak in any language, use any jargon, and examine any topic. Yet computer networks like America Online, CompuServe, and The WELL (Whole Earth 'Lectronic Link) bring together people from diverse cultures with very different customs, mores, and laws. Some cultures talk about religion or politics calmly; others might go to war over the slightest difference in opinion. Some cultures view eroticism as natural and healthy; others find "obscenity" under every rock. What standards should apply to cyberspace?

◆ **Social Security Numbers:**   When the Social Security Administration was created by the U.S. Congress, privacy advocates feared that the Social Security Number (SSN) would someday become a national ID. Social Security's creators ridiculed this fear, stating that the SSN would be used only for the Social Security system. Today, it is trivial to acquire someone's SSN — many institutions use the SSN as a "security password"! A great threat arises from the proposed use of the SSN for a national health-care system. This could open up our medical records to one and all.

- **Student Records:** State and federal governments are trying to increase the amount of information available in a student's files. In the old days, these files were mainly report cards. Proposed additions to the student's data-bank includes his employment history, extra-curricular activities, family financial records, personality tests, and voter-registration status. Lobbyists want to make it easier, if not compulsory, for schools to share this data with other institutions.

- **Video Conferencing:** As the price of video conferencing decreases, more people will begin to use it. These cyberspace meetings include more intimate details than telephone calls; namely, they supply a person's appearance and her body language. These conferences can be intercepted — thus, in effect, allowing snoops to place cameras in our rooms.

Participants in the Privacy Debate

Some information brokers and bureaucrats tell the public that only a "lunatic fringe" and a few "paranoids" care about privacy issues. These myth-makers add that all "mainstream" folk are so happy watching television sitcoms that they don't want to be bothered by academic or nerd talk that leads nowhere. Other data marketers belittle their critics as Anarchists, Democrats, Libertarians, Republicans, Socialists, or Vegetarians — the scapegoat of the day. In fact, a large and diverse mixture of individuals, groups, and businesses from all walks of life are deeply concerned about computer privacy. Here is a chance for you to scrutinize the evidence for yourself.

Jim Warren, under the auspices of the Palo Alto, California-based Computer Professionals for Social Responsibility, founded the Conferences on Computers, Freedom, and Privacy (CFP) in order to bring people who are passionate about computer privacy into the same room to talk with each other.

Bruce Koball, a San Francisco Bay Area computer consultant, organized the Third Conference (CFP'93), which was held in Burlingame, California, under the primary sponsorship of the Association for Computing Machinery. This conference met at the San Francisco Marriott Hotel in Burlingame, California. Below are partial lists of people and groups that made his conference possible. (This is all public information, published in a book that was distributed free of charge to all conference attendees). I attended CFP'93, and I can assure you that in the audience were people of all persuasions, from hackers to CIA agents to librarians.

Patrons, Supporters, and Sponsors

American Library Association

American Express Corporation

American Civil Liberties Union

Apple Computer, Inc.

Association for Computing Machinery

Computer Professionals for
Social Responsibility

Dun & Bradstreet Corporation

Electronic Frontier Foundation

Equifax, Inc.

Freedom to Read Foundation

Internet Society

Mead Data Central, Inc.

National Science Foundation

Pacific Bell

Privacy International

RSA Data Security, Inc.

The WELL (Whole Earth 'Lectronic Link)

Panelists and Speakers

These individuals' affiliations are listed only for the purpose of identification, so that you
can locate your colleagues. Of course, these individuals may hold opinions different from
those of their employers.

Sherri Alpert, Information Policy Analyst, U.S. Internal Revenue Service

John Perry Barlow, Co-Founder, Electronic Frontier Foundation

Dorothy Denning, Chair of Computer Science, Georgetown University

Donald P. Delaney, Senior Investigator, New York State Police

Robert Edgar, Producer, Paramount Technology Group

Mike Godwin, Legal Services Counsel, Electronic Frontier Foundation

Janlori Goldman, National Director, American Civil Liberties Union

Mark Graham, President, Pandora Systems

Sarah Gray, Operations Manager, We the People

Bruce Hartford, National Writers Union

Will Hill, Bell Communications Research

Lance Hoffman, Professor, George Washington University

Nicholas Johnson, former member of the Federal Communications Commission

James Packard Love, Director, Taxpayer Asset Project

Alan Robert McDonald, Technical Services, FBI

Judy Malloy, Co-Editor, Leonardo Electronic News

Gary Marx, University of Colorado

continued

Rob Mechaley, Vice President, McCaw Cellular Communications

Rebecca Mercuri, Research Fellow, University of Pennsylvania

Barbara Peterson, Staff Attorney, Florida Legislature

Jack Rickard, Publisher, *Boardwatch Magazine*

Ilene Rosenthal, General Counsel, Software Publishers Association

Roy G. Saltman, Computer Scientist, NIST (National Institute of Standards and Technology)

Daniel Sands, Center for Clinical Computing, Harvard Medical School

Barbara Simons, Researcher, IBM Corporation

Robert Ellis Smith, Publisher, *Privacy Journal*

David Sobel, Legal Counsel, Computer Professionals for Social Responsibility

Jacob Sullum, Associate Editor, *Reason* Magazine

Willis Ware, corporate research staff, Rand Corporation

Jim Warren, Columnist, *MicroTimes* and Entrepreneur, Autodesk, Inc.

A "Surveillance Age"

❝ *The principle that a man's home is his castle is under new attack. For centuries the law of trespass protected a man's lands and his home. But in this age of advanced technology, thick walls and locked doors cannot guard our privacy or safeguard our personal freedom.* **❞**

~ President Lyndon B. Johnson

Our computer-driven, high-technology world is a double-edged sword. The good side of the sword first: Economical desktop or laptop computers let us search encyclopedias, dictionaries, and vast databases by pressing a few buttons. We often label this positive power the "Information Age." Now the deadly side of the sword: The same computers permit credit agencies, insurance companies, and mobsters to collect, store, and sell data about us. So-called "confidential" files, such as medical records, move freely from computer to computer — invariably without our consent. Sometimes this data is erroneous. For example, one Californian's life became a nightmare after 12 strangers began using her Social Security number for credit scams. I call this dark side of computer technology the "Surveillance Age."

Today it can be profitable and prestigious to be a snoop. The American public elected George Bush, former Director of the CIA, to the White House. Spying, for Bush, was a patriotic stepping-stone to higher office. G. Gordon Liddy, a felon convicted for his actions in the Watergate scandal that forced President Richard Nixon's resignation, has a colorful history in surveillance and covert activities. Mr. Liddy, "G-Man" as he fondly calls himself, is one of America's most popular radio talk-show hosts. Finally, think about Colonel Oliver North, a specialist in covert activities, who played a central figure in the Irangate Scandal during President Ronald Reagan's regime. North's clandestine life in the spook underground made him a hero to millions of God-fearing patriots. This hero-worship enabled Mr. North to earn fabulous lecture fees and to nearly get elected to the U.S. Senate from the Commonwealth of Virginia. Bush, Liddy, and North demonstrate that spying has become as American and patriotic as grandma's good old-fashioned apple pie.

Surveillance has become a huge business. Almost all major corporations use private security forces. Visit skyscrapers in Los Angeles, Chicago, Miami, or just about any city. These buildings are fortresses guarded by visible personnel, as well as by semi-visible cameras and/or microphones that monitor the elevators, hallways, and garages. Two Hollywood movies focus upon this theme of high-surveillance buildings. *Sliver*, based on the novel by Ira Levin, stars Sharon Stone and William Baldwin (playing a wealthy computer-software designer), and depicts a New York residential building. *Rising Sun*, based on a novel by Michael Crichton, stars Sean Connery, and illustrates the inner workings of a Los Angeles corporate headquarters building.

To test our surveillance society, I performed a simple experiment. I entered the elevator of a famous hotel. After the door closed, I turned to my elevator companion and uttered something that I trusted would provoke eavesdroppers. When the elevator opened at a higher floor, a security officer greeted me. Clearly, the elevator was bugged. Reliable sources tell me that rooms are regularly bugged in those hotels that attract diplomats and other VIPs. As one Washington, D.C. colleague of mine noted, "This is common practice in Moscow and Cairo. Do you think America is different?"

America has many more private security officers than public police. Since New York's World Trade Center was bombed, employees at my favorite overnight courier service tell me that it is difficult for their carriers to deliver packages to New York corporate mailrooms. The courier must leave parcels with uniformed guards, who often X-ray the boxes in search of explosives. Search the Yellow Pages of any medium-size city under key words such as "security" or "surveillance". Advertisements that promise concealed wiring, executive escorts, mobile security patrols, motion-picture security, and strike coverage are commonplace. Shadier forms of surveillance are rarely stated openly.

These are great times for cloak-and-dagger enthusiasts. One day I opened my mail box and discovered an unsolicited yuppie catalog. Page one proudly hawked a book, *SpyGame: Winning Through Super Technology*. The gist of this book was simple: Everyone else is spying, so join in or you will be left behind. Big Brother, Big Business, and Big Neighbor are euphoric. They are prying into our secrets with small, inexpensive spy gadgets. These surveillance toys can be easily purchased throughout the United States. Let us explore the spy marketplace as it touches our lives.

High-tech surveillance is more widespread and insidious than President Johnson had anticipated 30 years ago. In particular, our privacy is under attack from at least four categories of surveillance: electronic, optical, managerial, and biological.

Electronic Surveillance

Electronic spying is rampant. This is not overly surprising in our Information Age. Millions of us are addicted to telephones, computers, and fax machines — all of which are easy targets for snoops.

I have asked private investigators and security experts to identify who is listening to us. They spoke with me only after they were confident that I was not "wired" (carrying a concealed microphone or transmitter) and that I would guard their anonymity. Typically, these people spend hours each week, if not each day, "sweeping" (electronically sniffing) for "bugs" (microphones that can be hidden almost anywhere) and other eavesdropping aids. Investigators painted a bleak picture in which half the world's landlords, salespeople, and wives seem to be secretly recording their tenants', competitors', and husbands' voices. The private eyes agreed on three points: 1) Fortune-500 companies are engaged in electronic warfare in pursuit of trade secrets. This is a common practice that everyone knows about but no one openly admits. 2) When illegal bugs or optical devices are discovered, they are rarely reported to the police. 3) Most private surveillance people are middle-class employees or entrepreneurs, who are trying to feed their families and pay their mortgages. Many of them come from law-enforcement backgrounds, and thus have unofficial access to "government-only" databases.

Two questions bothered me as I interviewed these private eyes. First, I asked them: "Isn't your job a police matter?" One detective laughed and confided, "Local cops have no electronics training. It's a waste of time telling them about surveillance. Clients hire me to deliver justice."

How does this justice work? Suppose you own Smith Architects and your detective discovers that Doe Builders has illegally wiretapped your phone in order to underbid you on jobs. Your investigator might: a) advise you to give false bids over the phone and thereby undermine Doe Builders' snooping; and/or b) say to Doe Builders, "Pay Smith Architects $40,000 or I'll report your felony wiretapping to the authorities. (Telephone companies take non-government taps seriously.) You'll be stuck with at least $50,000 in legal fees." I asked the detectives (who call themselves "counter-surveillance experts") a second question that puzzled me: "How can Doe Builders find someone to wiretap or to spy upon Smith Architects? You work in the field, yet you say that you don't know anybody who does illegal surveillance." Everyone I spoke with was vague on this issue. Author Doug Stewart solved this riddle in "Spy Tech," an article published in *Discover* Magazine. Stewart reports that federal agents impersonating business executives asked 115 detective agencies to tap phones. More than 33 percent of the agencies agreed to do the (illegal) work for fees between $30 and $5,000. Agencies that declined often suggested do-it-yourself phone taps. The federal government is not much better. A congressional survey indicates that 25 percent of federal agencies use electronic surveillance.

What kind of surveillance gadgets am I talking about? Here are sample items sold in mail-order catalogs. I will refrain from supplying names and addresses, because I do not want these devices to proliferate.

◆ FM telephone kits the size of a dime that broadcast *both* sides of anybody's telephone conversation, with crystal clarity, up to $1/8$ mile. Completely automatic, they use the telephone line's power. Telephone calls can be monitored on any FM radio.

◆ "Super mini-stethoscopes" that can hear a ticking clock or a conversation through thick wood or fiberglass walls. For less conspicuous use, you can detach the headset and snap in the single earpiece.

◆ "Voice changers" that slip over any telephone handset. A variable control allows the caller to pose as, say, a member of the opposite sex. In any case, the caller's voice is unrecognizable. It is pocket-sized and can be used anywhere in the world.

◆ "Computer interceptors" that allow you to tune in on any unprotected computer at ranges of up to a mile. You can reproduce anything appearing on the computer's screen.

People who market these Orwellian gadgets are attentive to language. Their first pitch is often realistic. I remember a very enthusiastic, back-slapping salesman who cornered me in Southern California. He winked: "You know, André, our voice changer is great for making gorilla calls" (i.e., for intimidating people), "or for keeping tabs on girlfriends" (i.e., for calling them while impersonating someone else)." Their second message is legalistic. The same guy reminded me, tongue in cheek: "Of course, it's illegal to use our voice changer for fraud or deception." Similarly, salespeople pretend that FM telephone kits are designed for high-school physics labs and that mini-stethoscopes are used by plumbers seeking leaky pipes. In the spirit of this cat-and-mouse legal game, many sellers print a disclaimer such as this:

```
WARNING: Not to be used for surreptitious
interception of oral communications. All
equipment is sold subject to public law
90-351, Title III, 18 U.S.D., Section 2511,
all local, state and federal ordinances,
rules, regulations, etc. It is the sole
responsibility of the buyer (not the seller)
to consult legal counsel for interpretation of
any laws applicable to the area of intended use.
```

Other catalogs, with more sophisticated spy equipment, state that their devices are perfect for military and police chores. The subliminal message is clear: "Our stuff is good enough for the Drug Enforcement Agency to listen to Colombian dope dealers, so it's good enough for you!" These items, like automatic weapons, can be purchased by almost anyone.

Before leaving this topic, it is worth noting how this marketplace resembles the famous *Mad* magazine "Spy versus Spy" cartoons: Many companies sell "counter-surveillance" items on one page to protect us from the surveillance devices on the next page. These businesses are like gun shops that sell bulletproof vests. Here is a fictitious catalog entry that is nonetheless typical of the genre:

```
        The Newest Business and
         Personal Security!

Get ahead of the game! Quit reacting to pri-
vacy attacks, violent crimes, and property
```

```
thefts. Act. Outsmart the criminals with our
latest in-house equipment.

Our company, run by an internationally noted
security expert, has designed counter-sur-
veillance methods and equipment to serve your
every need. For years, we have sold directly
to police agencies, major corporations, and
governments that require only the best
acoustic noise generators, alarm/bug detec-
tors, laser metal detectors, security tele-
phones, and tape recorder detectors. Now,
because of overwhelming popular demand, we
sell directly to individuals. If you wish, we
will come directly to your home or office and
in-stall state-of-the-art equipment so that
you can see who is trying to monitor you.
```

Optical Surveillance

Optical surveillance is on the rise. Since our society is so eager to hear evil, we may as well see it also. This impulse towards voyeurism is very popular in Hollywood movies, *Sliver* being one example. Here are some optical products that can be purchased with a little effort:

◆ X-Ray letter bomb detectors that make opaque paper temporarily transparent, allowing the user to view or read the contents of an envelope without opening it. Some 30 to 60 seconds after application, the liquid evaporates without leaving a trace.

◆ Night Invaders infrared optical systems that amplify existent starlight or other ambient light up to 75,000 times. These devices enable snoops to read license plates on moonless nights, and to peer into dark bedrooms. Some models come complete with a spot illuminator, a pistol grip, and a tripod designed for fast, stable setup for long-term surveillance.

◆ Miniature video cameras that are roughly the size of a small box of wooden matches.

◆ Cameras of all sorts that are disguised as clocks, photographs, plants, or attaché cases.

◆ Pinhole lenses. Designed for use on concealed cameras, these lenses provide minimal front exposure and ensure discreet observation. They are commonly used in clothing-store dressing rooms to safeguard against shoplifting — and to entertain the security staff and/or management.

Men and women who sell these products have a sense of humor. A can of "Letter-bomb detector spray" on sale in a discount store might be hyped with the catchy phrases "Distribution: Restricted" or "Formulation: Classified." An infrared camera might be sold as a unique gift to "Study owls in the dark." But there are disturbing waves beneath this humor. Sprays that peer through envelopes might prove useful in Israel or Ireland, where letter-bombs are a way of life. Night-vision optics were developed for soldiers and assassins to kill people under cover of darkness. It is arguable that these pro-death devices had a place, however gruesome, in war-torn countries. But why in the world should Americans need such assault-weapons against personal freedom and dignity?

Managerial Surveillance

Managerial spying is popular. Around 1900, Frederick W. Taylor, the "father of scientific management," urged employers to exercise greater control over workers — to the point of dictating the employee's smallest movements. Today, Big Manager's obsession with surveillance begins before we join the payroll. Corporations are using lie detectors, voice-stress analyzers, urinalysis tests, fingerprints, retina scans, blood tests — and, believe it or not, hand-writing analysis (very popular in France) and astrology (not only in California!) — to screen us from other applicants. To be fair, management claims that these pre-employment tactics are required because our society is full of phony résumés, chemically-dependent job applicants, and laws that pro-hibit former employers from talking candidly about deadbeat, disruptive employees. The workplace is clearly in an "Us versus Them" mind-set, which is antithetical to cooperation.

What happens once we are hired? Professor Alan Westin, a specialist in public law at Columbia University, has popularized the idea of "electronic privacy," and has written about the topic for several decades. For one study, Westin interviewed 650 managers and 1,100 workers at 110 organizations between 1982 and 1986. Westin discovered that two-thirds of government and private managers who monitor us practice a "Tayloresque" model. Here are some examples of Tayloresque monitoring, as reported in William Booth's *Science* editorial, "Big Brother Is Counting Your Keystrokes," and in other articles:

- ◆ A popular software package called Auto-AOC (for Advanced Office Controls) tells managers how quickly workers should move. After a supervisor queries it by pushing the proper buttons, the computer sage dictates that it should take 7.5 seconds to open envelopes and 2.9 seconds to staple papers.

♦ Reservation clerks at Pacific Western Airlines arrived at work one day to read this poster: "Compare yourself to your friends. Compare yourself with those who are not your friends. . .When the monthly statistics are published, ensure you are not dragging down your team and your office." Management determines these statistics by timing each incoming phone call and calculating the dollar sales per hour per clerk.

♦ Wonder what happened to telephone courtesy? In 1977, our calls to Bell operators lasted 85 seconds on the average. In 1986, with computer monitoring, the average call had been reduced to 27 seconds. Operators are now tempted to hang up on people with speech or hearing defects, in order to fulfill their robotic quotas. In 1994, telephone companies are trying to replace human operators altogether with pushbutton menus.

The increasing surveillance by company computers is unforgiving. Computer designer Stephen Hollander told a Canadian conference, "More than 100 pieces of equipment described by George Orwell in *1984* now exist." Rep. Barbara Pringle of Cleveland tried to outlaw this inhumane monitoring of people. However, her bill was killed by the business community. "It's crazy," she says. "You stop to sneeze, and the machine says you are behind."

Employer surveillance is within the spirit and the letter of the law. The 1986 Electronic Communications Privacy Act (ECPA), like many similar laws, leaves big loopholes. This particular act prohibits persons from tapping our telephone or datalines (fax, modem, etc.), with two notable exceptions: employers and law-enforcement officers. This is an immense loophole.

Believe it or not, the ECPA grants employers greater rights to infringe on our privacy than law-enforcement agents. The FBI or local police can tap telephone or data lines, but only with court approval. Officially, about 1,000 taps are authorized each year nationwide. Employers, however, can tap an employee's phones, monitor her e-mail, watch her on closed-circuit TV, and search her computer files, without giving her notice. The Communications Workers of America, a union that represents many telecommunications workers, figures that employers eavesdrop on more than 400 million employee and consumer calls each year. This astounding number boils down to 750 eavesdrops each minute. When we consider that many corporate security divisions are staffed by former law-enforcement people, it is hard to guess what volume of data from these legal employer taps is passed along to buddies in law enforcement. Likewise, we cannot know how many intercepted messages are used for purposes far above and beyond protecting the employer against theft, sabotage, and other legitimate concerns.

Ironically, managerial spying is being turned against many executives who value their own surveillance of underlings. Many Fortune-500 companies issue their executives (and employees lower on the totem pole) plastic, computer-linked ID cards that they need to open doors, to control entry into restricted areas, and to deduct the costs of meals in the company cafeteria. Some of these cards, attached to an employee's belt, activate sensors throughout the company buildings, so that a computer can track an employee's every move. Officially, this uninterrupted electronic surveillance allows the corporation to page an executive or other employee for, say, an incoming telephone call. The bottom line, however, is this: a manager's time of arrival, time in the washroom, time on the phone, time at lunch, and time of departure are being stored in computers. Historically, such strict surveillance has been reserved for the maximum security wings of asylums and prisons.

What can be done about this transformation of the workplace into a 9-5 mental institution or prison? According to a *Macworld* magazine survey, roughly 80 percent of all U.S. employers have no stated electronic-privacy policy. Thus, employees have no idea of whether they are being monitored, nor of what the company does with data about them. For example, I know employees at a supermarket chain who suspect that their company locker room is bugged, so that management can listen to them talk about a possible strike or whatever. Whether or not the room is under surveillance, the employees' suspicions decrease morale and increase anger. Here are a few rules that many privacy activists would welcome in the workplace:

- ◆ Management should use surveillance or secret searches only when credible evidence of criminal activity or other serious wrongdoing comes to light. For example, monitoring might be required to discover who is stealing laser printers.

- ◆ Employees should be guaranteed reasonable expectations of personal privacy on the job. For instance, employees should be able to use restrooms without fear of hidden cameras.

- ◆ Employers should be able to gather surveillance data only for clearly defined work-related purposes. For example, management has no right to monitor telephones to confirm or deny rumors about someone's vacations.

- ◆ Management should be prohibited from using surveillance data as the sole factor to evaluate employee performance. For example, suppose that management finds an open whiskey bottle in someone's desk. That person should not be demoted or fired for drinking on the job if nobody ever saw the person drunk.

♦ Management should be prohibited from releasing surveillance data to any third party, except to comply with legal requirements. For example, a manager must not read your stock portfolio and pass along that data to his sister, a broker.

♦ Employees or prospective employees must not be forced to waive their privacy rights as a condition for employment.

♦ Managers who violate these pro-privacy principles should be subjected to discipline or termination.

Frankly, it is sad that any society has to take the above list seriously. At best, the implementation of these rules will require more stifling bureaucracy and more attorneys in the workplace. How much saner it would be if, rather than reducing every person and every business to the lowest common denominator of mistrust, we could focus upon the best, most productive talents of everyone. How much freer it would be if we could see the "security race" as a self-destructive extension of the "arms race" (which has brought our society to the brink of bankruptcy), and call a truce.

Biological Surveillance

Biological surveillance is a newly fashionable enemy of privacy. Twenty years ago, any employer who insisted that we urinate in a bottle for him to examine would have been ridiculed as a petty tyrant or a pervert. Any government bureaucrat who demanded that we submit to voice-stress analyzers would have been judged a paranoid in need of therapy. Times have changed. Sam Diamond reports two examples in his *High Technology* article, "Biometric Security: What You Are, Not What You Know." First, a luxury hotel in White Plains, New York replaced the conventional lock-and-key on its wine room with a fingerprint reader. Locks have worked admirably well for centuries, but in some people's eyes, metal locks are inadequate for our brave new world of terrorists and wine thieves. We need real security: we need to place our fingers on the electronic line.

For other employers, fingerprints are too insecure. (Perhaps a black market for fingertips will develop, and wine thieves will be free to pilfer wine cellars at will.) EyeDentify, a company in Beaverton, Oregon, feels that we should not be judged and classified by our fingerprints alone. EyeDentify manufactures a retinal-scan system that measures the blood-vessel patterns at the back of our eyes. Why do we need such a device? So that intimate corporations ("We're all one big family," as the advertisements say) can see that you and I are different people.

Drug testing is a chic, and dangerous, form of biological invasion. Manufacturers of crude, inexpensive drug tests say they are doing a public service. What the manufacturers do not tell us is that their devices: a) produce many false "positive" readings, b) cannot distinguish between illicit drugs and over-the-counter substances, and c) cannot distinguish between one-time use and chronic abuse.

Here is one dramatic example, courtesy of Lee Hearn, chief toxicologist for the Dade County Medical Examiner Department in Miami. Hearn examined 135 bills, in denominations ranging from $1 to $100, obtained from banks in 12 cities across the United States. He found that 131 contained at least a trace of cocaine. The four cocaine-free bills were right off the press. Anybody who handles money, except perhaps for a few employees at the Federal Reserve mint, could test positively for cocaine!

Nobody is "innocent" once high technology is used to invade our bodies. Ronald K. Siegel, of the UCLA School of Medicine, proves this point with hair-raising seriousness. Siegel, author of *Intoxication*, has collected hair samples of famous people throughout history. He examines this hair with a process called RIAH (radioimmunoassay of hair), or "hair" spelled backwards. Siegel notes, "It is well known, for example, that Ulysses S. Grant used cocaine in the last years of his life." And Siegel discovered, from drugstore records, that Abraham Lincoln bought brandy liniment containing hemlock, and cough candy laced with opium. RIAH makes it possible to detect these chemicals many years after a person's death. Today, these American heroes could be tried as criminals because of drug tests.

How do illicit chemicals get into the body? RIAH tests confirm that Emperor Napoleon's hair contained arsenic. Does this mean that Napoleon committed suicide, or perhaps that he was murdered? Neither, according to researchers David E.H. Jones and Kenneth W.D. Ledingham. They noted that arsenic was an ingredient widely used in paints and wallpapers in the late 18th century. Damp wallpaper may have transmitted arsenic to Napoleon. My point is simple: Even the best technology, devoid of social understanding, leads to ambiguous conclusions. Cheap drug tests are pseudo-scientific assaults against human dignity.

Whatever the method employed, it is fashionable to snoop because it is unpopular to be an individual. Spies are always on the hunt for people who deviate from statistical norms. Hitler's agents used telephone-company records to track down enemies of his paradise on Earth. Dictator Papa Doc's henchman spied on Haiti's poor people to see who read which books. History has been, and still is, full of people who hide in the dark and spy on enlightened citizens. But at last the good news: Throughout history, humans have defeated tyrants and melted their spy toys. Respect for individual human dignity and privacy is the greatest weapon Americans have against the marketplace for our secrets. It is time we reaffirm that respect!

Why Privacy is Controversial

❝ Another person's secret is like another person's money: you are not so careful with it as you are of your own. ❞

~ Edgar Watson Howe, Country Town Sayings

❝ The hater of property and of government takes care to have his warranty deed recorded; and the book written against fame and learning has the author's name on the title-page. ❞

~ Ralph Waldo Emerson

~

Privacy is polemic for two reasons: 1) It invokes the power taboo, and 2) It evokes human double standards.

André Bacard, an author about whom I have mixed feelings, wrote this provocative passage to begin his book, *Hunger for Power: Who Rules the World and How*:

> *People are born to seek power. All that they hold dear, their justice, love, property, and wisdom, are subservient to their epic quest for power. Power is as necessary to the enjoyment of life as water is to the survival of life. Yet a tense silence surrounds this fact. Now that sex can be discussed openly, power remains the last dirty secret. Even the best and brightest persons are*

squeamish to acknowledge fully their attitudes towards power.
This taboo against candor arises from the popular myths that
all power is evil, all power is political, and all powerlessness is
righteous.

Privacy is, first and foremost, about power. Information, in the hands of people who know how to use it, is power. It always has been; it always will be. Cardinal de Richelieu, one of the great power brokers in French history, said "Secrecy is the first essential in affairs of the State." The Cardinal realized that power is, in large degree, the ability to control the flow of information. Microsoft, the computer software company, is powerful because it designs the operating system that millions of people use to organize and transmit data. The *Washington Post* is powerful because it screens, sorts, and defines "the news" for influential readers. The average TV couch-potato has little power, because he absorbs data from others rather than transmitting data to others.

The politics of privacy is a never-ending battle over who will control the two-way transmission of data. Who will get paid how much for which data bits? Who will be able to censor which files? Who will be able to control which passwords? Who will do the bidding of whom? Later, we will discuss anonymous remailers and encryption, two methods computer users can use to privatize their computer files and e-mail. These issues are controversial because they give us computer users power over data that other people want to sort, screen, and file.

Privacy is controversial for a second reason. Most of us have a double-standard about privacy. Vice-President Dan Quayle was upset when Jeffrey Rothfeder wrote in *Business Week* that Mr. Rothfeder had obtained Quayle's credit report. Was Quayle equally upset when his family newspapers investigated the finances of non-Quayles? President George Bush complained bitterly that the press snooped into his family affairs. Was Bush, as CIA director, morally repulsed by intruding into law-abiding people's lives? President Clinton criticized the tabloid sensationalists for writing about his extramarital sexual affairs. But at the same time, Clinton proposed the Clipper Chip, a form of national surveillance system, that could violate every American's privacy! Most of us feel it is our natural right to search our children's closets, but we do not like our children going through our belongings. Since few of us are totally innocent of privacy duplicity, we should occasionally step back from privacy arguments and laugh at ourselves. In the privacy-intrusion debate, there is plenty of blame (and credit) to go around.

The BBS (Bulletin Board System) corner of cyberspace provides several examples of the privacy double standard. A BBS is a computer service that one dials into by telephone. A typical BBS offers hundreds of *freeware* (no-cost) software programs that one can download (transfer to one's computer), and games that one can play online, and e-mail. The average BBS is a one-or two-telephone-line operation run by a computer hobbyist called a *sysop* (systems operator). Running a BBS gives a sysop a chance to sharpen his or her computer skills, to meet other users, and to pass out files espousing his favorite causes. Most sysops are computer fanatics who eagerly help novices learn about their own BBS and about computers in general. There are over 1,000 BBSs just in the San Francisco Bay Area. Many BBSs are free, whereas others cost maybe $10 per month. The BBS community is a loosely connected "grass-roots" subculture of the computer world.

Some BBS sysops are a bit confused about computer privacy. They passionately scold government snooping on computer networks, but they do not practice what they preach. When one dials a BBS for the first time, a programmed message typically asks for the newcomer's name, address, and telephone number. Some BBSs are programmed to automatically call back the given phone number to verify that it is legitimate. Some BBSs ask callers for their sexual orientation (heterosexual, homosexual, or bisexual), their physical description, etc. — even if the novice is calling just to secure general information about the BBS.

Sysops say they need this information to protect their computers from hackers. (A name and verifiable phone number should take care of this reasonable security step.) What would the same sysops say if the government asked them to provide biographical information in order to register as a BBS owner? There are two additional serious matters. First, some sysops — especially in so-called "adult" and "dating" BBSs — are voyeurs who read users' e-mail. Second, some BBS operators kick users off their computers if they catch them sending PGP-encrypted e-mail (encrypted, that is, so that the sysop can't read it!). Yet the same BBS might offer PGP, or other encryption programs, to its users to employ elsewhere!!

Here is a sample screen that I found on a BBS that offers encryption software to its users, but forbids its users to encrypt messages:

> Pursuant to the ELECTRONIC AND COMMUNICATIONS PRIVACY ACT OF 1986, TITLE 18, UNITED STATES CODE, Sections 2510 and following, Notice is hereby given that there are no facilities provided by this system for sending or receiving private or confidential messages. The System Operator can assign any/all users to be able to read Any Messages left by any User.

This is a good time to recall the old proverb from the Pogo comic strip: "I have seen the enemy, and he is us."

How Computers Help Snoops

❝ Our memories are card-indexes consulted, and then put back in disorder by authorities whom we do not control.❞

~ Cyril Connolly, The Unquiet Grave

❝ Memory is a net; one finds it full of fish when he takes it from the brook; but a dozen miles of water have run through it without sticking.❞

~ Oliver Wendell Holmes

The data peddler, the snoop, and the rumormonger (all closely related folk) have a long, if not illustrious, history. Prostitution is often said to be the world's oldest profession. Whomever revealed the first prostitute's address might have founded the world's second oldest profession, that of the data peddler. One might wonder how the electronic computer can help a business (I'm speaking about the snooping business, of course) that has been thriving for thousands of years.

Our computer-using society allows people to spy and intrude upon us more effectively than was practical in pre-computerized societies for four basic reasons.

1. **Computers are memory specialists.** The human brain has an awesome memory, in many ways far more awe-inspiring than any computer memory. We can recall smells and sounds from childhood: faces that we saw only once, years ago, and literally uncountable events, images, and feelings. In this sense, our biological memory is far more versatile and rich than any electronic computer memory. To put it another way, the DNA molecule is far more sophisticated than any silicon chip. Computers can only remember numbers. The largest computer storage disc, with all its billions of words

and pictures, is in the end a fancy bean counter that processes ones and zeroes. A rose's fragrance is far nobler than any number.

Computers, however, can remember far more numbers than can any human. It is trivial for a computer to remember every telephone number in a city, or every credit-card purchase. Herein lies one reason why snoops love computers. These electronic toys can store numbers, and in a world that revolves around money (a quantity reducible to ones and zeroes), this memory can be translated into sociopolitical power.

2. Computers are unforgiving.   One mark of civilization is people's ability to forgive and forget. We are all fallible, and if we rehash every error end-lessly, we will be paralyzed. There comes a time when we must say "Enough is enough" and move on. All of us are slighted and injured by other people. If we spend our lives seeking revenge, an eye for an eye and a tooth for a tooth, we will create a society of blind, toothless people. For example, our society is filled with divorced people. In order to give and receive affection in their remaining years, these people must soften, if not forget, disappointing memories from their previous marriage(s). We must forgive in order to grow.

Computers do not forget, much less forgive. They remember every gory detail of a divorce proceeding. Every legal payment, every property dispute, and every court filing has the same flat, unemotional, inhuman significance to a computer. A petty theft that someone committed in childhood has the same gravity, to a computer, as an armed robbery that occurred yesterday. For a computer, there is no difference between a birth certificate and a funeral notice. Snoops like this unforgiving, inhuman nature of computer memory because the data peddler, sitting in a comfortable chair, can dig up data about people that rekindles terrible memories, or that can be used to harass them. President Richard Nixon exemplified this use of power when he retrieved IRS files on members of his infamous "enemy list."

3. Computers permit sophisticated memory searches.   Computers make it easy for data peddlers to cross-reference, to search, and to index vast mem-ories quickly and cheaply. A wicked example was initiated in 1977 by President Carter's Secretary of Health, Education, and Welfare, a man named Joseph Califano. Califano started Project Match, at first to compare the computer lists of welfare recipients with computer lists of government employees. Anyone who showed up on both lists was a good candidate for prosecution. Needless to say, many people had their reputations ruined because the computer files were out of date, or otherwise in error. This pro-gram was popular — since there is little support for fraudulent double-dippers at the low end of the economic scale. (Retired governors who draw three government pensions tend to be highly esteemed). So the program was expanded to look for student loan defaulters and others. Again, virtually all the Washington insiders gave their blessings to this expanded Project Match.

Today, computer matching is big business. In 1982, Thomas McBride of the Department of Labor told the U.S. Senate that there were 500 or more government matching programs. One program existed to match Selective Service data files with ice-cream parlor birthday lists (a hunt for persons who don't register for the draft). An IRS matching program compared our tax forms with consumer lists (in order to find people with low reported incomes who bought items such as luxury cars). Other computer programs have searched video-store rental records (to tell police who rents "adult" movies) and library records (to tell the FBI who checks out books on certain topics). When we buy a computer or subscribe to a computer magazine, we often receive forms asking us for demographic information (age, occupation, income, etc.). How do we know that these forms are not matched with databases from the IRS or from our local realtors, or used to build police dossiers? How can the companies that distribute these questionnaires avoid telling us who will use them?

Data peddlers love computer matching because it enables them to go on fishing expeditions for suspicious behavior — which means behavior outside the norm. Notice that all these matching programs sought out criminals or deadbeats. I have not read about one computer matching system (except for dating agencies) that searched for the *positive* side of humanity! Where are the computer matches that look for local heroes? The sad fact is that data peddlers get paid more money to look for the dark side of humanity.

4. **Computer records are transferable.**   Human memory is not transferable. There is no way for me to download all of your recollections and place them in my mind. Computer memory, to the contrary, can be mailed on disks, sent over telephone lines, and communicated in a number of quick, inexpensive ways. Data peddlers love this aspect of computers, for obvious reasons.

The Dangers of a Cash-Free Society

❝ Never ask of money spent
Where the spender thinks it went.
Nobody was ever meant
To Remember or invent
What he did with every cent. ❞

~ Robert Frost, American poet

❝ I'm 80 years old and free because I never owed a dime. Young people are addicted to credit. Mark my words, André. Credit will lead to a police state in America. I hope I die before then. ❞

~ My grandfather

~

"Say, buddy, can you spare a quarter?" Suppose we lived in a society that had no quarters — and for that matter, that had no coins and no paper currency. What would happen to our daily lives?

Financial institutions, electronics firms, and law-enforcement agencies are leading the charge to replace metallic coins and paper currency with silicon chips and magnetic strips. They want to exchange all physical money for electronic money. We are moving in that direction quickly. Twenty years ago, only about 10 percent of all securities (stocks, bonds, etc.) were issued in "book entry" (electronic) form. Today, people who want to possess securities on paper are penalized. Some brokerage firms charge you a fee if you want a stock certificate in your name, and treat you as an undesirable alien for asking. Many hotels will not let us check in — even if we pay with cash in advance — unless we produce a plastic card showing that we are a bona fide member of consumer society.

This dramatic shift away from tangible currency to electronic dots might produce benefits and nightmares for all of us.

The Cash-Free Look

A cash-free society might evolve in many ways. For the sake of simplicity, let us examine one scenario. Let's imagine that on January 1 we were required by law to take all the cash in our wallets, in our safe deposit boxes, and in our piggy banks to an official bank. This bank would count all our money — let us say the total is $10,000 — and issue us a plastic "Money Card" with a balance of $10,000. This Money Card might also store our account numbers and financial records from various commercial banks, retail stores, and brokerage accounts. Suppose you want to pay me $1,000 (a fine, democratic idea). You might go to a "Money Machine" (an ATM look-alike) and press buttons that transfer $1,000 from one of your accounts to one of my accounts. You would receive a paper receipt for this transaction. These Money Machines would replace cash registers and would be located in all businesses — perhaps in all homes. We would receive paychecks, buy toothpaste, and give our children allowances by inserting our Money Cards into Money Machines.

Cash-free benefits

Here are a few arguments that Money Card enthusiasts, not André Bacard, use:

A Clean Wallet. We could toss out our dirty, germ-coated money and keep just one clean Money Card, plus a high-security photo ID card. This wallet would symbolize our cultural quest to make everything as "efficient" and "easy" as possible.

Abolish Cash Robberies. Muggings, liquor-store holdups, and cash crimes would vanish. Why would a thief force you to transfer money to his Money Card? The transaction would be computer-recorded and easily traced. Reduced crime would enable us to spend less money for police, courts, and prisons. Today, for example, we spend roughly $20,000 per year to incarcerate a felon and about $5,000 per year to educate a child.

Tax the Underground. The IRS reckons that millions of Americans operate outside our official economy. They run barter-based family businesses, or take cash payments that they do not report to the IRS. Money Cards would allow the IRS, for better or worse, to tax these evaders. This extra revenue might, at least in theory, help us pay our astronomical national debt.

Track Drug Dealers. Some people still have the illusion that the government will win the "War on Drugs" by tracking all monies, thus making it "impossible" to "launder" drug profits.

Curb Corruption. Some law-enforcement officers, bureaucrats, and elected politicians take bribes, kickbacks, or "legal fees" to cover up criminal enterprises or illegal lobbying activities. Jonathan Beaty and S.C. Gwynne provide chilling examples in their book, *The Outlaw Bank: A Wild Ride Into the Secret Heart of BCCI,* which portrays the Bank of Credit & Commerce International as a criminal enterprise aided by the highest levels of the American government. Perhaps Money Cards would make it easier for reporters such as Beaty and Gwynne to "follow the money" that greases corruption.

Abolish Counterfeiters. Printing fake currency, money orders, and financial papers is a big business aided by high-resolution computer scanners and laser printers. Money Card promoters allege that bogus Money Cards might be harder to manufacture than bogus paper monies.

Restore Accidental Loses. Many people lose their wallets, cash hordes, or valuable paperwork through carelessness, fire, or natural disaster. A lost Money Card could be easily replaced. This sense of security might decrease our blood pressure and help us enjoy life.

Simplify Accounting. We could place our Money Card into a Money Machine, press a couple of buttons, and get a "hard copy" (a paper record) of every cent that we earned and spent. This could save us endless hours of frustration balancing check books, and it might help us budget our finances better.

Help Business Efficiency. A cashless society would allow businesses to lay off bank tellers, clerks, and bookkeepers — thus passing on the savings to the rest of us.

Cash-free nightmares

Unfortunately, in an increasingly cash-free society, there is no free lunch. If Money Cards are poorly designed, without strict privacy built into the system, many people will be hurt. Here are a few thoughts and scenarios to think about:

Desecration of Family Privacy. Every time we gave our children pizza money, the IRS would know. Federal agents (and their friends) could see all monetary exchanges between family members — which could lead to new forms of "gift" and "family" taxes. In cases of divorce or family dispute, judges might instantly redistribute our family funds by altering our Money Cards.

In the former Soviet Union, and under many dictatorships, people have had only one place where they can speak and act freely — their home. What will happen to society's sanity if and when this last bastion of freedom, family privacy, comes under Big Brother surveillance?

Naive Labor Force.   Think about a few bank tellers you've met. In America today, many computer terminals are staffed by employees who have minimum education, minimum morale, and maximum data about you. Some of these people are easy to trick or bribe: they are minnows before data sharks. Do you want such people to "guard" even more data about yourself?

More Intrusive Taxes.   In a cash-free, high-surveillance society, Congress — which is increasingly desperate for more revenues to buy voters — might define almost any financial exchange as an "investment" and levy new "capital gains" taxes. Congress might go even further and tax a percentage of *all* human activity with a new "life tax." Far-fetched? One century ago, the idea of a national income tax was judged too outrageous to merit debate.

Marketable Dossiers.   Police could collect, store, and sort all of your economic transactions! The same police officers who take bribes from drug pushers could trade financial dossiers about business owners to competitors.

Credit Bureaus.   These businesses would be even more powerful than they are today. They could sell — openly or secretly — anything about us. Want an itemized list of every Christmas present Jane Doe purchased last year? Push a button. I'm reminded of a cartoon that shows two K.G.B. agents standing outside the Kremlin when the Soviet Union collapsed. One agent says, "What are we going to do now?" The other agent smiles, "No problem, we'll open a credit agency."

Hackers.   Computer experts, working for themselves or for hire, might find "loopholes" in the system. If so, they could alter our records, set up dummy companies, etc. In short, they could create an electronic underground that would be invisible to non-experts.

Secret Governments.   Intelligence agencies and secret police around the world could reprogram Money Cards to give themselves and their organizations almost unlimited, untraceable funds. This "black budget" bonanza might dwarf the money laundering and counterfeiting schemes that governments sponsor — and deny — today.

The technology to run a cash-free society already exists. It already has ardent advocates. Unless we awaken from our deep sleep, a Money Machine society might give Big Brother powers that even George Orwell did not imagine when he wrote *1984*.

Why Is Big Brother in Kindergarten?

The best way to educate anyone to become a healthy, productive person is to teach her critical thinking, curiosity, empathy, and knowledge when she is a child. Similarly, the most forceful way to propagandize or dominate a person is to start manipulating her when she is too young too escape.

Suppose you wanted to design a Surveillance Society in which computers tracked everyone. Naturally, you would start with kids. If you began monitoring everyone as children, only a few of us would grow into adults who were capable of imagining a non-surveillance world. Today, for example, many people who have been addicted to TV since childhood cannot imagine a world without TV. Big Brother is fully aware of this untapped potential. That is why he is returning to kindergarten.

The Seattle chapter of Computer Professionals for Social Responsibility wrote a fascinating and alarming document, *K-12 Student Records: Privacy at Risk*, which it distributed worldwide on the Internet. The basic theme of this document is that:

> *"The U.S. education system is rapidly building a nationwide network of electronic student records. This computer network will make possible the exchange of information among various agencies and employers, and the continuous tracking of individuals through the social service, education and criminal justice systems, into higher education, the military and the workplace."*

Most of this data collection and proliferation will be done *without* the knowledge and consent of either the students or their parents.

Here are a few items that are being either proposed or implemented:

◆ An electronic "portfolio" to be kept on each student, containing personal essays and other completed work.

◆ A requirement that enrolling kindergarten students must produce their Social Security numbers, which will be used to track them.

◆ An electronic network called WORKLINK that will send high school students' transcripts, plus their teachers' "confidential" ratings of them, to potential employers.

This national electronic student-records network would be coordinated by the federal government and adopted by the states with federal assistance.

CPSR/Seattle also quotes from a report by the National Education Goals Panel, a federally appointed body established by the "Goals 2000" bill to oversee restructuring of our national education system. This group's *Publication 93-03* recommends that school districts and/or states collect expanded data about individual students. According to the panel, these data should include the young person's:

prenatal care records
birth weight
preschool history
poverty status
physical, emotional, and other status at ages 5 and 6
health- and dental-care records
extracurricular activities
community-service record
post-secondary institution records
post-secondary degree or credential
current employment status
employer's name
voter registration status

The National Education Goals Panel also notes other "data elements useful for research and school management purposes." Samples include:

highest level of education of student's "primary care-givers"
names of people living in student's household
relationship of those people to the student
nature and ownership of family dwelling
number of moves in the last five years
family's public assistance status and years of benefits
total family income

Many of these data categories were, CPSR reports, also recommended in the public draft of the *Student Data Handbook for Elementary and Secondary Schools*. This publication was written by the Council of Chief State School Officers in order to standardize student records across the nation. In theory, state and local agencies can design their own information systems. However, the handbook encourages agencies to collect as much personal data about students as is feasible — including:

attitudinal test
description of employment permit
evidence verifying date of birth
military service experience
personality test
Social Security number
telephone number of employer
type of dwelling

Who would have access to this dossier about your child and you? CPSR answers:

> *"Officers, employees and agents of local, state and federal educational agencies and private education researchers may be given access to individual student records without student or parent consent, according to the federal Family Educational Rights and Privacy Act of 1974 (20 USC 1232g) and related federal regulations (34 CFR 99.3)."*

This move to share your family business with virtually every bureaucrat in the nation is described in *Together We Can*, a book published jointly by the U.S. Department of Education and the U.S. Department of Health and Human Services. CPSR reports that this book speaks hopefully of "overcoming the confidentiality barrier."

What do you think Big Brother will do with this information about you and your children? Here is one example, again provided by CPSR:

"In Kennewick, Washington, over 4,000 kindergarten through fourth graders were rated by their teachers on how often they lie, cheat, sneak, steal, exhibit a negative attitude, [and] act aggressively, and whether they are rejected by their peers. The scores, with names attached, were sent to a private psychiatric center under contract to screen for 'at-risk' students who might benefit from its programs. All of this was done without the knowledge and consent of the children or their parents."

It is easy to imagine school officials interviewing children about their parents' sexual, political, and economic views — then giving the resulting data to whomever they wish. According to recent polls, only about 20 percent of the American people have confidence in the United States Congress. If we do not trust the people whom we vote into office, why should we give faceless local, state, and federal bureaucrats more power over our personal lives than we give our elected officials?

The authors of the CPSR/Seattle report believe that schools and other agencies should minimize the collection, distribution, and retention of personal data. Students and/or their parents should decide who has access to detailed personal information.

The FBI's Digital Telephony Proposal

Starting in 1991, the FBI (Federal Bureau of Investigation) began publicly stating that technological changes might hinder law enforcement's ability to conduct authorized wiretapping. For instance, the FBI questioned its own capability to monitor telephone calls transmitted over fiber-optic cables using new digital protocols. In response, the FBI began lobbying Congress for new legislation to make it easier for law enforcement to wiretap American citizens. The FBI called this "Digital Telephony" legislation.

On September 18, 1992, the Electronic Frontier Foundation (EFF) issued a now-historic report called *An Analysis of the FBI Digital Telephony Proposal*. Prepared in coalition with organizations ranging from the American Civil Liberties Union to AT&T, and Sun Microsystems.

This report concluded that:

> *"Although the FBI proposal is described as relating to 'digital telephony,' it actually applies to all forms of communication, including all computer networks. The proposal requires that equipment be designed to give access to communications on a "concurrent" basis, regardless of the mobility of a target, in isolation from messages being exchanged by any other persons. These requests may have complex and differing application in different contexts, but they would certainly introduce additional costs and substantial uncertainties for both equipment manufacturers and everyone who offers messaging service to others."*

How big would such a re-engineering job be? The EFF report suggests that the statutory language of the FBI proposal could turn out to require redesign or expensive alteration of:

1. Public electronic-mail systems, like those offered by MCI, AT&T, and a host of other companies and individuals.

2. All telephone switches, and the sophisticated equipment used by long-distance carriers.

3. Software used by online information services like Prodigy, GEnie, CompuServe, America Online, and many others.

4. Local area networks linking all kinds of computers — operated by small businesses, colleges and universities, and many other types of organizations — including links into these systems from other homes and offices.

5. PBXs owned by small and large businesses.

6. High-speed data networks that connect workstations with mainframes and supercomputers — as well as those carrying message traffic across the Internet.

7. Radio-based and cellular communications systems, including pocket telephones, and computers with radio-based modems.

8. The thousands of small personal computers-owned by businesses, hobbyists, local governments, and political organizations — that exchange communications with others via computer bulletin boards.

9. Private metropolitan "wide-area communications systems" used by businesses such as large banks.

10. Satellite uplink and downlink equipment, supporting radio and television transmissions, and other communications.

11. Air-to-ground equipment serving general-aviation and commercial aircraft.

In short the "Digital Telephony" proposal, as existed in 1992, would have required that we (taxpayers and manufacturers) pay to redesign large parts of the telecommunications industry in order to aid FBI wiretaps. All this for roughly 1,000 authorized wiretaps per year? This would make wiretapping one of the most expensive enterprises on Earth! Surely we can find more cost-effective solutions to satisfy the legitimate hunt for a thousand thugs.

Would this "Digital Telephony" proposal really help protect our security and privacy? Suppose that every electronics manufacturer had to design a "back door" to let the FBI monitor the Sicilian Mafia, the Medellin cocaine cartel, or the Texas Vegetarian Party. Imagine how many people would know about that back door. How long would it take before a black market developed to peddle keys to the back door? The military invented automatic weapons to "protect" us; now hoodlums drive around our city streets with these guns, shooting law-abiding citizens like flies. The government invented nuclear weapons to "protect" us; now the world is living under an umbrella of fear that psychotics will get these weapons. And now we are told that potential surveillance of 250 million Americans will "protect" us. From whom? Who will use this surveillance against us tomorrow as they use guns and bombs against others today? This central issue needs to be part of any real-world legislation.

In Summer 1994, the Electronic Privacy Information Center (EPIC) obtained a copy of a new draft (July 19, 1994) of the FBI's Digital Telephony proposal. This draft was written by staff members of the House and Senate Judiciary Committees and was the result of negotiations between telephone companies and the FBI. In EPIC's view:

> *The first major change over earlier drafts is its expanded scope. The bill now covers "telecommunications carriers," which is defined as "any person or entity engaged in the transmission or switching of wire or electronic communications for value for unaffiliated persons, but does not include persons or entities engaged in providing information services." This would appear to be far broader than an earlier draft which covered only common carriers. This bill would cover everything from small BBSs that charge fees to large online services like AOL and Prodigy.*

Here are a few highlights of the latest draft of the FBI's proposal:

◆ The Attorney General would tell carriers the government's specific needs for electronic surveillance. Service providers would have four years to either provide such surveillance capabilities or face civil fines for non-compliance.

◆ Carriers are not compelled to decrypt communications that you have encrypted unless the carrier provided you with the encryption method and has the key to decrypt the message.

◆ The Attorney General and other law-enforcement agencies will meet with industry associations to develop standards for surveillance capabilities. If there is a dispute over standards, or if the bodies fail to issue standards, any person can petition the Federal Communications Commission (FCC) to establish standards. The FCC can impose fees for conducting such rule-making.

◆ The courts could impose civil fines of up to $10,000 per day for non-compliance.

◆ To pay for the mandated redesigns, taxpayers will be billed $500 million for fiscal years 1995 through 1998. After 1999, "sums as may be necessary to carry out the purposes" will be charged to the taxpayers.

As of this writing, negotiations are continuing between the FBI, industry representatives, and Congressional staff over the text of the bill. If you want to participate in this debate, see the Appendix to find out how to contact EFF or EPIC.

(Update: *After this book was written, a Digital Telephony Bill was passed by the United States House of Representatives and by the Senate. This is by no means the end of the war to limit your privacy. Funding, and probably legal, battles will surround this legislation. Get involved!*)

Do You Want a National ID?

Imagine a world in which a Washington, D.C. bureaucrat has "fingertip" access to your entire employment history, medical records, vacation itineraries, and video-rental choices, just by pushing one button.

In Summer, 1994, the *CBS Evening News* reported that the National Commission on Immigration endorsed a national identity card. This commission, headed by former Texas Congresswoman Barbara Jordan, was established by the 1990 Immigration Reform Act. The proposed card would be used to validate work eligibility and to simplify transactions with the government. Earlier, in 1993, President Clinton had proposed a national health card — although the White House claimed that it did not want this document to be used as a general identification card.

Once again, the idea of an American ID card has surfaced. Roughly 80 nations — including Iraq and North Korea — have national ID cards. This popularity is not much of a recommendation. Many countries are de facto police states in which anyone accused of a crime is considered *guilty until proven innocent*. National identity cards are forced upon their citizens, not chosen by them! Some countries such as Australia, Canada, New Zealand, Sweden, and the United Kingdom do *not* have national ID cards. It is worth noting that these countries have the best tradition for assuming that people are *innocent until proven guilty*.

Who wants a national ID card? Illegal immigration is the latest rallying point for supporters of such a document. U.S. Senator Dianne Feinstein of California, a Democrat, and California Governor Pete Wilson, a Republican, have flirted with a national ID. California is said to be overflowing with illegal immigrants; some people estimate that 1,500,000 illegal immigrants live in the state — twice the population of San Francisco — with the total growing daily. California taxpayers, who have no control over federal immigration policies, must pay medical, educational, and welfare bills for noncitizens. This situation has created a great deal of anger. Feinstein and Wilson hope that a national ID will help American agencies identify illegal immigrants and stop them from getting such taxpayer-supported benefits. This opinion is shared by ID-card advocates in New York, Texas, Florida, and other states heavily populated with illegal aliens.

There is a lot of irony involved in this issue. The U.S. government has shown no resolve to keep illegal immigrants from crossing the border into America. Now that millions of men, women, and children are here illegally in search of freedom, Washington wants to restrict American citizens' privacy in order to hunt down and prosecute noncitizens.

What might a national ID card look like? California Democratic Congressman Anthony Beilenson submitted legislation that would create a "counterfeit-proof" Social Security card. This card might include your photograph and your fingerprints. Barbara Jordan, chair of the National Commission on Immigration Reform, notes that currently, "For $25, any illegal immigrant can purchase a counterfeit driver's license and documentation card." Advocates want high-tech "smart" cards that include all kinds of data about you and are therefore harder to forge.

Why Would You Use an Identity Card?

Advocates claim you would use it only for a specific function — say, to prove your work eligibility to a prospective employer. Skeptics point out that the original Social Security number was ushered in with similar promises. Martin Anderson, a senior fellow at the Hoover Institution, notes: "Once you've got this handy card set up, the temptation will be to use it." David Banisar, a policy analyst with EPIC (Electronic Privacy Information Center) adds: "In every instance where these cards have been tried, we've seen a process of 'function creep,' in which the card begins to serve a range of new and unintended purposes." Anderson of the Hoover Institution continues:

```
"[Suppose] one has to present an ID to buy a
gun. By linking the national ID card to com-
puterized criminal records, we could do
instant background checks to weed out felons
who can't legally buy a gun. . .One can think
of any number of purposes that sound worthy
to someone, that these cards can be used for,
if we're willing to sacrifice privacy."
```

Will these ID cards stop criminals, or just invade the privacy of law-abiding people? The Social Security Administration admits that high-quality counterfeits will be on the streets in short order. The Secret Service admits that high-quality counterfeit currency is common around the globe. Bankers admit that bogus charge-cards are commonplace. The State Department admits that making phony passports is a lucrative business. In short, the idea that identity cards will stop crime is an adolescent illusion.

Clearly, identity cards will threaten law-abiding citizens' privacy. I suspect that if a national ID is introduced, even millions of law-abiding citizens will help create an underground market for fake cards. David Banisar of EPIC expresses a mainstream sentiment when he observes:

```
"I can see instances where I would want a fake
card, not because I'd do anything illegal, but
simply because I want to protect my privacy. I
```

```
don't see that it's anyone's business which
hotels I stay in or what stores I shop at."
```

Why don't we have a national ID card in America now? The basic reason is that America is a nation of immigrants. People came here from all over the world to escape their pasts and to build a better future.

When Russian dishwashers came to the U.S., they changed their last names and dreamed of starting their own restaurants. They did not want people telling them, "You're just a dishwasher from Russia," for the rest of their lives. They wanted to define *themselves*. When settlers moved from New England to the West, they did so to improve their lives. We do not have a national ID because we do not want everyone to define us by our grandparents and our childhoods. We want the chance to make our own mistakes and to create our own successes. The vast majority of all new businesses fail.

The vast majority of all successful people have failed many times. The entrepreneurial, risk-taking spirit that has *made* America will not survive if we have to carry around a national ID, hooked into computers, that records every mistake that we have made — and makes records of all those errors available to every non-risk-taking bureaucrat who is following the politically-correct fashions of the minute.

Money magazine (July 1994) published an article entitled "Escape from America," which revealed that one-fourth of all Americans who earn more than $50,000 a year have thought about leaving the U.S. for better opportunities elsewhere! According to the U.S. Immigration and Naturalization Service, roughly 250,000 people *emigrate* from the U.S. each year. These people tend to be much better educated than the people who *immigrate* into the U.S. For example, a 1990 U.S. — Canada government study shows that American immigrants to Canada were nearly 50 percent more likely to hold college degrees than the general U.S. population or than Canadian immigrants moving to America. *Forbes* magazine did a recent cover story about some of America's wealthiest people who are fleeing America for more opportunities elsewhere.

If America adopts a national ID (and continues its escalating attack against privacy), Uncle Sam will be saying loudly and clearly, "The American frontier spirit is over." This might lead to a further "brain drain" on America that will accompany the ongoing flight of capital and jobs away from America. Such flights of talented citizens happened to Germany in the 1930s, to England in the 1960s, and is happening to Russia in the 1990s. It can happen here!

There have been many attempts over the decades to sneak a national ID past the American public. For instance, Congress rejected proposals by Senator Alan Simpson of Wyoming (in 1986 and 1990) to require ID cards for employment. In addition, Martin Anderson of the Hoover Institution — who is a former aide to President Reagan, reports that Reagan considered and rejected a similar card in 1981.

If you are interested in this issue, you might contact EPIC in Washington, D.C. (see the Appendix). This organization is working to stop a national ID card in coalition with Privacy International, a group that has led successful campaigns to stop identity cards in Australia, New Zealand, and the Philippines.

A Prototypical National ID:

Your Social Security Number and How to Protect It

Although Congress has rejected attempts to explicitly introduce a national ID card, these victories for privacy have been only partial. To find a prototype of a national ID, you need look no further than the Social Security card in your wallet.

At this moment, the government is tracking every law-abiding American citizen of working age by his or her Social Security number (SSN). The SSN has also become a de facto universal identifier for other institutions to use in collecting data about us. In addition, many institutions use the number as our "security" password, even though an individual's SSN is trivial to intercept.

What shall we do to prevent abuse of the information linked to our SSNs? For answers, I have turned to Chris Hibbert, an activist at CPSR who has studied the SSN issue (See "Chris Hibbert of CPSR Speaks Out" sidebar).

(Note: *The accompanying sidebar about Social Security numbers was written — and is regularly circulated on the Internet — by Chris Hibbert, not by André Bacard.*)

Chris Hibbert of CPSR Speaks Out

Many people are concerned about the number of organizations asking for their Social Security Numbers. They worry about invasions of privacy and the oppressive feeling of being treated as just a number. Unfortunately, I can't offer any hope about the dehumanizing effects of identifying you with your numbers. I can try to help you keep your Social Security number from being used as a tool in the invasion of your privacy.

Surprisingly, government agencies are reasonably easy to deal with; private organizations are much more troublesome. Federal law restricts the agencies at all levels of government that can demand your number, and a fairly complete disclosure is required even if use of your number is voluntary. There are no comparable Federal laws restricting the uses non-government organizations can make of it, or compelling them to tell you anything about their plans. Some states have recently enacted regulations on collection of SSNs by private entities. With private institutions, your main recourse is refusing to do business with anyone whose terms you don't like. They, in turn, are allowed to refuse to deal with you except on those terms.

Short History

Social Security numbers were introduced by the Social Security Act of 1935. They were originally intended to be used only by the Social Security program. In 1943, Roosevelt signed Executive Order 9397, which required federal agencies to use the number when creating new record-keeping systems. In 1961, the IRS began to use it as a taxpayer ID number. The Privacy Act of 1974 required authorization for government agencies to use SSNs in their databases, and required disclosures (detailed below) when government agencies request the number. Agencies which were already using SSN as an identifier before January 1, 1975, were allowed to continue using it. The Tax Reform Act of 1976 gave authority to state or local tax, welfare, driver's-license, or motor-vehicle registration authorities to use the number in order to establish identities. The Privacy Protection Study Commission of 1977 recommended that Executive Order 9397 be repealed, after some agencies referred to it as their authorization to use SSNs. I don't know whether it was repealed, but no one seems to have cited EO 9397 as their authorization recently.

Several states use the SSN as a driver's-license number, while others record it on applications and store it in their database. Some states that routinely use it on the license will make up another number if you insist. According to the terms of the Privacy Act, any states that have a space for it on the application forms should have a disclosure notice. Many don't, and until someone takes them to court, they aren't likely to change. (Though New York recently agreed to start adding the notice on the basis of a letter written by a reader of this blurb.)

The Privacy Act of 1974 (Pub. L. 93-579) requires that any federal, state, or local government agency that requests your Social Security number has to tell you four things:

continued

1: Whether disclosure of your Social Security number is required or optional,

2: What statute or other authority they have for asking for your number,

3: How your Social Security number will be used if you give it to them, and

4: The consequences of failure to provide an SSN.

In addition, the Act says that only Federal law can make use of the Social Security number mandatory. So anytime you're dealing with a government institution and you're asked for your Social Security number, just look for the Privacy Act Statement. If there isn't one, complain and don't give your number. If the statement is present, read it. If it says giving your Social Security number is voluntary, you'll have to decide for yourself whether to fill in the number.

Private Organizations

The guidelines for dealing with non-governmental institutions are much more tenuous. Most of the time, private organizations that request your Social Security number can get by quite well without your number, and if you can find the right person to negotiate with, they'll willingly admit it. The problem is finding that right person. The person behind the counter is often told no more than "get the customers to fill out the form completely."

Most of the time, you can convince them to use some other number. Usually the simplest way to refuse to give your Social Security number is simply to leave the designated space blank. One of the times when this isn't a strong enough statement of your desire to conceal your number is when dealing with institutions which have direct contact with your employer. Most employers have no policy against revealing your Social Security number; they apparently believe that it must be an unintentional slip when an employee doesn't provide an SSN to everyone who asks.

Public utilities (gas, electric, phone, etc.) are considered to be private organizations under the laws regulating SSNs. Most of the time they ask for an SSN, and aren't prohibited from asking for it, but they'll usually relent if you insist. Ask to speak to a supervisor, insist that they document a corporate policy requiring it, ask about alternatives, ask why they need it, and suggest alternatives.

Lenders and Borrowers

Banks and credit-card issuers, and various others, are required by the IRS to report the SSNs of account holders to whom they pay interest or charge interest, and to report it to the IRS. If you don't tell them your number, you will probably either be refused an account or be charged a penalty such as withholding of taxes on your interest.

Most banks send your name, address, and SSN to a company called ChexSystems when you open an account. ChexSystems keeps a database of people whose accounts have been

continued

terminated for fraud or chronic insufficient funds in the past five years. ChexSystems is covered by the Fair Credit Reporting Act, and the bank is required to let you know if it refuses to open your account and a report from ChexSystems was a factor. You can also send a letter to ChexSystems directly and request a copy of your report.

Many banks, brokerages, and other financial institutions have started implementing automated systems to let you check your balance. All too often, they are using your SSN as the Personal Information Number (PIN) that lets you access to your personal account information. If your bank does this to you, write them a letter pointing out how common it is for the people with whom you have financial business to know your SSN. Ask them to change your PIN, and if you feel like doing a good deed, ask them to stop using the SSN as a default identifier for their other customers. Some customers will believe that there's some security in it, and will be insufficiently protective of their account numbers.

Sometimes banks provide for a customer-supplied password, but are reluctant to advertise it. The only way to find out is to ask if they'll let you provide a password. (This is reportedly true of Citibank Visa: e.g., they ask for a phone number, but are willing to accept any password.)

When buying (and possibly refinancing) a house, most banks will now ask for your Social Security number on the Deed of Trust. This is because the Federal National Mortgage Association recently started requiring it. The fine print in their regulations admits that some consumers won't want to give their number, and allows banks to leave it out when pressed to. [It first recommends getting it on the loan note, but then admits that it's already on various other forms that are a required part of the package, so they already know it. The Deed is a public document, so there are good reasons to refuse to put it there, even though all parties to the agreement already have access to your number.]

Insurers, Hospitals, Doctors

No laws require medical service providers to use your Social Security number as an ID number (except for services provided under Medicare, Medicaid, etc.). They often use it because it's convenient or because your employer uses it to identify employees to its group health plan. In the latter case, you have to get your employer to change their policies. Often, the people who work in personnel departments assume that the employer or insurance company requires use of the SSN, when that's not really the case. When a previous employer asked for my SSN for an insurance form, I asked them to try to find out if they had to use it. After a week, they reported that the insurance company had gone along with my request to substitute a different number, and told me what number to use. Blood banks also ask for the number, but are willing to do without if pressed on the issue. After I asked politely and persistently, the blood bank I attend agreed that they didn't have any use for the number. They've now expunged my SSN from their database, and they seem to have taught their receptionists not to request the number.

continued

Most insurance companies share access to old claims through an organiation called the Medical Information Bureau (MIB). If your insurance company uses your SSN, other insurance companies will have a much easier time finding out about your medical history. You can get a copy of the file MIB keeps on you by writing to Medical Information Bureau, P.O. Box 105, Essex Station, Boston, MA 02112. Their phone number is (617)426-3660.

If an insurance agent asks for your Social Security number in order to "check your credit," point out that the policy will automatically be invalid anyway if your check bounces or your payment is late. They don't need to know what your credit is like, just whether you've paid them.

Children

The Family Support Act of 1988 (Pub. L. 100-485) requires states to require parents to give their Social Security Numbers in order to get a birth certificate issued for a newborn. The law allows the requirement to be waived for "good cause," but there's no indication of what may qualify.

The IRS requires taxpayers to report SSNs for dependents over one year of age, but the requirement can be avoided if you're prepared to document the the child's existence by other means, if challenged. The law on this can be found at 26 USC 6109. The penalty for not giving a dependent's number is only $5. Several people have reported that they haven't provided SSNs for their dependents for several years, and haven't been challenged by the IRS.

Universities and Colleges

Universities that accept federal funds are subject to the Family Educational Rights and Privacy Act of 1974 (the "Buckley Amendment"), which prohibits them from giving out personal information on students without permission. There is an exception for directory information, which is limited to names, addresses, and phone numbers; and another exception for release of information to the parents of minors. There is no exception for Social Security numbers, so covered Universities aren't allowed to reveal students' numbers without their permission. In addition, state universities are bound by the requirements of the Privacy Act, which requires them to provide the disclosures mentioned above. If they use the SSN in ways that aren't covered by the disclosure, they are in violation of the Act.

Why SSNs Are a Bad Choice for UIDs in Databases

Database designers continue to introduce the Social Security Number as the key, or universal identifier (UID), when putting together a new database or when reorganizing an old one. Some of the qualities that are (often) useful in a key — qualities that people think they are getting from the SSN — are Uniqueness, Universality, Security, and Identification. When designing a database, it is instructive to consider which of these qualities are actually important in your application; many designers unwisely assume that they are all useful for every application, when in fact each is occasionally a drawback. The SSN provides

continued

none of these qualities, so designs predicated on the assumption that it does provide them will fail in a variety of ways.

Uniqueness

Many people assume that Social Security Numbers are unique. They were intended by the Social Security Administration (SSA) to be unique, but the SSA didn't take sufficient precautions to ensure that they would be so. They have several times given a previously-issued number to someone with the same name and birth date as the original recipient, thinking it was the same person asking again. There are a few numbers that were used by thousands of people because they were on sample cards shipped in wallets by those wallets' manufacturers. (One is given below.)

The passage of immigration reform legislation in 1986 caused an increase in the duplicate use of SSNs. Since the SSN is now required for employment, illegal immigrants must find a valid name/SSN pair in order to fool both the INS and the IRS long enough to collect a paycheck. When you can't cross-check your database with the SSA, using the SSN as an identifier means you can count on getting some false numbers mixed in with the good ones.

Universality

Not everyone has a Social Security Number. Foreigners are the primary exception, but many children don't get SSNs until they're in school. The numbers were only designed to cover people who were eligible for Social Security.

Identification

Few people ever ask to see anyone's Social Security card; they believe whatever number you recite. The ability to recite the number provides little firm evidence that you're associated with the number in anyone else's database.

There's little reason to carry your card with you anyway. It isn't a good form of identification, and if your wallet is lost or stolen, it provides another way for the thief to hurt you — especially if any of your banks use the SSN as your PIN.

Security

The card is not at all forgery-resistant, even assuming anyone did ask to see it. The numbers don't have any redundancy (no check-digits), so any nine-digit number in the range of numbers that have been issued is a valid number. It's relatively easy to inadvertently copy the number incorrectly, and there's no automatic way to tell that you've done so.

In most cases, there is no cross-checking whatsoever that a Social Security number is valid. Credit-card and checking-account numbers are checked against a database almost

continued

every time they are used; and if you write down someone's phone number incorrectly, you find out the first time you try to use it.

Why You Should Resist Requests for Your SSN

When you give out your number, you are providing access to information about yourself. You're providing access to information that you don't have the ability or the legal right to correct or rebut. You're providing access to data that is irrelevant to most transactions, but that will occasionally trigger prejudice.Worst of all, since you provided the key (and did so "voluntarily") all the information discovered under your number will be presumed to be true, to really be about you, and to be relevant.

A major problem with using SSNs as identifiers is that this makes it hard to control levels of access to personal information. Even assuming that you want someone to be able to find out some things about you, there's no reason to believe that you want to make all records concerning yourself available. When multiple record systems are all keyed by the same identifier, and all are intended to be easily accessible to some users, it becomes difficult to allow someone access to some of the information about a person while restricting them from other information.

Unfortunately, far too many organizations assume that anyone who presents your SSN must be you. When more than one person uses the same number, it clouds up the records. If someone intended to hide their activities, it's likely that the results will look bad on whichever record they show up on. Even when this SSN confusion happens accidentally, its discovery can be unexpected, embarrassing, or worse. How do you prove that you weren't the one using your number when the record was made?

What You Can Do to Protect Your Number

If, despite your having written "Refused" in the box for Social Security Number, your SSN still shows up on the forms someone sends back to you (or worse, on the ID card they issue), your recourse is to write letters or make phone calls. Start politely, explaining your position and expecting them to understand and cooperate. If that doesn't work, there are several more things to try:

1: Talk to people higher up in the organization. This often works simply because the organization has a standard way of dealing with requests not to use the SSN, and the first person you deal with just hasn't been around long enough to know what it is.

2: Enlist the aid of your employer. You have to decide whether talking to someone in Personnel, and possibly trying to change corporate policy, is going to get back to your supervisor and affect your job.

3: Threaten to complain to a consumer-affairs bureau. Most newspapers can get a quick response. Ask for their "Action Line" or equivalent. If you're dealing with a local govern-

continued

ment agency, look in the state or local government section of the phone book under "Consumer Affairs." If it's a federal agency, your congressmember may be able to help.

4: Insist that they document a corporate policy requiring the number. When someone can't find a written policy or doesn't want to push hard enough to get it, they'll often realize that they don't know what the policy is, and that they've just been following tradition.

5: Ask what they need it for and suggest alternatives. If you're talking to someone who has some independence, and who would like to help, they will sometimes admit that they know the reason the company wants it — and you can satisfy that requirement a different way.

6: Tell them you'll take your business elsewhere (and follow through if they don't cooperate).

7: If it's a case where you've gotten service already, but someone insists that you have to provide your number in order to have a continuing relationship, you can choose to ignore the request, in hopes that they'll forget or find another solution before you get tired of the interruption.

If someone absolutely insists on getting your Social Security number, you may want to give a fake number. There are legal penalties for providing a false number when you expect to gain some benefit from it. A federal court of appeals ruled that using a false SSN to get a driver's license violates federal law.

There are a few good choices for "anonymous" numbers. Making one up at random is a bad idea, as it may coincide with someone's real number and cause them some amount of grief. It's better to use a number like 078-05-1120, which was printed on "sample" cards inserted in thousands of new wallets sold in the '40s and '50s. It's been used so widely that both the IRS and SSA recognize it immediately as bogus — while most clerks haven't heard of it.

There are several patterns that have never been assigned, and that therefore don't conflict with anyone's real number. These include numbers with any field all zeroes, and numbers with a first digit of 8 or 9. For more details on the structure of SSNs and on how they are assigned, Internet users can use anonymous ftp to retrieve the file:

```
/cpsr/privacy/ssn/SSN-structure from the
machine cpsr.org.
```

Giving a number with an unused pattern. rather than your own number, isn't very useful if there's anything serious at stake — since it's likely to be noticed. The Social Security Administration explicitly recommends that people showing Social Security cards in advertisements use numbers in the range 987-65-4320 through 987-65-4329.

If you're designing a database (or have an existing one) that uses SSNs, and want to use numbers other than SSNs, you should make your identifiers use some pattern other than nine digits. You can make the numbers longer or shorter than that, or can include letters somewhere inside. That way no one will mistake the identifier for an SSN.

continued

The Social Security Administration recommends that you request a copy of your file from them every few years to make sure that your records are correct (i.e., that your income and "contributions" are being recorded for you, and that no one else's are.) As a result of a recent court case, the SSA has agreed to accept corrections of errors when there isn't any contradictory evidence, where SSA has records for the year before or after the error, and where the claimed earnings are consistent with earlier and later wages. (*San Jose Mercury News*, May 14, 1992, p. 6A) Call the Social Security Administration at (800)772-1213 and ask for Form 7004 (Request for Earnings and Benefit Estimate Statement).

When All Else Fails (Getting a Replacement Number)

The Social Security Administration (SSA) will occasionally issue a replacement SSN. The most common justification is that the SSA or the IRS has mixed together earnings records from more than one person, and that since one of the people can't be located, it's necessary to issue a new number to the other. The SSA tries very hard to contact the person who is using the number incorrectly before resorting to this process.

There are a few other situations that the SSA accepts as justifying a new number. The easiest is if the existing number contains the sequences 666 or 13, which some people consider objectionable or unlucky. (These digits need to be consecutive, according to SSA's policy manual, but may be separated by hyphens.) You apparently don't have to prove that your religious objection is sincere. Other commonly accepted complaints include harassment, sequential numbers assigned to family members, or serious impact on your credit history that you've tried to clear up without success.

In all cases, the process includes an in-person interview, at which you have to establish your identity and show that you are the original assignee of the number. The decision is normally made in the local office. If the problem is with a credit bureau's records, you have to show that someone else continues to use your number, and that you tried to get the credit bureau to fix your records but were not successful. When the SSA does issue a new number, the new records are linked to the old ones. (Unless you can convince them that your life might be endangered by such a link.)

There are a few justifications that the SSA doesn't accept at all: attempting to avoid legal responsibilities, poor credit record which is your own fault, lost SSN card (without evidence that someone else has used it), or use of the number by government agencies or private companies.

The only justification the SSA accepts for canceling the issuance of an SSN is that the number was assigned under their Enumeration at Birth program (wherein SSNs are assigned when birth certificates are issued) without the parent's consent. In this case, the field officer is instructed to try very hard to convince the parent that getting the number revoked is futile, but to give in when the parent is persistent.

continued

US Passports

The application form for U.S. passports (DSP-11 12/87) requests a Social Security number, but gives no Privacy Act notice. There is a reference to "Federal Tax Law" and a misquotation of Section 6039E of the 1986 Internal Revenue Code, claiming that the section requires that you provide your name, mailing address, date of birth, and Social Security number. The referenced section only requires "TIN (SSN)," where "TIN" is a "Taxpayer Identification Number"; and it requires that it be sent to the IRS and not to the Passport office. It appears that when you apply for a passport, you can refuse to reveal your SSN to the passport office, and instead mail a notice to the IRS giving only your SSN (other identifying info. optional) and notifying them that you are applying for a passport.

Aren't Computer Files and E-Mail Already Safe?

" E-mail is more like a postcard than a sealed letter."

~ Mark Rotenberg, Director, Electronic Privacy Information Center

~

Our personal computer files are not really very safe. Anybody can break into our home or office, turn on our computer, and copy our files. People who use laptop computers are particularly at risk, because these small machines are easy to steal or lose. The only way to protect these files, before they fall into the wrong hands, is to routinely encrypt files on your computer. Then, if someone steals your material, the thief will find nothing but unintelligible garbage. I'll discuss encryption in great detail later.

E-mail is notoriously unsafe. It is truly mind-boggling that millions of people use e-mail without realizing or caring about this simple fact. Typical e-mail travels through many computers. The people who run these computers can read, copy, and store our mail. Many voyeurs get their kicks out of intercepting mail. As a result, sending business, legal, and personal mail through computers is even less confidential (with all due respect to my colleague Marc Rotenberg) than sending the same material on a postcard.

Charles Piller, in his excellent *Macworld* article entitled "Bosses With X-Ray Eyes," reports on a study of Macintosh software that reached the following conclusions:

If your office network runs on a full-featured network operating system, like Novell NetWare or Microsoft LAN Manager, and is run by a technically astute manager, then your Macintosh and all data transferred from it is an open book. Working from an office across the room or across the country, a network manager — particularly in server-based local area networks — can eavesdrop on virtually every aspect of your networked computing environment with or without your approval or even knowledge. The manager can view the contents of data files and electronic-mail messages, overwrite private passwords, and audit your time and activities on the network.

All the major electronic-mail and groupware products that combine messaging, file management, and scheduling (such as WordPerfect Office) allow the network administrator to change passwords at any time, then read, delete, or alter any messages on the server. With few exceptions, network-monitor programs, such as AG Group's LocalPeek, Farallon Computing's Traffic Watch II, and Neon Software's NetMinder, allow astute managers to read files transmitted over the net. In short, these tools are only slightly less invasive than others specifically designed for surveillance and used primarily on mainframe systems.

How much e-mail surveillance occurs? In a *Macworld* survey, roughly twenty five percent of the businesses contacted admitted that they eavesdrop on employees' computer files, e-mail, or voicemail. It is reasonable to assume that e-mail monitoring is widespread in corporations, on Bulletin Board Systems, on college-campus systems, on commercial information services, and on Internet hookup providers.

It is important to note that e-mail can be scanned for key words much more easily than can intercepted telephone calls. Many outspoken Internet users are fully aware of this scanning power. In order to taunt, overwork, or amuse potential eavesdroppers, they sign their messages in ways calculated to set off the maximum number of red flags. Here, in typical cyberspace humor, is an example:

```
John Doe,

President of Doe Associates

[crypto, Kennedy assassination, sex, Warren
Report, terrorism, dope, money laundering,
Mafia, kidnapping, bombs, bribery, CIA, hack-
ers, crackers, KGB, and books.]
```

E-mail is, in short, an ideal invention for mass surveillance. The Eavesdrop Establishment — plus free-lance snoops everywhere — must be thrilled by e-mail; it is their dream come true.

Password Protection: What They Don't Tell You

❝ *LTPass and XLPass were picked as Expert's Favorite Utilities for 1992. This is great news for the absent-minded...* **❞**

~ Richard Scoville, *PC World*

~

Millions of computer users live with the illusion that their word processor or spreadsheet files are "safe" because these software files are protected by a password. This fantasy can be dangerous for your privacy.

Computer companies often voluntarily build *weak* password systems. They do this for two simple reasons: 1) to rescue absent-minded customers and 2) to protect themselves from irate customers. What happens if a WordPerfect or a Paradox user forgets his password? Ultimately, he is unlikely to blame himself. More likely, he will call WordPerfect or Paradox and yell for help. Would you like to explain to a furious customer that he has lost his files because you neglected to foresee his forgetfulness and devise a "back door" to retrieve his lost files? Many first-rate companies take the prudent legal route — rightfully so — and create easy-to-break security systems.

Some computer firms capitalize on this weak security. They market password-recovery software. Typical advertising literature for these software firms uses testimonials from 1) the firms that make weak password systems, 2) customers who lose their passwords, and 3) law-enforcement agents who read confiscated files. In other words, recovery software is marketed to individuals who forget their passwords and to people who want other people's passwords. Ironically, break-your-password ads often say things like this: "Now that our product exists, you can feel perfectly safe using your password!"

Password-recovery products are effective and popular. No doubt, these programs save many people and companies from data disaster. Therefore, it is wise for all intelligent computer users to know about such software. But you should also know that these products can help snoopers "retrieve" passwords that unlock your files.

If you use DataPerfect, Lotus 1-2-3, Microsoft Excel, Microsoft Money, Microsoft Word, Novell Netware, Paradox, PKZip, Professional Write, Quattro Pro, Symantec's Q & A, Symphony, or WordPerfect, you especially might want to contact Access Data Corporation.

RESOURCE BOX

AccessData Corporation

125 South 1025 East
Lindon, Utah 84042
801-785-0363

The Guardians of Cyberspace

Fortunately for democracy, there are many guardians of cyberspace. Thousands of individuals are working to defend and expand computer privacy.

Macworld, MicroTimes, the *New York Times, Playboy, Omni, Scientific American, Wired*, and other periodicals publish pro-privacy articles. In addition, the American Civil Liberties Union, the Association for Computing Machinery, the *Financial Privacy Report*, the Oxford Club, Privacy International, the Privacy Rights Clearinghouse, the Software Publishers' Association, and the Taxpayer Assets Project work on specific aspects of privacy.

This book is written for computer users. Therefore, in the Appendix, I have included detailed descriptions of three guardians of cyberspace that are 1) computer experts, 2) activists, 3) easy to contact, and 4) eager to hear from you. These groups are Computer Professionals for Social Responsibility (CPSR), Electronic Frontier Foundation (EFF), and Electronic Privacy Information Center (EPIC). In addition, I have included the *Privacy Journal* for people who want to know about privacy in a broader context.

I urge you to contact these groups. From them, you can learn everything you ever wanted to know about privacy. Better yet, you can join forces with these colleagues, improve the quality of your life, and help mold history!

Anonymous Remailers

❝Anonymity represents for many people a liberating even more than a threatening phenomenon. ❞

~ Harvey Cox, *The Secular City*

❝You don't have to wait for cryptography to secure complete anonymity on the Net. All you need is the address of a remailer. ❞

~ *Wired* magazine

~

One easy way to privatize your e-mail is to use an *anonymous remailer*. Steven Levy, who writes the "Iconoclast" column for *Macworld* magazine, refers to remailers as a way to "launder" your e-mail. A remailer is a free service that allows you to send anyone an e-mail message without the recipient knowing who sent the message. Let us take an example. Suppose you are surfing the Usenet news groups and you come across one of the following (fictitious) screens:

```
Thu, 20 Oct 1994  06:15:12           alt.privacy           Thread 5 of 8
wi.123@wizvax.com                    Anonymous Contact Service @ Wizvax

I am a battered woman in St. Louis looking for help. Please contact "Victim".
Thank you.

wi.admin@wizvax.com                          (non anonymous mail)
wi.0@wizvax.com        (anonymous mail, no replies)
uunet!wizvax.com!{wi.admin,wi.0}

Alt-Z FOR HELP | ANSI-BBS | FDX | 9600 N81 | LOG CLOSED | TERMINAL | ON-LINE
```

or:

```
Thu, 20 Oct 1994 10:48:21       alt.privacy        Thread 7 of 8
an123@anon.penet.fi             Anonymous contact service

I am a battered woman in St. Louis looking for help. Please contact "Victim".
Thank you.

To find out more about the anon service, send mail to help@anon.penet.fi.
Due to the double-blind, any mail replies to this message will be
anonymized,
and an anonymous id will be allocated automatically. You have been warned.
Please report any problems, inappropriate use etc. to admin@anon.penet.fi.

Alt-Z FOR HELP  |  ANSI-BBS  |  FDX  |  9600 N81  |  LOG CLOSED  |  TERMINAL  |  ON-LINE
```

You have just encountered an anonymous remailer. The latter service, run by Johan Helsingius, is the most popular anonymous service on the Internet. Mr. Helsingius is the president of Penetic, a Helsinki, Finland company that helps businesses connect to the Internet. Note that the "fi" in his address stands for Finland. His "an@anon.penet.fi" return addresses are common in controversial conferences and where anonymity is required. For example, it could be suicidal for Victim, the battered woman, to post her real name.

Suppose you want to respond to the (fictitious) battered woman calling out for help. You can write her a message and e-mail it to <an123@anon.penet.fi>. Helsingius' computer will strip away your real return address (the header at the top of your e-mail), replace it with a dummy address like <an345@anon.penet.fi>, and forward your message to Victim. Also, Helsingius' computer will notify you that <an345@anon.penet.fi> is your new anonymous address. You can use Helsingius' service to forward letters to anyone, even to persons who do not choose to use his service. Helsingius' computer sends each recipient and mailer detailed information about his system.

Currently there are about 20 active public remailers on the Internet. These remailers tend to come and go. One reason for this is that they take work to set up and maintain; for another, they bring in zero revenue. Some people are perplexed that anonymous services are free. There is a simple answer. How are they going to collect money from people who want maximum secrecy? Ask for a Visa number? It is fair to assume that people set up remailers for personal reasons, which they may or may not care to share with the rest of us. *Wired* magazine interviewer, Joshua Quittner, co-author of the high-tech thriller *Mother's Day*, asked Mr. Helsingius why he runs an anonymous service. Helsingius replied:

"It's important to be able to express certain views without everyone knowing who you are. One of the best examples was the great debate about Caller ID on phones. People were really upset that the person at the receiving end would know who was calling. On things like telephones, people take for granted the fact that they can be anonymous if they want to and they get really upset if people take that away. I think the same thing applies for e-mail."

"Living in Finland, I got a pretty close view of how things were in the former Soviet Union. If you actually owned a photocopier or even a typewriter there you would have to register it and they would take samples of what your typewriter would put out so they could identify it later. That's something I find so appalling. The fact that you have to register every means of providing information to the public sort of parallels it — like saying you have to sign everything on the Net. We always have to be able to track you down."

I have experimented with Helsingius' system, talked with other users, and have no reason to doubt his sincerity.

How safe are anonymous remailers? Clearly, they are probably safer than using your real e-mail address. For most low-security tasks, such as responding to personal advertisements, remailers create little need for paranoia. However, all the best made plans of mice and men have weaknesses. Suppose, for example, that you are a government employee who has just uncovered a nasty bribery scheme in your department. Is it safe to use an anonymous remailer to send evidence to a government whistleblower's e-mail hot line? Here are a few points to consider.

◆ The person who runs your e-mail system might intercept your secret messages to and from the anonymous remailer. This gives him or her evidence that you are an honest employee — which could get you into deep trouble. Honesty can be very expensive. Worse, if the person who runs your e-mail system can demonstrate that your are an anonymous identity, he may be able to use that directly against you.

◆ It is possible that the anonymous remailer is a government sting operation designed to entrap people, or a criminal enterprise designed for blackmail. The person who runs this service might be your boss' tennis partner, or worse. In addition, many privacy proponents assume that the United States government records all e-mail (100%) that crosses U.S. borders. This includes *all* e-mail going to and from remailers such as anon.penet.fi.

◆ Hackers can do magic with computers. One day I received a strange letter from Cambridge, England. This letter had been routed through an anonymous remailer. I say *strange* because this e-mail had very complex headers. Normally, when you answer mail from an anonymous remailer, the remailer will convert your real address into an anonymous address. In ways I do not understand, the Cambridge hacker circumvented this system so that, if I had answered the letter, the hacker would get my real name and address. Fortunately, the guy who runs this remailer posted a note at the bottom of my mail warning me about this security break. It is always possible that hackers (who they're working for, only they know) have broken a remailer security system without anyone's knowledge.

Hard-core privacy freaks do not trust individual anonymous remailers. They write programs that send their secret messages through a dozen or more remailers. This way only the first remailer knows their real address, and the first remailer cannot know the final destination of the e-mail message. In addition, these messages are encrypted so that nobody along the line can read them. If you want to become an expert on remailers, or just to learn the addresses of remailers, go to the **alt.privacy.anon-server** Usenet news group.

Here is a sample screen from that news group:

```
  alt.privacy.anon-server (22T 41A 0K 0H R)              h=help

    1  + 2      Update on my mg5n+alias remailer      Matthew J Ghio
    2  + 2      Remailer shutdown                     Eric Frias
    3  + 5      Annon Remailers Compromised!!         Nate
    4  +        remailer@ds1.wu-wien.ac.at            Steve Harris
    5  +        Please Help!                          shoshana@spider.ll
    6  +        Need Assistance With anon.penet.fi    shoshana@spider.ll
    7  + 3      "New World Order" Remailed Spam       L.Detweiler
    8  +        mail->usenet                          Matthew Ghio
    9  + 2      failed posting                        an144379@anon.pene
   10  +        second test message                   Jim Brophy
   11  + 5      Forgot my password, what do i do ?    Blair F. Joudrey
   12  + 2      List of reliable remailers            Raph Levien
   13  +        ignore testing tomaz's remailer       Anonymous
   14  +        Remailer meeting on IRC..             John A. Perry
   15  +        Anon service at anon@vox.xs4all.nl    Alex de Joode
   16  +        chaos.bsu.edu                         Matthew Ghio

  Alt-Z FOR HELP | ANSI-BBS | FDX | 9600 N81 | LOG CLOSED | TERMINAL | ON-LINE
```

PART TWO

Cryptology:

Roots of the Clipper Chip Controversy

What Is Cryptology ("Crypto")?

❝ *Cryptology has gone public. A field that was once the exclusive domain of governments has become a concern of businesses and individuals.* **❞**

~ David Kahn, *Kahn on Codes*

~

The word *cryptograph* stems from the Greek words *kryptos* and *graphos*, which literally mean "secret" and "writing" respectively. Let us familiarize ourselves with some terminology. *Cryptography* is the art and science of sending disguised messages so that only select people can see through the disguise. For everyone else, the message appears as gibberish. *Cryptanalysis* is the art and science of figuring out what the gibberish means, especially when nobody wants you to do so. *Cryptology* is the study of both cryptography and cryptanalysis. In this non-technical book, I use the word *crypto* as shorthand for cryptology and to refer to cryptographic algorithms and software such as DES and PGP (which we will discuss later).

Here is an example of gibberish that was generated by a computer crypto system.

```
Hdwc6uwcomuvkoebaycesa1yelzwhkkrjhczzyvb09xx7wi0ywn8zu6tk+UjTAO6
DeGhPJf6JLzZHmk0bRSmAAAC7SxTfVUjjgErvWYcfflXh6EbdrFosu3jJ15n0+97
hIS04TNK6+lt4m0zdQ88bsbdlwJVsZA4v+7gzL27WvACFH7PiwBLi3BwtXeYW1
HVBPkVLXjk6P4JThtv8xaSvDpZmpbKBm0/zcx/8m1GQgtzUUFNoTC1ULMoIFZ
0uqcjTJlDzQ3YMoKfy5fxhH2X4KK2RHdyzXrcdJ6du/BnO0nvtKGW+EDUW2ZG
FAB7MBR4/VAEfcQ8QBIysMoNQ2gm/ZHDr489aeB7drgC1YcMdgFDUBkCeDji6
RrV3PqSXkWW
```

To the naked eye, this appears to be a collection of random alpha-numeric characters with a few assorted symbols added. A skilled cryptographer might be able to uncover the logic behind this block of characters and convert this garble back into a message of great value.

A *cryptosystem* is a procedure that allows a person to *encrypt* (scramble) regular writing, called either *cleartext* or *plaintext*, into gobbledygook called *ciphertext*. By reversing the technique, one can *decrypt* (unscramble) the gobbledygook back into the original cleartext. The mathematical formula, or the rules, that allow a person to switch back and forth from cleartext to ciphertext is called a *cipher* or an *algorithm*.

Let us illustrate this terminology with a very easy cipher called simple substitution. Many of us played this substitution game when we were children. Suppose that you and I agree to use the following cipher, algorithm, or formula.

Cipher: a=z, b=x, c=j, d=m, é=b, n=4, r=5

This cipher means that whenever you see the letter "a" you replace it with the letter "z"; you replace the letter "b" with the letter "x", etc.

Suppose we start with the following cleartext.

Cleartext: André Bacard

If you encrypt this cleartext by using the agreed upon cipher, you will generate the following ciphertext.

Ciphertext: Z4m5b xzjzrm

If we decrypt this ciphertext by reversing the cipher (that is by replacing the letter "z" with the letter "a", etc.), we will go back to our cleartext.

Cleartext: André Bacard

The crypto universe is, in a nutshell, a cat-and-mouse game. The sender (the mouse) tries to find a cipher that will enable him to send secret messages (sneak past the cat to eat the cheese). Meanwhile, other clever people (the cats) try to build better mousetraps that will break the mouse's communications system, if not his neck. Over the centuries, people have invented countless ciphers of every imaginable type with inviting names like ENIGMA, IDEA, and LUCIFER. Bruce Schneier's popular technical book, *Applied Cryptography: Protocols, Algorithms, and Source Code in C*, examines many of these algorithms for the mathematically advanced reader.

Cryptology has been around for thousands of years. In fact, written language is cryptic to an illiterate and, for much of human history, only a tiny elite was literate. To depict the intimate relation between language and crypto, here is a brain-teaser. Is the following passage a cleartext or a ciphertext message?

Jean et moi te remercions de ton aimable attention.

If you read French, this sentence is a cleartext message. If you do not read French, you might need a *cryptoanalyst* (in this case, a Parisian with nothing better to do) or MicroTac Software's French Assistant 5 to decrypt (translate) this ciphertext into the English cleartext:

Jean and I thank you for your kind thought.

In World War II, United States intelligence officers employed this crypto/language bond by using American Indians to discuss secrets over telephones. Imagine a German or Japanese spook trying to make sense of an intercepted conversation in Navajo.

Language, and its cousin crypto, has always been a favorite tool for the elites to keep their thoughts away from the masses. In ancient Egypt, there were two well-defined written languages. The priests communicated secretly with hieratic writing, whereas the non-elite used demotic writing. Ancient Romans and Greeks used secret writing — including shorthand. Xenophon, the Greek who wrote Socrates' memoirs, played with rudimentary shorthand four centuries before Christ. Tullius Tyro, who lived in the same house as the immortal Stoic philosopher Cicero, helped spread the use of shorthand in the Roman Empire one century before Christ. For more than a thousand years after Christ, the ruling elite of Europe communicated in Latin, which was indecipherable to the masses, who used "vulgar" languages such as English, French, and German. Fast forwarding to today, one can argue that our technological elite speaks in mathematics, a language that is ciphertext to the common person.

There is nothing intrinsically sinister about using language or crypto to protect sociopolitical power. If it is diabolic, who is going to cast the first stone? Almost everyone uses cryptic language. Computer programmers, lawyers, and professors use jargon to communicate amongst themselves. These professionals also employ obscure language in order to make themselves sound profound. For instance, many of us have read "scholarly" sentences such as this in text books:

```
"Human beings are completely exempt from unde-
sirable behavior patterns only when certain
prerequisites, not satisfied except in a small
percentage of actual cases, have, through some
fortuitous concourse of favorable circum-
stances, whether congenital or environmental,
chanced to combine in producing an individual
in whom many factors deviate from the norm in
a socially advantageous manner."
```

Bertrand Russell, the British thinker, translated this pretentiousness into plain English; "All men are scoundrels, or at any rate almost all. The men who are not must have had unusual luck, both in birth and in their upbringing." On the lower end of the totem pole, the criminal underworld has a rich slang, both so that criminals can network and so that police eavesdroppers will be hard pressed to decipher their crime plans. Additionally, every generation of young people invents their own slang to separate the *in crowd* from outsiders and to be distinct from their parents.

Cryptography as a formal discipline took root in Europe during the Middle Ages. Because crypto is so rooted in language, it was given a big boost by Johann Gutenberg's method of utilizing movable type and the printing press to print large varieties of written material quickly and accurately. The first Gutenberg Bible appeared around 1454. The first book devoted to cryptology was written by Johannes Trithemius, a Benedictine abbot. Called *Polygraphiae* (note the resemblance to the English word "polygraph"), it was published in 1499. David Kahn, the premier expert on the history of cryptology, writes:

> *Johannes Trithemius (1462-1516) seemed to intermingle cryptosystems with angel-assisted methods of long-distance instant communication. In its religious origin, cryptology resembled many other activities, such as drama and music.*

This metaphysical origin of cryptology is in line with Auguste Comte's (he was a founder of sociology) idea that useful human theories pass through three stages: "first, the theological or fictitious, which is provisional; secondly, the metaphysical or abstract, which is transitional; and thirdly, the positive or scientific, which alone is definitive." In any case, *Polygraphiae* was popular enough to merit republishing in Latin in 1518 and in French in 1541. No doubt this book influenced European leaders, who started using formalized crypto to safeguard secrets, especially in diplomatic circles.

Interest in cryptography spread to early America. Thomas Jefferson, the third President of the United States, was an ardent amateur cryptographer. He jointly developed a private crypto system with James Madison, and he invented an elaborate "wheel cypher" that was way ahead of its time. The next time you hear someone say that cryptography should be illegal, or that it is only used for criminal purposes, remember this fascinating fact. Thomas Jefferson has earned the title "Father of American Cryptography"! Another eager cryptographer was Edgar Allan Poe, famous for his macabre short stories. Poe wrote several newspaper articles about riddles, anagrams, and puzzles. In addition, he challenged readers to send him encoded messages, most of which he solved. Poe even wrote a famous story, "The Gold-Bug," about cryptograms. In this story, a South Carolina naturalist finds sketches of a golden beetle on a piece of paper. It turns out that this paper contains a secret message, written in invisible ink, which leads to a pirate's hidden treasures.

Cryptography played a vital role in World War II. By the time this war began, secret writing machines (cipher machines) existed. These machines, which look like fancy typewriters with lots of gears, could produce more complex, reliable ciphertexts than people (prone to error) could make in previous eras. Adolph Hitler's Germany invented and used a famous device, called the Enigma machine, to pass secret messages within in all branches of the Third Reich's military, as well as within its government bureaus. The British knew about the Enigma machine ciphers and secretly built a line of quasi-computers to logically attack the Enigma system. Fortunately for the Allies, the British succeeded. They referred to this captured data by the code name ULTRA. It turns out that ULTRA data greatly helped the allies combat German submarines, Field Marshall Rommel's forces in North America, and in diverse operations after the Normandy invasion in 1944. The Americans were equally adept to break Japanese ciphers, JADE and CORAL, in particular. These crypto breakthroughs largely affected the outcome of battles of the Coral Sea and Midway.

Note that these ciphers were broken by proto-computers. It is widely known that development of computers paralleled rocketry. It is less known, but perhaps as important, that the battle to break cipher machines led to much government support for the creation of our computer world. It is no mere coincidence that the National Security Agency, which is in charge of monitoring and decoding all foreign communications that might impact United States security, is, by some measures, the world's largest buyer of computer hardware. It is also worth noting that many eminent cryptographers were recruited amongst professional linguists.

In the last forty years, as computers have evolved at a breath-taking clip, cryptology has become a highly mathematical field. Computers are so fast, that many ciphers of yesterday can easily be broken by "brute force." Take a simple example of a password (a combination lock, if you will) such as "567345". A computer can guess your passcode by starting at "000001" and trying *every number* until it gets the right one!

Until about 20 years ago, cryptography was used on a systematic ongoing basis by governments only. Both dictators and democrats used crypto to protect military and diplomatic secrets. In recent years, with the rise of computers, many companies have begun to use crypto — mainly to protect trade & financial secrets. Now, the personal computer allows all of us law-abiding citizens to use high-powered crypto to safeguard our computer records and e-mail from criminals, stalkers, and voyeurs.

Crypto is vital to privacy and democracy. Many people use Schwab software to trade stocks over the telephone, use the Internet to send electronic mail, and use electronic voting machines. Crypto can help all of these functions.

First-rate crypto is on the market right now. In the long term, we might need a crypto infrastructure to insure that we have financial, medical, and communications privacy. In the short term, every person reading this page can help protect his or her electronic privacy easily and cheaply.

Where to Meet Cryptologists

Secret codes and ciphers excite many people. A good way to network with knowledgeable individuals who care about cryptography and cryptanalysis is to contact the American Cryptogram Association (ACA). The ACA, founded in 1929, appeals to hobbyists, mathematicians, and computer scientists at all levels. ACA bestows awards, maintains historical archives, and publishes *The Cryptogram* newsletter.

Another place to find cryptographers is to go to the sci.crypt Usenet news group. Here is a sample screen from that news group:

RESOURCE BOX

American Cryptogram Association (ACA)

Contact: William G. Sutton
1 Pidgeon Drive
Wilbraham, MA 01095
413-596-6635

```
sci.crypt (22T 27A 0K 0H R)              h=help

   1 +   Kwik-Crypt                        Ctty Nul
   2 +   safer algo                        Thomas Yip
   3 +3  HDD Encryption?                   Ben Humphreys
   4 +2  IACR Members Please Read          IACR Membership Se
   5 +2  "Enhanced" passwords in WordPerfect  heath@iinet.com.au
   6 +2  Take back the streets             CCLAPP
   7 +   Excel encryption                  Scott Greer
   8 +   IEEE Seminar: Internet Security   Scott Corcoran
   9 +   PGP 2.6.2 now available from MIT    (for U.S. us merriman@metronet.
  10 +   reccomendations for encryping embedded licen  Michael Paul Johns
  11 +   Richard Outerbridge?              W. Kinney
  12 +   long integer                      Roger Simmons
  13 +   source: class longint             Roger Simmons
  14 +   Encryption Books                  Douglas Stieber
  15 +   Need to break StuffIt passwd protection  Lemieux Sebastien
  16 +   Interesting Bookstore             Jim Gillogly

Alt-Z FOR HELP I ANSI-BBS I FDX I 9600 N81 I LOG CLOSED I TERMINAL I ON-LINE
```

The Powers and Limitations of Crypto

Crypto, such as PGP which I shall discuss shortly, never has been, is not, and never will be a Genie to solve all of society's ills. All the encrypted data in the world cannot magically cure cancer, eradicate illiteracy, or end corruption. More to the point, crypto cannot completely solve our privacy problems. Encrypted data cannot stop a greedy bank employee, who can decrypt the data, from selling confidential records. Widespread use of encryption cannot magically force our legislatures to pass pro-privacy laws or our courts to enforce the law.

Realistically, encryption can and will be able to provide users with the following powers:

◆ Authentic, unforgeable digital signatures

◆ Private data files

◆ Private electronic mail

◆ Private financial transactions

◆ Private telephone conversations

All of these powers are practical, important steps towards the reinstatement of our personal privacy.

Most importantly, when people consciously use crypto they tend to think about privacy in other areas of their lives. A Wells Fargo bank ATM in my town recently installed cameras that take full face photographs of every person who uses the ATM. This enables Wells Fargo to match photographs with account numbers. Who do you think will be more likely to understand (and protest) this Orwellian move? A person who uses encryption? Or a person who is oblivious to the computer world? I suspect the former.

What Is High-Quality Crypto?

This section of the book is written as a practical guide to crypto for the average computer user. This user wants results, not esoteric mathematics or polysyllabic jargon. For him or her, high quality crypto software (or hardware), must be:

Error Free and Loss Free. High quality crypto must be able to encrypt cleartext into ciphertext that it can always decrypt back into the identical cleartext. Nobody wants software with "just a few glitches" that loses one file in a hundred, or that picks up or loses a few characters during each encryption\decryption cycle. Thus, high-quality software is thoroughly tested before given to end users.

Easy to use. High quality crypto makes life easier, not harder. A reasonably intelligent user should be able to learn the basic keystroke procedures in a matter of minutes. Some cryptosystems may look beautiful to a mathematician or a software designer, but they are of no practical use to anyone except their inventors. Nobody (more accurately, only a few programmers) wants to spend all day encrypting a file. For one thing, the more complex the software, the easier it is to make a user error.

Produce random ciphertext. High quality crypto produces ciphertext which appears random to all standard statistical tests. Cryptanalysts, with the help of computers, have compiled incredible detailed frequency charts about the English and other languages. For example, they know the frequency patterns for all vowels, consonants, and syllable pairs. In English, the most common letters are (in order) "e", "t", "a", "o", and "n". The least frequent letters are "q", "x", and "z". The first thing a "code breaker" will do with your encrypted message is to count the letters, numbers, and other symbols used and to note with which other letters, numbers, or symbols they occur. If you use a weak program that, say, substitutes one letter for another, the snoop will "break" (decipher) your secret message in a few seconds. Sophisticated cryptographers realize this and choose systems that stump snoops with frequency charts.

"Impossible" to break. High-quality crypto may be breakable in theory, but nobody has been able to break it in practice. To be more precise, nobody has been able to *publicly* demonstrate how to break this crypto. The non-government crypto world is a small circle. You can be sure that if one person demonstrates a way to break John Doe's secret messages, other cryptanalysts will learn the trick shortly thereafter. Sadly, many people use encryption software, which they download from Bulletin Board Systems or that they purchase in software stores, that *does not* protect their files from sophisticated snoops!

(Note: *It is possible that the National Security Agency, the super-secret agency that undoubtedly leads the world in crypto expertise, can break codes that everyone else believes are "impossible" to break.*)

Data Encryption Standard (DES)

The Data Encryption Standard (DES) is the most well-known and a central cryptographic algorithm. Its stature is derived, in part, because DES has been the United States Government's official data encryption standard for use in protecting "sensitive but unclassified" data since late 1976. The government uses other systems for classified data. DES is a "single-key" system, which means that DES uses *the same key* (for instance, "12345") to encrypt and to decrypt a message. DES plays a role in all of our lives, even if we do not know that fact until this moment. In particular, DES is used when banks wire money amongst themselves and when ATM machines communicate with their central computer.

In 1972, the National Bureau of Standards (now called the National Institute of Standards and Technology [NIST]) decided to develop a national cryptographic standard. This bureau had sound reasons. Standards benefit from the economy of scale. It costs much less to build 10,000 encryption devices that do the same thing than to assemble 10,000 unique encryption devices. Also, communications standards are necessary, in some instances, to avoid chaos. Most of us know the nightmare of buying "compatible" computer parts that are incompatible. Anyway, back to DES. The banking system, for example, would be hobbled if the Bank of America and Citicorp used different encryption systems.

The National Bureau of Standards (NBS) solicited proposals for this first-ever, public standard in the May 15, 1973 issue of the *Federal Register*. The NBS stipulated that the standard must be:

- Able to provide a high level of security
- Adaptable for use in diverse applications
- Available to all users
- Completely specified
- Easy to understand
- Efficient to use
- Exportable

The NBS also required something vital. Namely, the security of the standard algorithm must reside in the key; the security should not depend on the secrecy of the algorithm. The NBS wanted a *public standard* that was a *public algorithm* that anybody, including non-government mathematicians and cryptologists could investigate at will. We shall see later that the Clinton White House wants to reverse this earlier public spirit and replace DES with a *secret algorithm* — which forms the cryptographic guts of the notorious Clipper Chip.

The National Bureau of Standards picked DES as its winning algorithm. In 1975, the NBS published the details of DES in the *Federal Register,* and the NBS announced that IBM (which developed DES) would grant a nonexclusive, royalty-free license to make, use, and sell devices that implemented the DES algorithm. On November 23, 1976, DES was authorized for use on all *unclassified* government communications. The word "unclassified" worried many experts who feared that the National Security Agency had an "invisible hand" in creating DES, so that the NSA could break DES from the start. These experts preferred LUCIFER, an algorithm which they considered safer than DES. In any case, DES became and remains the standard. Note that DES has another name, DEA (Data Encryption Algorithm).

DES uses a 56-bit key. What does this mean in English? Think of each bit as a combination lock with two numbers on the lock, zero and one. With 56 such bits, the total number of combinations possible is 2 to the 56th power— which means 2 multiplied by itself 56 times. The first ten numbers in this series are 2, 4, 8, 16, 32, 64, 128, 256, 512, and 1024. Two to the 56th power is an enormous number (roughly 72,058,000,000,000,000). If a computer can try one million combinations per second, it will take that computer over *1,000 years* to try all the possible DES combinations!

In 1976, DES seemed very safe from "brute force" attempts to try every combination. Today, it might be possible for super-computers in the hands of experts to break a 56-bit key in a timely, affordable manner. Because of this possibility, some high-security organizations change their key every hour! I asked Professor Martin Hellman, a cryptologist in the Electrical Engineering Department at Stanford University, about DES in an interview for Computer Professionals for Social Responsibility. Hellman suggested that one way to save DES, to overcome the 56-bit limitation, is to *double* encrypt data with DES. One reason to save DES is that so much hardware and so much data already uses it. Any conversion would be expensive. Other experts insist that DES must be replaced by a new standard. Full information about DES can be ordered from the U.S. Department of Commerce.

The relative documents are:

FIPS PUB 46-2
Data Encryption Standard

FIPS PUB 74
Guidelines for Implementing
and Using the NBS DES

RESOURCE BOX.

U.S. Department of Commerce
National Technical Information service
Springfield, VA 22161

FIPS PUB 81   DES Modes of Operation

FIPS PUB 113   Computer Data Authentication (using DES)

(FIPS means "Federal Information Processing Standard.")

What Is RSA?

RSA is a public-key algorithm which is gaining worldwide acceptance. Unlike the Data Encryption Standard (DES), RSA uses a public key to encrypt data and a second (secret) key to decrypt the same data. This double key permits you to distribute your public key openly, the way you can list your telephone number. Anybody can send encrypted e-mail to you using your public key, but nobody can read your encrypted e-mail without your secret key and an accompanying secret "pass phrase." Similarly, anybody can call your telephone number, but only you can answer your telephone number. This double key feature makes RSA very practical and popular. RSA is essential to PGP (Phil Zimmermann's Pretty Good Privacy software), which I'll discuss in great detail. Once you practice using PGP, you will discover that public keys, private keys, and pass phrases are very practical tools.

The biggest security dilemma in cryptology has been how to secretly transfer and store keys. Suppose that you and I agree to use DES in order to exchange encrypted business correspondence. How do we swap the key? Historically, governments have swapped keys by paying a trusted courier to carry the key in a briefcase. This is a very expensive method. What if I mail you the key? The postal service is neither safe nor fast. What if I e-mail you the key? As we have seen, it is trivial to intercept e-mail. It is hard enough to get one key safely to you. If I desire to carry on encrypted correspondence with ten other persons, I could spend half of my life trying to get the right keys safely to the correct persons. This is very unpractical. RSA solves this problem.

In 1976, Professor Martin Hellman and researcher Whitfield Diffie at Stanford University published an article which proposed a revolutionary cryptosystem. This public-key system, which was independently invented by Ralph Merkle, allowed each user to create a unique two-key pair — a public key and a secret key. One beauty of this system is that the public key cannot be used to figure out the secret key.

RSA is very popular because it is the easiest public-key system to understand and to use. It is also extremely strong. RSA was first announced in 1977 by its inventors, Ronald Rivest of MIT (Massachusetts Institute of Technology), Adi Shamir of the Weizmann Institute in Israel, and Leonard Adelman of USC (University of Southern California). Note that RSA was named after its inventors (**R**ivest, **S**hamir, and **A**delman).

The mathematics of RSA is beyond the scope of this book. In a few words, RSA builds its security upon the difficulty of factoring large numbers into prime numbers. A prime number is a number that can be divided only by itself and by the number one. The numbers 3 and 13 are examples of prime numbers. The number 6 is not a prime number, because it can be divided by the prime numbers 2 and 3. Consider the following number:

```
1,234,587,458,297,345,786,123,178,987,236,234,
567,128,543
```

How do you factor this number, much less a far larger number, into prime numbers? It is very difficult. Therein lies the mathematical strength of RSA.

RSA, because it involves so much computation, is very slow. On a 486-based personal computer, RSA with a 1,000-bit key takes roughly 1,000 times longer than DES to encrypt a message that is 100,000 bytes long! Thus, people do not use RSA to encrypt love letters to each other, much less to encrypt lengthy spreadsheets. In real-world cryptosystems, RSA is not usually used to encrypt bulk data, since it can be too slow. Instead, a faster single-key system (such as DES or IDEA) is used to encrypt the bulk data. A random key is made up for each "session" or message (for instance, an encrypted phone call or e-mail letter) and that key is then encrypted using RSA and the recipient's public key. The recipient uses RSA and his secret key to decrypt the single "session" key with which he may then decrypt the bulk data.

The RSA algorithm is patented in the United States. Being a computer user, you may wonder how a U.S. government bureaucrat can award a patent for a mathematical equation. You may ponder whether someone with White House contacts will someday get the patent for "2+2=4". Is a math patent absurd? In a Woody Allen movie, the star was asked what he thought of God.

Woody Allen quipped something like, "What do I think of God? I don't even know how a refrigerator works!" Whether algorithm patents make sense to anybody but lawyers and patent holders is beyond the scope of this book. In the real world of dollars and cents, patents do exist.

Public Key Partners, a consortium of several groups including Stanford University and MIT, hold the patent for RSA (among other patents). Patents are good for 17 years. This means that RSA, which was patented in 1983, will enter the public domain in the year 2000.

If you want details about how to obtain a license to use RSA before the millenium, you can contact Public Key Partners or RSA Data Security, Inc.

Thomas G. Donlan, an editor at *Barron's* (a weekly financial publication related to *The Wall Street Journal*), articulated RSA's growing importance in a full-page editorial in the April 25, 1994 *Barron's*. The editorial was entitled "Privacy and Security: Computer Technology Open Secrets, And Closes Them."

RESOURCE BOX
RSA Data Security, Inc.
10 Twin Dolphin Drive Redwood City, CA 94065 (415) 595-8782

RESOURCE BOX
Public Key Partners
130 B Kifer Court Sunnyvale, CA 94086 (408) 735-6779

Mr. Donlan wrote, in part:

> *RSA Data Security, the company founded by the three inventors, has hundreds of satisfied customers, including Microsoft, Apple, Novell, Sun, AT&T, and Lotus. Versions of RSA are available for almost any personal computer or workstation, many of them built into the operating systems. Lotus Notes, the network communications system, automatically encrypts all its messages using RSA. Other companies have similar products designed around the same basic concept, and some versions are available for free on computer bulletin boards.*

Donlan continues:

> *Without security, the Internet is little more than the world's biggest bulletin board. With security, it could become the information supermarket of the world. RSA lets people and banks feel secure putting their credit-card numbers on the public*

network. Although it still seems that computers created an age of snoopery, the age of privacy is at hand.

Donlan clearly voices the mainstream, corporate view that RSA in specific and data encryption in general are necessary for the expanding business world.

International Data Encryption Algorithm (IDEA)

The International Data Encryption Algorithm (IDEA) was first announced in 1990 by Xuejia Lai and James Massey. IDEA has a 128-bit key (compared with the DES 56-bit key). This means that IDEA is far more difficult to crack by "brute force" than DES. In spite of IDEA's longer key, it runs just about as quickly as DES. IDEA is too complex to discuss in this book. I mention it for two reasons: 1) Cryptology expert Bruce Schneier says, "In my opinion, it is the best and most secure block algorithm available to the public at this time." and 2) IDEA is used in ViaCrypt PGP.

Digital Signatures

Digital signatures are computer generated strings of data that are attached to a computer document. The purpose of this extra data is to provide *authenticity* (to help convince the recipient that the document was indeed generated by the alleged sender) and to insure *integrity* (to attest that the document was not altered since it was signed). It is easy to clarify this abstract talk with a concrete example from PGP.

Here is a sample screen from the **alt.privacy** news group:

```
Thu, 20 Oct 1994 10:48:21     alt.privacy      Thread 7 of 8
               —--BEGIN PGP SIGNED MESSAGE—--

One vital tool for YOUR e-mail privacy could be anonymous remailers
(aka "servers"). The bad news... Few people are aware of remailers.
The good news... First, the news group ALT.PRIVACY.ANON-SERVER
exists. Second, Raph Levien <raph@kiwi.cs.berkeley.edu> keeps an
up-to-date list of remailers which he generously shares with us.
```

continued

Here is a direct quote from Levien:

****

I have written and installed a remailer pinging script which
collects detailed information about remailer features and
reliability.

To use it, just finger remailer-list@kiwi.cs.berkeley.edu
There is also a Web version of the same information, at:
http://www.cs.berkeley.edu/~raph/remailer-list.html
Please let me know about any other remailers which I missed. I've
only included remailers which can mail to arbitrary addresses, so
I already know chop and twwells are missing.

****

Please tell other people about these remailers. Thanks to Raph
Levien for his work!

See you in the future,
André
===

André Bacard | Bacard, author of "Hunger for Power:
P.O. Box 3009 | Who Rules the World and How," has been
Stanford, CA 94309 | a guest on hundreds of radio talk shows.
abacard@well.com | His NEW book, "The Computer Privacy
PGP Key Fingerprint= | Handbook," is forthcoming. [write for
93 E7 97 56 42 FA ... | further details].
===

————BEGIN PGP SIGNATURE————-
Version: 2.7

iQCVAwUBLrEXCN6pT6nCx/9/AQGgLwP/bhHKdYmwaiLf2GFuVPYPoLmuHhJ1l5
Si5pyvMVufrl3bCrs28sRYugr50xLZ3zLJtlAlUihW0BYV8BWiDTDMhSgW7JEtPK
CAAzSOBKhjvIk+zFMdHb97P09W7R5zCY2FnF67kqTaoRM0mJnYrT68IQ9HMVOX
=96g1
————END PGP SIGNATURE————-
Alt-Z FOR HELP | ANSI-BBS | FDX |9600 N81 | LOG CLOSED | TERMINAL | ON-LINE

I generated the above digitally signed note in two steps. First, I wrote the note about Raph Levien and anonymous remailers. Second, I used PGP software to "sign" the letter. Anyone on the Internet who has my PGP public key and who uses PGP software can verify that my signature is correct. Note that I signed this letter with my *secret* key, which nobody else has. Even if somebody stole my secret key, with fraud in mind, he or she would need to guess my complicated pass phrase.

Digital signatures can be very useful. Philip Zimmermann, the inventor of PGP, often issues Internet "press releases" about new developments in the

PGP world. Mr. Zimmermann signs these posts so that the rest of us will know that his message is legitimate, not the work of a practical joker. All PGP users have access to Phil's public key, so this system works very well.

Can a digital signature be fraudulent? A criminal sender would need, in the case of PGP software at least, a secret key plus a secret pass phrase. Those are difficult to come by, unless the person who guards these secrets is extraordinarily careless. The more likely problem is old-fashioned lying. Suppose Jane sends me a signed letter and, later, decides that the letter was a mistake. She can always claim that someone broke into her computer and stole her secret key and also found her secret pass phrase written on a piece of paper (Jane is sobbing with sorrow by now), which the criminal used to write me a phony letter. How did the criminal know about me and what to say? An imaginative Jane could come up with something.

Are digital signatures legally valid? As of this writing, digital signatures are in legal limbo in America. They have not been tested in the courts, for two reasons. First, digital signatures are rarely used. Very few legislators, lawyers, or judges have ever seen a digital signature. Second, there is no digital signature standard. A court cannot rule on the validity of a digital signature, if the judge cannot understand the signature! These conditions must change as cyberspace becomes more commercial, and as citizens realize their need to protect their privacy. The current situation, whereby people give their Visa or MasterCard number and expiration date to strangers over the telephone, or on computer networks, is reckless and dangerous.

Popularizing Digital Signatures

Ultimately, digital signatures will become popular when there is an economic incentive to use them. When they can be used to sign checks and contracts, they will become an essential part of our society. Nobody knows when this will take place. In the meantime, there are small, important steps that each of us can take.

The best way to popularize digital signatures, ice cream bars, or anything else is to publicly use them! It is especially helpful for high-profile persons and groups to set examples.

Computer Professionals for Social Responsibility (CPSR), the Electronic Frontier Foundation (EFF), and the Electronic Privacy Information Center (EPIC), are three ideal groups to get the digital signature movement going. These groups have four valuable assets in common:

◆ They are well-known and respected in cyberspace.

◆ They post announcements regularly on the Internet conferences.

◆ Their members include technical and legal experts.

◆ They have a tradition of setting bold precedents.

I urge all three organizations (and anyone else!) to start digitally signing all your official announcements with PGP. Your digital signatures, which are easy and inexpensive to implement, will accomplish five valuable social services.

1. **Educate the public about cryptology.** When people see your digital signatures, they will wonder what these strange symbols mean. In order to fathom your signatures, they will have to learn something about public-key cryptography. Their learning process will enrich the public debate about how citizens in the United States and other nations can safeguard our privacy as cyberspace inevitably becomes a more intrusive part of everyday life.

2. **Affirm the legality of PGP versions.** As of this writing, two popular versions of PGP are legal in the U.S. and Canada, MIT PGP Version 2.6.2, and ViaCrypt PGP Version 2.7. Many people are afraid to use PGP, because they think it is illegal. Your use of PGP will educate people that this privacy software is legal.

3. **Protect yourself from fraud.** At least one of the above groups has been victimized by a phony press release. Your digital signatures can help reduce this chance in the future.

4. **Encourage non-computer groups to follow your lead.** In order for digital signatures and public-key cryptography to reach critical mass, it must (by definition) be accepted and used by people other than a computer elite. The American Civil Liberties Union, Amnesty International, and the National Football League are three groups among thousands that can and will benefit from digital signatures. These groups need you to start the digital ball moving.

5. **Suggest alternatives to the Clipper Chip.** The U.S. wants to standardize a secret cryptographic algorithm that creates the potential for unlimited government surveillance. People need a *practical alternative*. When the public understands public-key crypto, people will be able to understand and articulate options to Clipper.

You (any organization) might be reluctant to use digital signatures because you foresee administrative obstacles. For example, you may worry that you will be overwhelmed with requests for information about how to use digital signatures. This is good fortune, not a problem! As computer experts, you can easily set up an automated response to these queries. You may also shy away from deciding which staff members will have access to your secret key. You make the same decision every time you give one staff member, instead of another, the key to your office and add a staff member to your checking account's signature card. It is important for you, cyberspace leaders, to work out these problems. If not you, who? Last, you may be scared of junk PGP — lots of encrypted trivia that takes precious time to decrypt — if you make your public key truly public. You can reduce this problem by distributing a note such as:

```
We use PGP encryption for legal contracts,
financial transactions, and confidential let-
ters. Please observe PGP etiquette. Do not
use PGP for trivial matters.
```

I urge all persons reading this section to ask your friends and employers to *learn about and use digital signatures*. If you do so, we will change society!

What Are DigiCash and Blind Signatures?

" *I have developed an extension of digital signatures, called blind signatures, that can restore privacy.* "

~ Dr. David Chaum, DigiCash

~

In the section "The Dangers of a Cash-Free Society." I posed many potential problems about how cash-free transactions can create intrusive dossiers. Fortunately, there is good news in this cash-free area. Dr. David Chaum, who earned his doctorate in computer science at the University of California, has created a clever, usable way to preserve our electronic privacy. He has invented *cryptographic blind signatures* which permit numbers to act as electronic cash, or to replace conventional identification. The full details of his system are presented in "Achieving Electronic Privacy," an article that he published in *Scientific American* in August 1992.

Let us get a nontechnical feeling for how Chaum's digital cash works. (Don't get discouraged if this process seems too subtle at this point. After you have played with PGP public keys, the Chaum method will be much clearer.) Suppose your bank wants to send you two electronic bank notes (credit vouchers, deposit receipts, or IOUs), one worth $20 and the other worth $100. The bank can encrypt a message with your public key and sign it with one of the bank's private keys. For example, a message signed with one secret bank key might be worth $20; an encrypted message signed with a second key being worth $100. These electronic bank notes could be authenticated by using the bank's *public* key, which it makes public. These messages could be stored on a *smart card* that belongs to you.

Now suppose that you want to buy a pizza at Pizza Palace. You place your smart card into Pizza Palace's card reader. The Pizza Palace clerk pushes a few buttons and transfers, say, one of your $20 bank notes from your smart card (i.e. bank account) to Pizza Palace's bank account. In the midst of this electronic transfer, which only takes seconds, computer software automatically verifies the bank's digital signature. When the card reader finishes its job, the Pizza Palace clerk hands you a digitally signed receipt.

The preceding scenario, using digital signatures, stops all three parties from cheating. The bank cannot deny that it placed $20 in your account, or that it transferred $20 from your account to Pizza Palace. You cannot deny that you spent the $20 at Pizza Palace. Finally, Pizza Palace cannot deny that it received $20 payment from you. In short, this system provides security. However, the cost of this system is lack of privacy. Anyone with access to computer records can tell that you spent $20 at Pizza Palace at a specific date and time.

David Chaum has found a way to provide security while safeguarding your privacy. He has invented an extension of digital signatures called *blind signatures*. Before you send a note number to the bank, Chaum's encryption software makes your transaction as private as a cash transaction. The details of Chaum's method are beyond the scope of this book. What is important is that Chaum's system can restore the privacy that has been destroyed by the current banking and business system.

Let us stop for a moment to breathe. Unless you are a computer expert who gets paid for writing programs, you might be asking "Why in the hell do we need such a complicated system? Why don't we just keep paper money that everyone can understand?" Whether you and I like it or not, computer companies have spent billions of dollars deifying the computer. Many people reading this book have become addicted to their machines, such as people who are hooked on TVs. One practical result of this computer proliferation and deification is that computer nerds are taking over our financial world, whether we are talking about designing ATMs or trading pork belly options. Why banking? As a famous bank robber said, "That's where the money is!" In this cultural context, Chaum's blind signature system helps us restore privacy that other computer people have taken away. God giveth as God taketh.

Chaum is one of the founders of DigiCash, a company based in the Netherlands that develops electronic cash payment systems. On a recent trip to Palo Alto, California, Dr. Chaum telephoned me about this book. I asked him what we, normal citizens, can do to help get his anonymous cash system adopted by our institutions. He told me that, by the time this book is published in early 1995, he will be free to announce certain steps that we might take. The following press release has been reprinted here because it may become an historical document as the first computer network, electronic cash payment system. At the end of the release, you will find the e-mail address to secure up-to-date information about private digital cash.

DIGICASH PRESS RELEASE

World's first electronic cash payment over computer networks.

FOR IMMEDIATE RELEASE

(Release Date: May 27, 1994)

Payment from any personal computer to any other workstation, over email or Internet, has been demonstrated for the first time, using electronic cash technology. "You can pay for access to a database, buy software or a newsletter by email, play a computer game over the net, receive $5 owed you by a friend, or just order a pizza. The possibilities are truly unlimited" according to David Chaum, Managing Director of DigiCash TM, who announced and demonstrated the product during his keynote address at the first conference on the World Wide Web, in Geneva this week.

Electronic cash has the privacy of paper cash, while achieving the high security required for electronic network environments exclusively through innovations in public key cryptography. "It's the first software only solution. In the past we've pioneered such cash for chip cards and electronic wallets, always with a tamper-resistant chip for storing the value — now all you have to do is download the software and you're up and running" continues Dr. Chaum.

The product works with Microsoft(R) Windows TM, Macintosh TM, and most UNIX TM platforms. It was shown integrated with Mosaic, the most popular software for people accessing databases, email, or other services on the Internet and World Wide Web. The graphic user interface allows intuitive "dragging and dropping" of icons representing stacks of coins, receipts, record books, etc.

continued

The company will be supplying the technology through other firms who will release the products, under various cooperation and trial programs. The user software, which allows both paying and receiving payment, will be distributed free of charge.

The product was developed by DigiCash TM Corporation's wholly owned Dutch subsidiary, DigiCash TM BV. It is related to the firm's earlier released product for road pricing, which has been licensed to Amtech TM Corporation, of Dallas, Texas, worldwide leader in automatic road toll collection. This system allows privacy protected payments for road use at full highway speed from a smart card reader affixed to the inside of a vehicle. Also related is the approach of the EU supported CAFE project, of which Dr. Chaum is Chairman, which uses tamper-resistant chips inserted into electronic wallets.

The underlying 'blind signature' technology was described in the article "Achieving Electronic Privacy," by David Chaum, Scientific American, August 1992.

For more information contact:

DigiCash bv   info@digicash.nl

Kruislaan 419   tel +31 20 665 2611
1098 VA Amsterdam   fax +31 20 668 5486

The Netherlands

Steganography

❝ To know that one has a secret is to know half the secret itself. ❞

~ Henry Ward Beecher, *Proverbs from Plymouth Pulpit*

~

The word *steganography* comes from the Greek language and literally means "covered writing." Steganography, a close cousin of cryptography, is a form of secret communications that involves covering or hiding secret messages. The messages are "secret" in the sense that nobody, except the intended receiver, can find them. For instance, one can hide messages inside a pen. The Nazis added to steganography technology by developing the microdot, which hid full-size typewritten letters on miniature dots the size of a punctuation mark. Smugglers have perfected the art of concealment in other ways. These hidden messages may or may not be encrypted for additional security.

Fred B. Wrixon, author of *Codes and Ciphers: An A to Z of Covert Communication from the Clay Tablet to the Microdot*, provides a delightful example of steganography:

> *The Histories of Herodotus, A Greek historian of the 5th century B.C., contains an account of a revolt against Persian rule that directly benefitted from steganography. Two regional strongmen communicated secretly by shaving a slave's head and tattooing it with a secret message. After his hair grew back, the slave was sent to co-conspirators, who shaved his head again and read the message. The communication was successful, and the revolt became a reality.*

In this case the slave was lucky. Early tyrants sometimes wrote secret messages on the backs of slaves. They covered these messages with shirts. After the messages were read, the slaves were killed so that no unauthorized person could see their backs. To this day, secret couriers often risk life and limb.

In our computer age, the basic lesson of steganography remains true. Namely, it is hard for anyone to intercept a secret message, if they do not know it exists. Suppose you want to pass along the following secret message to 10 people:

```
America is at war. Perhaps not your standard
definition of war, but a very real war
nonetheless. We are at war economically.
```

One way to pass this secret message (which should be broadcast to everyone) is to give all ten people a copy of Harry E. Figgie's book *Bankruptcy 1995: The Coming Collapse of America and How to Stop It* and tell them, secretly, to read the first three sentences of Senator Warren Rudman's Foreword. Anyone who intercepts *Bankruptcy 1995* will have no idea that it contains your secret message. In World War II, German agents used Daphne du Maurier's novel, *Rebecca*, in this manner. The Germans distributed *Rebecca* to its agents and prearranged to use certain texts on certain days. You can test this form of steganography by telling all of your friends to purchase this book to perform a vital experiment!

These literary examples suggest computer examples. Suppose you want your secret lover to phone you at a telephone booth for a rendezvous. You can e-mail her a list of one hundred computer generated phone numbers (secretly agreeing that the third item from the bottom of the list is the real one). What good is this list to an e-mail snoop? Not much. Even if the snoop is ambitious enough to call all hundred numbers, he will get nothing but busy signals, wrong numbers, and ringing phones because he does not know the time of your call.

Hiding in Pictures: Stego

We live in a highly visual world. Millions of us spend our lives addicted to television and computer screens. Madison Avenue spends a small fortune to develop a 30-second broadcast commercial or a one-page color magazine advertisement. Ad designers try to put the maximum emotional impact into every second and each square inch in order to sell us products. Sometimes their messages are overt; sometimes they are hidden ("subliminal"). George Lucas' special-effects movie company, Industrial Light and Magic, has entranced the entire world with computer graphics in films such as "Jurassic Park." *Time* and other publications digitally retouch photographs, so that the reader cannot tell whether these photos are fact or fiction. In addition, superb computer graphics software and hardware are available to anyone with a few thousand dollars.

Our cultural obsession with graphic images provokes a natural question. Since people rely so much upon graphics to relay data, when will people use graphics to hide data? This question sets the stage for Stego.

Stego is computer software developed by Romana "Cypherella" Machado of Paradigm Shift Research. Stego 1.0a2 (the current version) is the first steganography tool widely available on Macintoshes for hiding data in graphics images. Nobody knows what will happen to Stego as the years unfold. However, Stego's underlying logic might lead privacy preservation in new directions.

Stego is a program that lets the user embed and retrieve data from Macintosh PICT format files without altering the appearance or the size of the PICT file. In plain English, this means that Stego will enable you to print a picture of, say, yourself that contains hidden data, say, your resumé. Anybody who looks at your picture will have no idea that the images in front of his eyes contain your resumé. Stego hides messages inside digitized pictures that do not look like secret codes. This is the beauty and power of steganography!

How is this possible? Stego alters pixel values. Let us turn to Robin Williams' invaluable *Jargon* for further guidance:

> *Pixel is short for picture element. The computer screen is composed of hundreds of thousands of tiny little spots of light. Each one of these spots is a pixel and is the smallest element that a screen can display. Everything you see on your monitor (screen) is created using those tiny spots. On a color monitor, each pixel is actually made up of a varying number of triads, three separate dots of color — one red, one green, and one blue — placed immediately adjacent to one another. The color you see from a given pixel is a blend of the light from those three dots."*

> *"Each pixel is controlled by information stored in your computer. If a pixel is controlled by just a single on-or-off unit of information — one bit — it can only display one of two 'colors': it can either be on (white, green or amber, depending on what kind of monitor you have) or off (black). If a pixel is controlled by two bits, the pixel can appear as any of four colors or shades of gray. With four bits you can see sixteen colors or shades of gray. And so on."*

Stego uses the least significant bit in each pixel to hold one bit of a hidden message. In half of the pixels, the least significant bit remains the same. In the other half, the shade of the pixel will be altered very slightly. This change is too subtle for the naked human eye to detect.

Note that Stego is compatible with encryption, but it is not encryption. Anyone with a copy of Stego can retrieve your data from your PICT file. However, Stego can be used as an "envelope" to obscure a previously encrypted data file so that nobody will know they are looking at an encrypted file.

Romana Machado announced in a recent form letter sent to all

RESOURCE BOX

Romana Machado

Paradigm Shift Research
19672 Stevens Creek Blvd Suite 127
Cupertino, CA 95014
romana@apple.com

e-mail queries: "I plan to release the code for Stego, but it is not fully groomed yet. In the meantime, it is available on request. Stego may be expanded to handle other image formats, and other digital media: audio, video, etc."

As of this writing, work is underway to develop Stego versions for the PC and other platforms. You can get full technical details by contacting Romana Machado.

Should Crypto Be Software or Hardware?

Hardware are the parts you can kick. Software is the stuff you can swear at.

~ Clay Gordon in, *Jargon: An Informal Dictionary of Computer Terms*

~

Cryptographic systems come in two forms, hardware and software. People who manufacture encryption chips tend to praise them at the expense of software programs, and software producers tend to return the favor. Let us try to clear our eyes of business competition and look at the pros and cons of each.

What is encryption hardware? Look at the back of your personal computer. You will probably find a series of expansion slots. Some PCs have as many as eight slots. Computer stores sell electronic boards (also called *cards*) that fit into these slots and give our computer extra powers. For example, we can buy a sound card to enable our computer to generate music, or an internal modem board that allows our computer to communicate over telephone lines. We can also buy encryption boards for our computer, or encryption boxes for our facsimile machine. These boards or boxes are, by definition, hardware. They are parts that you can kick, though I do not recommend doing so.

Encryption hardware has several advantages over software.

Speed. Cryptographic chips are designed to perform one task: to encrypt and decrypt data. Therefore, they do this job much faster than all-purpose computer micro-processors, which must manipulate software in addition to the encrypted data. This speed may be vital, if you run a bank that encrypts thousands of ATM and wire transfers daily. This speed is one reason that commercial and military institutions prefer hardware encryption. However, what does this speed mean to you? Suppose hardware can encrypt your financial records in 10 seconds, while software takes 30 seconds. What are you going to do with the extra 20 seconds of your life? How often will you run the encryption? Many users, obsessed with speed, never address this question.

Physical Security. Computer chips can be made "tamper-proof." The little chips are coated with a chemical so that, if anyone tries to break into the chip, the chip's logic is destroyed. By comparison, it is possible for somebody to modify software encryption without the user ever knowing it. This security might be important, if you own a missile company and world-class experts are trying to break your security system. However, what does this security mean to you and your personal computer? Anybody with access to your personal computer can steal your pass phrase or secret key much easier than he or she can rewrite your software!

Mindless Operation. Cryptographic hardware allows a user to encrypt and decrypt data mindlessly. For instance, the hardware might automatically encrypt everything that goes onto your hard drive and decrypt everything that comes back to your screen. Hardware advocates love this mindless feature. Their favorite maxim is: "Encryption must be transparent. It must be invisible to the user."

Software has several advantages over hardware.

Transportable. Crypto software programs, such as PGP, fit on a floppy disk. You can put it in your pocket, drive across down, and install an unregistered, freeware version in the computer of your choice. If you prefer, you can transfer the software to your mother-in-law over telephone wires. To be sure, hardware can be shipped but with more difficulty.

Educational. Software permits the user to exercise his or her brain. Not only is this good for mental health, but it encourages users to understand something about encryption and, therefore, add intelligent comments to the national cryptographic debate. Software encourages activity, whereas hardware promotes passivity. (See the Clipper Chip section. The Eavesdrop Establishment wants you to use hardware, whereas the pro-privacy forces want you to learn about encryption.)

Freedom from Trap Doors. PGP privacy software (and other crypto software) are written in computer code. The PGP code is available to the public. It has been investigated, line by line, by computer experts of every political persuasion to insure that the software has no *trap-doors*. Some software and hardware systems have trap doors (think of a stage magician with his hidden doors that allow rabbits to appear and disappear) built into them so that the company that manufactures them can (secretly) break the security. Some customers actually prefer trap doors so that, if they lose their pass phrase, the company that markets the product can decrypt their lost files. Suppose you use a cryptographic chip (hardware). How do you know if anyone can read your encrypted data without your knowledge? Do you think the chip manufacturer will be able or willing to tell you, if there is a (secret) trap door? The proper software eliminates this need for worry.

Piggyback Security.   Crypto software permits you to piggyback on top of crypto hardware or software built into an operating system. Suppose your employer uses a hardware system that automatically encrypts all e-mail sent from one employee to another. However, you suspect that your employer can read this mail. You may be able, depending on the computer system used, to encrypt your messages on top of the company encryption system.

Crypto Is a "Munition" and Export Controlled!

❝ Making cryptographic software equivalent to munitions is just as foolish as making addictive crossword puzzles equivalent to drugs. ❞

~ Lennart Benschop, Eindhoven University of Technology

❝ Just as in the case of tele-communications, the National Security Agency is attempting to put the genie back in the bottle. It won't happen; and a vibrant and productive sector of American industry may be sacrificed in the process. ❞

~ Sam Gejdenson (D-Conn), House Foreign Affairs Committee

~

The United States government, as of this writing, defines crypto as a munition. A *munition*, according to my dictionary, is a "material used in war, such as guns, ammunition, and bombs." Indeed, the U.S. government treats cryptography in the same category as jet fighters or missiles. What does this have to do with us ordinary users? The bottom line is this: It is *illegal to export crypto* (and nuclear bombs for that matter) overseas without the proper export license. It is also *illegal to give non-American citizens crypto on US soil* without the proper export license. Personally, I do not even think about exporting crypto overseas or giving it to foreign visitors! I let my correspondents get their crypto in England, New Zealand, or in other countries that are more pro-privacy than the United States. Life is difficult enough without punching alligators in the nose.

How does this export policy impact the computer industry? For a start, U.S. manufacturers are not permitted to export their top-flight crypto without a license. In the real world, these licenses are nearly impossible to get. Therefore, American computer firms have three choices. First, they can forgo sales outside the United States and Canada (for reasons beyond the scope of this book, the U.S. seems to view Canada as our only safe crypto ally in the world). This decision is an economic disaster for American firms and a bonanza for foreign competitors. Note that first-rate crypto is sold by foreign companies! Second, American firms can market two crypto products, one outside the U.S. and Canada, the other inside the U.S. and Canada. This choice is ludicrous. In a world of trans-national corporations, how can offices in America operate with a different cryptosystem than offices in Hong Kong? Third, American firms can sell the same weak crypto to customers abroad and to us in America. This is the most popular choice. Foreign companies can market top-quality products; whereas the U.S. government forces Americans to market watered-down products!

Michel Kabay, the director of education with the National Computer Security Association, is one opponent of the U.S. policy. In *Network World* (November 8, 1993), he penned an angry editorial entitled "ITAR Sticks Users with Unfair Encryption Restrictions." Here is a short excerpt:

> *"U.S. taxpayers have been paying bureaucrats' salaries to apply the International Traffic in Arms Regulation (ITAR) to encryption software. According to ITAR, the Office of Defense Trade Controls of the U.S. Department of State can define anything it wants as equivalent to munitions. There is nothing to stop the bureaucrats from adding the decoder rings found in popcorn boxes to the U.S. Munitions List and designating them as a restricted export."*

"Trying to restrict the export of encryption programs in this age of the global Internet is about as useful as trying to keep cigarette smoke from drifting into the no-smoking zone in your favorite restaurant. Trying to control the flow of information via diskette or paper when data can travel unimpeded through the Internet is just plain dumb. How can a government official stop international users from using anonymous File Transfer Protocol to get a copy of any encryption algorithm found on a file server anywhere in the world?"

Addressing Crypto Export Controls

The Software Publishers Association is one of many groups that wants to see American companies remain competitive in a tough global marketplace that has cost Americans millions of well-paying jobs. The Third Conference on Computers, Freedom, and Privacy sponsored a panel discussion of "Digital Telephony and Crypto Policy." One of the panel members was Ilene G. Rosenthal, General Counsel for the Software Publishers Association. Here are a few thoughts from a position paper that she presented at the conference.

"These [export] controls significantly harm the legitimate export prospects and impede the competitiveness of America's software publishers. Apart from the time and expense of the licensing process, software publishers face a Hobson' Choice: either they market a single program worldwide with reduced encryption capabilities to meet U.S. Government restrictions; or they have to incur the time and expense of marketing two separate programs, as well as the reduced appeal of an export version which clearly has reduced security."

"This outdated export control policy:"

♦ "Keeps strong encryption out of the hands of legitimate users concerned about their business and personal privacy thereby making them vulnerable to spying and tampering;

♦ Forces American companies to compete against pirated copies of their own programs; and

♦ Gives a huge advantage to *foreign* software companies willing and able to sell encryption products abroad."

American industry has been crippled by U.S. bureaucrats and global competitors for the last 20 years. Export regulations are the latest assault against the computer industry, one of our few ongoing success stories. U.S. Congressional Representatives Maria Cantwell and Sam Gejdenson are two of many people in Congress trying to reverse this destructive cycle. If you care about computers, be sure to contact the guardians of cyberspace listed in the Appendix of this book for the latest developments.

What Is The Clipper Initiative?

" Any sound that Winston made, above the level of a very low whisper, would be picked up by it... There was of course no way of knowing whether you were being watched at any given moment... You had to live — did live, from habit that became instinct — in the assumption that every sound you made was overheard and, except in darkness, every movement scrutinized. "

~ George Orwell, *1984*

" The 'clipper chip' — aptly named, as it clips the wings of individual liberty... "

~ William Safire, *New York Times*

~

The *Clipper Initiative* may be the boldest, practical technological assault against privacy ever proposed by a government. Its scope is the stuff of science-fiction novels. The Clipper Initiative, a brainstorm of the United States government, has created a hurricane of opposition from law-abiding citizens all over the world. However, as of this writing, it is unclear whether the Eavesdrop Establishment or the American people will win this epic battle. In either case, it is vital for every pro-democracy person to learn about the Clipper Initiative — and how to fight against this and future naked power grabs. In short, the Clipper Initiative consists of the *Clipper Chip*, the *Capstone Chip*, and the *Skipjack algorithm*.

The infamous Clipper Chip is a tamper-resistant, cryptographic computer chip. It encrypts phone calls, making them unintelligible to most others, such as competitors and mothers-in-law. The United States government alleges that Clipper's purpose is twofold: 1) to prohibit (non-government) citizens and companies from eavesdropping on our voice communications, and 2) to permit U.S. law enforcement agents to eavesdrop on all voice communications, if these agents have "legal authorization." Basically, the Eavesdrop Establishment in Washington, D.C. is telling the American people:

> ```
> "Trust us. If you give Uncle Sam complete
> power to monitor all your voice and computer
> communications whenever he wants for whatever
> reason he wants, Uncle Sam will insure that
> your mother-in-law will not electronically
> monitor you. If you don't grant us that
> authority, we plan to take it anyway."
> ```

While the Clipper Chip would be used in digital telephones, Capstone (a similar electronic micro-chip) would be used in personal computers and digital appliances other than telephones. Both Clipper and Capstone are based on a secret algorithm called Skipjack.

Many privacy specialists assert that the Clipper Initiative is a smoke screen. They do not trust that Clipper is designed to protect America from cocaine dealers and mothers-in-law. Clipper was built, officially, because the FBI and other law enforcement agencies urged its creation. These agencies claim that the availability of strong encryption programs will interfere with their power to conduct wiretapping. No evidence in support of these claims has been released. In fact, Computer Professionals for Social Responsibility has obtained FBI documents (through litigation) which indicate that no such encryption difficulties have been reported by FBI field offices, or other federal law enforcement agencies. In 1992, fewer than 900 wiretap warrants were issued to state and federal law enforcement agencies. Does the Eavesdrop Establishment want the power to electronically eavesdrop on 250,000,000 Americans, so that it can monitor 900 criminal suspects more efficiently? To the privacy experts who have marshaled this evidence, the real purpose of Clipper and Capstone is crystal clear: to provide the technological means for a total Surveillance State in America.

The Skipjack algorithm was developed by the National Security Agency (NSA) (aka "No Such Agency" and "No Sounds Allowed"). NSA is a super-secret intelligence agency responsible for intercepting foreign government communications and breaking the codes that protect such transmissions. In 1987, Congress passed the Computer Security Act, a law intended to limit NSA's role in developing standards for the civilian communications system. In spite of that legislation, the agency has played a leading role in the Clipper Initiative and other civilian security proposals. NSA has classified the Skipjack algorithm on national security grounds, thus stopping independent cryptographers from evaluating the system's strength. Computer Professionals for Social Responsibility has filed suit under the Freedom of Information Act seeking the disclosure of the secret algorithm and other information concerning the Clipper plan. Stewart A. Baker, the NSA top lawyer, articulates the NSA's position in the article "Don't Worry. Be Happy. Why Clipper Is Good for You" in the June 1994 issue of *Wired* magazine.

How would the Clipper (the *key-escrow system*) work in your kitchen? Suppose you buy a telephone that has the Clipper Chip built into it. Your chip has a serial number, a unit key, and a family key. The serial number and the unit key are unique to your chip, whereas the family key for all similar chips is known (in theory) only by the government. When a chip is "programmed," two random numbers are generated and sent along with the serial number to two government escrow agencies, currently the Commerce Department and the Treasury Department. The two random numbers are then used by the chip to produce its unit key.

The first thing you must do is report your serial number to the government (perhaps the salesperson will do this for you) much the way you must register your automobile. When you start to make a phone call (to another Clipper Chip based phone), both phones automatically create a one-time *session key* so that both phones scramble and unscramble your voices in the same manner. The Clipper Chip takes this session key and encrypts it with the unit key. This result is mathematically combined with the serial number and encrypted with the family key to produce the Law Enforcement Access Field (LEAF). This LEAF is transmitted prior to the actual encrypted data. (This may sound complicated, but remember that computer chips are very sophisticated, fast devices.)

Suppose that a law enforcement agent, or someone else, wants to tap your Clipper encrypted conversation. First, the eavesdropper records your conversation and decrypts the LEAF with the family key to get the serial number and the encrypted session key. Next, he or she sends a request to two escrow agencies. Under current guidelines, a law enforcement agency must certify that it has a valid court order for a wiretap in order to get your two escrow-keys. With these escrow-keys, the eavesdropper can decrypt your phone calls. Currently, the procedure for intelligence agencies to obtain a key are classified.

The Clipper Chip raises many perplexing problems. What happens if a spy, such as CIA mole Aldrich "Rick" Ames, gains access to the escrow data banks? Will his government also be able to monitor every American? Will "intelligence" people like Oliver North or the Watergate Plumbers have access to their favorite escrow keys? Who will stop them? Suppose a federal agent gets a court order to wiretap a Mafia assassin but, in reality, requests the escrow keys for the Democratic, Libertarian, or Republican's office phone? Who will know the difference? Today, government agents regularly pass along database information to their friends in private practice. Will a lucrative black market develop for escrow keys? Suppose someone gets your escrow keys for a one-time investigation. Will he be able to use them to monitor you for the rest of your life? Who will stop him? What corporation or government outside the United States will buy any electronic product that enables the U.S. government to monitor its activities? Will the U.S. government try to ban all other encryption if and when the Clipper and Capstone chips reach mass acceptance? Will the U.S. government try to ban all imports of foreign electronics that contains other cryptographic standards? What happens if someone breaks the Skipjack algorithm once it has been installed in millions of systems? The U.S. government wants the Escrowed Encryption Standard (based on the Skipjack algorithm) to replace the Data Encryption Standard (DES). The first rule of a top-rate cryptographic algorithm is that its strength is not compromised by revealing the algorithm. If Skipjack is the electronic privacy messiah, why is it classified? Finally, why has the White House fought so hard to keep the Clipper Chip debate in the dark? Whatsamatter, does the government have something to hide? All of these questions, and many more, need to be openly debated in the bright of day by informed persons.

What is the present status of Clipper Chip? During President George Bush's regime, the United States Congress tried to pass Digital Telephony laws to require all domestic telecommunications systems to make FBI wiretaps easier. These results failed, in part because they were opposed by virtually everyone in the computer world. When Clinton was elected, pro-privacy activists and civil libertarians tried to persuade Clinton (himself the victim of vicious rumormongering and privacy invasions) to oppose Digital Telephony and Clipper. As of this writing, it appears that Clinton still supports a total Surveillance State. Here are several instructive steps that have occurred in the Clipper battle.

Crypto Experts Oppose Clipper

Here is a letter sent to President Clinton, and widely circulated on the Internet, about Clipper. This letter was coordinated by Computer Professionals for Social Responsibility (CPSR), which had long sought to open the issue of cryptography policy to public debate.

This letter was circulated at a crucial point in the debate on cryptography policy. An internal Administration review of the issue was near completion, and the National Security Agency (NSA) was moving forward with efforts to deploy Clipper technology in civilian agencies, including the Internal Revenue Service.

CPSR, by this time, had sponsored several public conferences on cryptography and privacy and had litigated Freedom of Information Act cases seeking the disclosure of relevant government documents.

January 24, 1994

The President
The White House
Washington, DC 20500

Dear Mr. President,

We are writing to you regarding the "Clipper" escrowed encryption proposal now under consideration by the White House. We wish to express our concern about this plan and similar technical standards that may be proposed for the nation's communications infrastructure.

The current proposal was developed in secret by federal agencies primarily concerned about electronic surveillance, not privacy protection. Critical aspects of the plan remain classified and thus beyond public review.

The private sector and the public have expressed nearly unanimous opposition to Clipper. In the formal request for comments conducted by the Department of Commerce last year, less than a handful of respondents supported the plan. Several hundred opposed it.

If the plan goes forward, commercial firms that hope to develop new products will face extensive government obstacles. Cryptographers who wish to develop new privacy enhancing technologies will be discouraged. Citizens who anticipate that the progress of technology will enhance personal privacy will find their expectations unfulfilled.

Some have proposed that Clipper be adopted on a voluntary basis and suggest that other technical approaches

continued

will remain viable. The government, however, exerts
enormous influence in the marketplace, and the likelihood that competing standards would survive is small.
Few in the user community believe that the proposal
would be truly voluntary.

The Clipper proposal should not be adopted. We believe
that if this proposal and the associated standards go
forward, even on a voluntary basis, privacy protection
will be diminished, innovation will be slowed, government accountability will be lessened, and the openness
necessary to ensure the successful development of the
nation's communications infrastructure will be threat-
ened.

We respectfully ask the White House to withdraw the
Clipper proposal.

Sincerely,

Public Interest and Civil Liberties Organizations

Marc Rotenberg, CPSR
Conrad Martin, Fund for Constitutional Government
William Caming, privacy consultant
Simon Davies, Privacy International
Evan Hendricks, US Privacy Council
Simona Nass, Society for Electronic Access
Robert Ellis Smith, Privacy Journal
Jerry Berman, Electronic Frontier Foundation

Cryptographers and Security Experts

Bob Bales, National Computer Security Association
Jim Bidzos, RSA Data Security Inc.
G. Robert Blakley, Texas A&M University
Stephen Bryen, Secured Communications Technologies, Inc.
David Chaum, Digicash

continued

George Davida, University of Wisconsin
Whitfield Diffie, Sun Microsystems
Martin Hellman, Stanford University
Ingemar Ingemarsson, Universitetet i Linkvping
Ralph C. Merkle, Xerox PARC
William Hugh Murray, security consultant
Peter G. Neumann, SRI International
Bart Preneel, Katolieke Universiteit
Ronald Rivest, MIT
Bruce Schneier, Applied Cryptography (1993)
Richard Schroeppel, University of Arizona
Stephen Walker, Trusted Information Systems
Philip Zimmermann, Boulder Software Engineering

Industry and Academia

Andréw Scott Beals, Telebit International
Mikki Barry, InterCon Systems Corporation
David Bellin, North Carolina A&T University
Margaret Chon, Syracuse University College of Law
Laura Fillmore, Online BookStore
Scott Fritchie, Twin-Cities Free Net
Gary Marx, University of Colorado
Ronald B. Natalie, Jr, Sensor Systems Inc.
Harold Joseph Highland, Computers & Security
Doug Humphrey, Digital Express Group, Inc
Carl Pomerance, University of Georgia
Eric Roberts, Stanford University
Jonathan Rosenoer, CyberLaw & CyberLex
Alexis Rosen, Public Access Networks Corp.
Steven Zorn, Pace University Law School

(affiliations are for identification purposes only)

White House Press Release on Clipper

Pro-privacy people were unable to persuade Clinton and/or his advisors. The Clinton White House simply took a different path than the Bush regime. In early 1994, the White House announced that the United States government was making the Clipper Chip a Federal Information Processing Standard.

Here is a copy of the White House Press Release.

THE WHITE HOUSE   CONTACT: 202 156-7035

OFFICE OF THE PRESS SECRETARY

EMBARGOED UNTIL 3 PM (EST) FRIDAY, February 4, 1994

STATEMENT OF THE PRESS SECRETARY

Last April, the Administration announced a comprehensive interagency review of encryption technology, to be overseen by the National Security Council. Today, the Administration is taking a number of steps to implement the recommendations resulting from that review.

Advanced encryption technology offers individuals and businesses an inexpensive and easy way to encode data and telephone conversations. Unfortunately, the same encryption technology that can help Americans protect business secrets and personal privacy can also be used by terrorists, drug dealers, and other criminals.

In the past, Federal policies on encryption have reflected primarily the needs of law enforcement and national security. The Clinton Administration has sought to balance these needs with the needs of businesses and individuals for security and privacy. That is why, today the National Institute of Standards ant Technology (NIST) is committing to ensure a royalty-free, public-domain Digital Signature Standard. Over many years, NIST has been developing digital signature technology that would provide a way to verify the author and sender of an electronic message. Such technology will be critical for a wide range of business applications for the National Information Infrastructure. A digital signature standard will enable individuals to transact business electronically

continued

rather than having to exchange signed paper contracts. The Administration has determined that such technology should not be subject to private royalty payments, and it will be taking steps to ensure that royalties are not required for use of a digital signature. Had digital signatures been in widespread use, the recent security problems with the Internet would have been avoided.

Last April, the Administration released the Key Escrow chip (also known as the "Clipper Chip") that would provide Americans with secure telecommunications without compromising the ability of law enforcement agencies to carry out legally authorized wiretaps. Today, the Department of Commerce and the Department of Justice are taking steps to enable the use of such technology both in the U.S. and overseas. At the same time, the Administration is announcing its intent to work with industry to develop other key escrow products that might better meet the needs of individuals and industry, particularly the American computer and telecommunications industry. Specific steps being announced today include:

— Approval by the Commerce Secretary of the Escrowed Encryption Standard (EES) as a voluntary Federal Information Processing Standard, which will enable government agencies to purchase the Key Escrow chip for use with telephones and modems. The department's National Institute of Standards and Technology (NIST) will publish the standard.

— Publication by the Department of Justice of procedures for the release of escrowed keys and the announcement of NIST and the Automated Services Division of the Treasury Department as the escrow agents that will store the keys needed for decryption of communications using the Key Escrow chip. Nothing in these procedures will diminish the existing legal and procedural requirements that protect Americans from unauthorized wiretaps.

— New procedures to allow export of products containing the Key Escrow chip to most countries.

In addition, the Department of State will streamline export licensing procedures for encryption products

continued

that can be exported under current export regulations in order to help American companies sell their products overseas. In the past, it could take weeks for a company to obtain an export license for encryption products, and each shipment might require a separate license. The new procedures announced today will substantially reduce administrative delays and paperwork for encryption exports.

To implement the Administration's encryption policy, an interagency Working Group on Encryption and Telecommunica-tions has been established. It will be chaired by the White House Office of Science and Technology Policy and the National Security Council and will include representatives of the Departments of Commerce, Justice, State, and Treasury as well as the FBI, the National Security Agency, the Office of Management and Budget, and the National Economic Council. This group will work with industry and public-interest groups to develop new encryption technologies and to review and refine Administration policies regarding encryption, as needed.

The Administration is expanding its efforts to work with industry to improve on the Key Escrow chip, to develop key-escrow software, and to examine alternatives to the Key Escrow chip. NIST will lead these efforts and will request additional staff and resources for this purpose.

We understand that many in industry would like to see all encryption products exportable. However, if encryption technology is made freely available worldwide, it would no doubt be used extensively by terrorists, drug dealers, and other criminals to harm Americans both in the U.S. and abroad. For this reason, the Administration will continue to restrict export of the most sophisticated encryption devices, both to preserve our own foreign intelligence gathering capability and because of the concerns of our allies who fear that strong encryption technology would inhibit their law enforcement capabilities.

continued

At the same time, the Administration understands the benefits that encryption and related technologies can provide to users of computers and telecommunications networks. Indeed, many of the applications of the evolving National Information Infrastructure will require some form of encryption. That is why the Administration plans to work more closely with the private sector to develop new forms of encryption that can protect privacy and corporate secrets without undermining the ability of law-enforcement agencies to conduct legally authorized wiretaps. That is also why the Administration is committed to make available free of charge a Digital Signature Standard.

The Administration believes that the steps being announced today will help provide Americans with the telecommunications security they need without compromising the capability of law enforcement agencies and national intelligence agencies. Today, any American can.purchase.and.use.any.type of encryption product. The Administration does not intend to change that policy. Nor do we have any intention of restricting domestic encryption or mandating the use of a particular technology.

This White House press release sent immediate shock waves throughout the computer world. The following is one response that has been widely-circulated on the Internet.

CPSR's Clipper Chip Petition

The following petition was signed by 50,000 computer people, from universities, corporations, and government agencies all over America.

Electronic Petition to Oppose Clipper

Please Distribute Widely

On January 24, many of the nation's leading experts in cryptography and computer security wrote President Clinton and asked him to withdraw the Clipper proposal.

The public response to the letter has been extremely favorable, including coverage in the *New York Times* and numerous computer and security trade magazines.

Many people have expressed interest in adding their names to the letter. In response to these requests, CPSR is organizing an Internet petition drive to oppose the Clipper proposal. We will deliver the signed petition to the White House, complete with the names of all the people who oppose Clipper.

To sign on to the letter, send a message to:

    Clipper.petition@cpsr.org

with the message "I oppose Clipper" (no quotes)

You will receive a return message confirming your vote.

Please distribute this announcement so that others may also express their opposition to the Clipper proposal.

CPSR is a membership-based public interest organization. For membership information, please email cpsr@cpsr.org. For more information about Clipper, please consult the CPSR Internet Library

FTP/WAIS/Gopher CPSR.ORG /cpsr/privacy/crypto/clipper

The Association of Computing Machinery Speaks Out

Here is a press release issued by a major computer organization.

---

* PRESS RELEASE *

Thursday, June 30, 1994

COMPUTER POLICY COMMITTEE CALLS FOR
WITHDRAWAL OF CLIPPER COMMUNICATIONS PRIVACY "TOO
IMPORTANT" FOR SECRET DECISION-MAKING

WASHINGTON, DC !! The public policy arm of the oldest
and largest international computing society today urged
the White House to withdraw the controversial "Clipper
Chip" encryption proposal. Noting that the "security
and privacy of electronic communications are vital to
the development of national and international information infrastructures," the Association for Computing
Machinery's U.S. Public Policy Committee (USACM) added
its voice to the growing debate over encryption and
privacy policy.

In a position statement released at a press conference
on Capitol Hill, the USACM said that "communications
security is too important to be left to secret processes and classified algorithms." The Clipper technology
was developed by the National Security Agency, which
classified the cryptographic algorithm that underlies
the encryption device. The USACM believes that Clipper
"will put U.S. manufacturers at a disadvantage in
the global market and will adversely affect technological development within the United States." The technology has been championed by the Federal Bureau
of Investigation and the NSA, which claim that
"non-escrowed" encryption technology threatens law
enforcement and national security.

"As a body concerned with the development of government
technology policy, USACM is troubled by the process
that gave rise to the Clipper initiative," said Dr.
Barbara Simons, a computer scientist with IBM who
chairs the USACM. "It is vitally important that privacy protections for our communications networks be
developed openly and with full public participation."

continued

The USACM position statement was issued after completion of a comprehensive study of cryptography policy
sponsored by the ACM (see companion release). The
study, "Codes, Keys and Conflicts: Issues in U.S Crypto
Policy," was prepared by a panel of experts representing various constituencies involved in the debate over
encryption.

The ACM, founded in 1947, is a 85,000 member non-profit educational and scientific society dedicated to the
development and use of information technology, and to
addressing the impact of that technology on the world's
major social challenges. USACM was created by ACM to
provide a means for presenting and discussing technological issues to and with U.S. policymakers and the
general public. For further information on USACM,
please call (202) 298-0842.

USACM Position on the Escrowed Encryption Standard

The ACM study "Codes, Keys and Conflicts: Issues in U.S
Crypto Policy" sets forth the complex technical and
social issues underlying the current debate over widespread use of encryption. The importance of encryption,
and the need for appropriate policies, will increase as
networked communication grows. Security and privacy of
electronic communications are vital to the development of
national and international information infrastructures.

The Clipper Chip, or "Escrowed Encryption Standard"
(EES) Initiative, raises fundamental policy issues that
must be fully addressed and publicly debated. After
reviewing the ACM study, which provides a balanced discussion of the issues, the U.S. Public Policy Committee
of ACM (USACM) makes the following recommendations.

1. The USACM supports the development of public policies and technical standards for communications security in open forums in which all stakeholders — government, industry, and the public — participate.Because
we are moving rapidly to open networks, a prerequisite
for the success of those networks must be standards for
which there is widespread consensus, including international acceptance. The USACM believes that communications security is too important to be left to secret
processes and classified algorithms. We support the

continued

principles underlying the Computer Security Act of 1987, in which Congress expressed its preference for the development of open and unclassified security standards.

2. The USACM recommends that any encryption standard adopted by the U.S. government not place U.S. manufacturers at a disadvantage in the global market or adversely affect technological development within the United States. Few other nations are likely to adopt a standard that includes a classified algorithm and keys escrowed with the U.S. government.

3. The USACM supports changes in the process of developing Federal Information Processing Standards (FIPS) employed by the National Institute of Standards and Technology. This process is currently predicated on the use of such standards solely to support Federal procurement. Increasingly, the standards set through the FIPS process directly affect non-federal organizations and the public at large. In the case of the EES, the vast majority of comments solicited by NIST opposed the standard, but were openly ignored. The USACM recommends that the standards process be placed under the Administrative Procedures Act so that citizens may have the same opportunity to challenge government actions in the area of information processing standards as they do in other important aspects of Federal agency policy making.

4. The USACM urges the Administration at this point to withdraw the Clipper Chip proposal and to begin an open and public review of encryption policy. The escrowed encryption initiative raises vital issues of privacy, law enforcement, competitiveness and scientific innovation that must be openly discussed.

5. The USACM reaffirms its support for privacy protection and urges the administration to encourage the development of technologies and institutional practices that will provide real privacy for future users of the National Information Infrastructure.

Dr. Matt Blaze Finds Clipper Flaw

The Clipper Initiative, government officials have promised, is so secure that it is futile for non-government experts to look for glitches. Suppose someone did find a defect? This discovery would clearly indicate that Clipper is less than "perfect." It would also highlight the value of having an open, unclassified algorithm for the best minds to investigate.

Dr. Matt Blaze of AT&T Bell Laboratories found a flaw. Here is the Abstract from his June 3, 1994 paper, entitled "Protocol Failure in the Escrowed Encryption Standard," which is available in full from the Electronic Frontier Foundation's superb archive.

The Escrowed Encryption Standard (EES) defines a US Government family of cryptographic processors, popularly known as "Clipper" chips, intended to protect unclassified government and private-sector communications and data. A basic feature of key setup between pairs of EES processors involves the exchange of a "Law Enforcement Access Field" (LEAF) that contains an encrypted copy of the current session key. The LEAF is intended to facilitate government access to the cleartext of data encrypted under the system. Several aspects of the design of the EES, which employs a classified cipher algorithm and tamper-resistant hardware, attempt to make it infeasible to deploy the system without transmitting the LEAF. We evaluated the publicly released aspects of the EES protocols as well as a prototype version of a PCMCIA-based EES device. This paper outlines various techniques that enable cryptographic communication among EES processors without transmission of the valid LEAF. We identify two classes of techniques. The simplest allow communication only between pairs of "rogue" parties. The second, more complex methods permit a rogue application to interoperate with legal EES users. We conclude with techniques that could make the fielded EES architecture more robust against these failures.

Blaze's publication sent yet another round of shock waves throughout the computer world, clouding the Clipper scheme with more distrust. In non-technical terms, Blaze found a method that would enable two persons to have a secret conversation that law enforcement agents could not unscramble.

The June 2, 1994 *New York Times* featured a front page story about Blaze's breakthrough. The newspaper article, called "Flaw Discovered in

Federal Plan For Wiretapping: 'Clipper Chip' is at Issue." Columnist John Markoff asked Blaze the significance of his discovery.

> *"Nothing I've found affects the security of the Clipper system from the point of view of people who might want to break the system. This does quite the opposite. Somebody can use it to circumvent the law-enforcement surveillance mechanism."*

Government officials do not deny Blaze's findings. Rather, they try to put a good face on the matter. When I ask computer experts if anybody outside Washington D.C. supports Clipper, they inevitably name the same person: Professor Dorothy Denning — though they note that she is a computer scientist at Georgetown University in Washington D.C. Dr. Denning, part of a team that advises the government, told Mr. Markoff: "I don't think this undermines the Clipper. But it's good to know what the vulnerabilities are." Thanks to Dr. Blaze, even Denning acknowledges the value of outside help!

The Clipper Chip reminds me of an old parable. One sunny day, an oak tree and a fern were talking. The oak tree was feeling very proud. He was bragging that his limbs were so strong that he had lived one hundred years. Nothing, he assured the fern, could stop him. The fern, by comparison, admitted that he looked rather weak but he was flexible. The oak tree laughed at the slender little fern. That winter a huge storm struck. The oak tree growled that it was indestructible and challenged the wind. The wind and rain came harder and harder until it broke the oak's branches and uprooted the tree. In spring the once mighty oak tree was dead, while the fern said nothing and rocked gently in the breeze. The Clipper Chip, if made universal, would convert the United States into one oak tree with millions and millions of ferns. When the social storm comes, as it did in Colonial America or in the once mighty Soviet Union, the oak tree will break.

Vice-President Gore's Letter to Representative Cantwell

On July 21, 1994 the American media reported that the White House had changed its policy towards Clipper. A typical newspaper headline was: "White House Retreats on Clipper." On July 20, 1994 Vice-President Albert Gore wrote a letter to United States Congressional Representative Maria Cantwell, who was holding hearings in order to pass a law making it possible for American computer companies to export high-quality crypto abroad. The Gore letter [see below] refers to a possible White House retreat on the Clipper/Capstone/Skipjack suite of applications. The Gore letter does *not* explicitly retreat on the Clipper Chip itself, nor on the key "escrow" ideas behind Clipper. Here is the Gore letter:

July 20, 1994

The Honorable Maria Cantwell
House of Representatives
Washington, D.C., 20515

Dear Representative Cantwell:

I write to express my sincere appreciation for your
efforts to move the national debate forward on the issue
of information security and export controls. I share your
strong conviction for the need to develop a comprehensive policy regarding encryption, incorporating an
export policy that does not disadvantage American software companies in world markets while preserving our
law enforcement and national security goals.

As you know, the Administration disagrees with you on
the extent to which existing controls are harming U.S.
industry in the short run and the extent to which their
immediate relaxation would affect national security.
For that reason we have supported a five-month
Presidential study. In conducting this study, I want to
assure you that the Administration will use the best
available resources of the federal government. This
will include the active participation of the National
Economic Council and the Department of Commerce. In
addition, consistent with the Senate-passed language,
the first study will be completed within 150 days of
passage of the Export Administration Act reauthoriza-
tion bill, with the second study to be completed within one year after the completion of the first. I want
to personally assure you that we will reassess our
existing export controls based on the results of these
studies. Moreover, all programs with encryption that
can be exported today will continue to be exportable.

On the other hand, we agree that we need to take action
this year to assure that over time American companies
are able to include information security features in
their programs in order to maintain their admirable
international competitiveness. We can achieve this by
entering into an new phase of cooperation among government, industry representatives and privacy advocates
with a goal of trying to develop a key escrow encryption

continued

system that will provide strong encryption, be acceptable to computer users worldwide, and address our national needs as well.

Key escrow encryption offers a very effective way to accomplish our national goals, That is why the Administration adopted key escrow encryption in the "Clipper Chip" to provide very secure encryption for telephone communications while preserving the ability for law enforcement and national security. But the Clipper Chip is an approved federal standard for telephone communications and not for computer networks and video networks. For that reason, we are working with industry to investigate other technologies for those applications.

The Administration understands the concerns that industry has regarding the Clipper Chip. We welcome the opportunity to work with industry to design a more versatile, less expensive system. Such a key escrow system would be implementable in software, firmware, hardware, or any combination thereof, would not rely upon a classified algorithm, would be voluntary, and would be exportable. While there are many severe challenges to developing such a system, we are committed to a diligent effort with industry and academia to create such a system. We welcome your offer to assist us in furthering this effort.

We also want to assure users of key escrow encryption products that they will not be subject to unauthorized electronic surveillance. As we have done with the Clipper Chip, future key escrow systems must contain safeguards to provide for key disclosure only under legal authorization and should have audit procedures to ensure the integrity of the system. Escrow holders should be strictly liable for releasing keys without legal authorization.

We also recognize that a new key escrow encryption system must permit the use of private-sector key escrow agents as one option. It is also possible that as key escrow encryption technology spreads, companies may established layered escrowing services for their own products. Having a number of escrow agents would give individuals and businesses more choices and flexibility in meeting their needs for secure communications.

continued

```
I assure you the President and I are acutely aware of
the need to balance economic and privacy needs with law
enforcement and national security. This is not an easy
task, but I think that our approach offers the best
opportunity to strike an appropriate balance. I am
looking forward to working with you and others who
share our interest in developing a comprehensive
national policy on encryption. I am convinced that our
cooperative endeavors will open new creative solutions
to this critical problem.

Sincerely,


Al Gore
AG/gcs
```

The White House has clearly been forced to reassess its Clipper Initiative because of overwhelming opposition from almost all parties involved. Much of the credit goes to Rep. Cantwell (D-WA), who has been engaging the White House in debate on these topics for over a year, to the 50,000 CPSR petition signers, to the people at EPIC and EFF, and to many online activists.

EFF Analysis of Vice-President Gore's Letter

The Electronic Frontier Foundation has been intimately involved in the battle to stop the Clipper Chip. Here is EFF's interpretation of Gore's letter.

```
July 22, 1994

Two days ago, Vice-President Al Gore signaled a major
setback in the Administration's Clipper program, and a
willingness to engage in serious negotiations leading
to a comprehensive new policy on digital privacy and
security. Many questions remain about the future, but
one thing is certain: Clipper is a dead end, and those
of us who are concerned about digital privacy have won
a new opportunity to shape a better policy.
```

continued

The Vice-President's letter to Rep. Maria Cantwell (D-WA) made it clear that while Clipper might have a small place in the telephone security market, it has no future in the digital world. "...[T]he Clipper Chip is an approved federal standard for telephone communications and not for computer networks and video networks. For that reason, we are working with industry to investigate other technologies for those applications.... We welcome the opportunity to work with industry to design a more versatile, less expensive system. Such a key escrow system would be implementable in software, firmware, hardware, or any combination thereof, would not rely upon a classified algorithm, would be voluntary, and would be exportable." Clipper does not meet most of these criteria, so, according to the Vice-President, it is a dead end.

End of the Line for Clipper—Long-Run Effort to Drive Market Will Fail

The premise of the Clipper program was that the government could drive the market toward use of encryption products which incorporated government-based key escrow agents. A series of subtle and not so subtle government actions would encourage private citizens to use this technology, thus preserving law enforcement access to encrypted communications.

Clipper was originally announced as the first element of a family of hardware-based, government key escrow encryption devices that would meet security needs for both voice and data communications on into the future.

Clipper itself was purely a voice and low-speed data product, but other members of the Skipjack family, including Tessera and Capstone, were to be compatible with Clipper and were intended to lead the way from escrowed encryption in voice to escrowed encryption for data. Plans are already announced, in fact, to use Tessera and Capstone in large government email networks. At the time, the hope was that government use of this technology would push private sector users toward key escrow systems as well.

Now, the announcement that the Administration is re-thinking plans for data encryption standards leaves Clipper a stranded technology. No one wants to buy, or

continued

worse yet, standardize on, technology which has no upgrade path. As a long-run effort to force the market toward government-escrowed encryption standards, Clipper is a failure.

We Still Must Work for Voluntary, Open, Exportable Standards

The fight for privacy and security in digital media is by no means over. Though the Administration has backed away from Clipper, and expressed willingness to talk about other solutions, we are pursuing serious progress on the following issues:

Improved telephone encryption standards. For the reasons listed by the Vice-President, in addition to the inherent problems of making copies of all your keys available, Clipper is a poor choice for telephone encryption. Industry should develop a standard for truly secure and private telephones, make them available from multiple manufacturers worldwide, and make them interoperate securely with audio conferencing software on multimedia PC's.

Truly voluntary standards. Any cryptographic standard adopted by the government for private sector use must be truly voluntary. Voluntary means, to us, that there are statutory guarantees that no citizen will be required or pressured into using the standard for communications with the government, or with others. No government benefits, services, or programs should be conditioned on use of a particular standard, especially if it involves government or private key escrow.

Open standards Standards chosen must be developed in an open, public process, free from classified algorithms. The worldwide independent technical community must be able to create and evaluate draft standards, without restriction or government interference, and without any limits on full participation by the international cryptographic community.

No government escrow systems Any civilian encryption standard which involves government getting copies of all the keys poses grave threats to privacy and civil liberties, and is not acceptable in a free society.

Liberalization of export controls Lifting export controls on cryptography will make the benefits of strong cryptography widely available to our own citizens. U.S.

continued

hardware, software and consumer electronics manufacturers will build encryption into affordable products once they are given access to a global marketplace.

Today's widespread availability of "raw" cryptographic technology both inside and outside the United States shows that the technology will always be available to "bad guys". The real question is whether our policies will allow encryption to be built into the fabric of our national and international infrastructure, to provide significantly increased individual privacy, improved financial privacy, increased financial security, enhanced freedom of association, increased individual control over identity, improved security and integrity of documents, contracts, and licenses, reduced fraud and counterfeiting, the creation of significant new markets for buying and selling of intellectual property, and a lessened ability to detect and prosecute victimless crimes.

These benefits are not free, however. EFF does recognize that new communications technologies pose real challenges to the work of law enforcement. Just as the automobile, the airplane, and even the telephone created new opportunities for criminal activity, and new difficulties for law enforcement, encryption technology will certainly require changes in traditional investigative techniques. We also recognize that encryption will prevent many of the online crimes that will likely occur without it. We further believe that these technologies will create new investigative tools for law enforcement, even as they obsolete old ones. Entering this new environment, private industry, law enforcement, and private citizens must work together to balance the requirements of both liberty and security.

Finally, the export controls used today to attempt to control this technology are probably not Constitutional under the First Amendment; if the problems of uncontrolled export are too great, a means of control must be found which does not restrict free expression.

Congressional Leadership Toward Comprehensive Policy Framework Is Critical

The efforts of Congresswoman Maria Cantwell, Senator Patrick Leahy, and other members of Congress, show that

continued

comprehensive policies on privacy, security and competitiveness in digital communication technologies can
only be achieved with the active involvement of
Congress. Unilateral policy efforts by the Executive
branch, such as Clipper and misguided export control
policies, will not serve the broad interests of
American citizens and businesses. So, we are pleased to
see that the Vice-President has pledged to work with
the Congress and the private sector in shaping a for-
ward-looking policy. We see the Vice-President's letter
to Congresswoman Cantwell as an important opening for
dialogue on these issues.

The principles of voluntariness and open standards
announced in the Vice-President's letter, as well as
those mentioned here, must be incorporated into legislation. We believe that under the leadership of Senator
Leahy, Reps. Cantwell, Valentine, Brooks and others,
this will be possible in the next congress. EFF is eager
to work with the Congress, the Administration, along
with other private sector organizations to help formu-
late a new policy. EFF is also pleased to be part of
the team of grass roots activism, industry lobbying,
and public interest advocacy which has yielded real
progress on these issues.

For More Information Contact:

Jerry Berman, Executive Director <jberman@eff.org>

Daniel J. Weitzner, Deputy Policy Director <djw@eff.org>

Current Status of the Clipper Initiative

Up-to-the-moment information about the Clipper Initiative can be found
on the **alt.privacy.clipper** Internet news group:

Here is a sample screen from that news group:

```
alt.privacy.clipper (7T 12A 0K 0H R)   h=help
1 +     What is Clipper?        Moss A D
2 + 5 Crypto ban still a possibility, Clipper alive     Pat Myrto
3 +     CA Visual Objects                               Andréas@ast.ping.d
```

continued

```
4 +  2  Crypto ban still a possibility, Clipper alive     bbass@fcw.com
5 +     *NEW SUG SECURITY CD-ROM*                          J. Mickevich
6 +     More boots are dropping; Denning suggests ban  Shabbir J. Safdar
7 +     looking for clipper info              Sean Murphy

*** End of Articles ***

Alt-Z FOR HELP | ANSI-BBS | FDX | 9600 N81 | LOG CLOSED | TERMINAL | ON-LINE
```

In addition, you can download files about the Clipper Initiative by searching the EFF and CPSR archives at:

> gopher gopher.eff.org
> gopher gopher.cpsr.org

Where Can You Read the Latest Crypto News?

The computer world changes quickly. By the time we get used to one software program, a new version is released. Similarly, laws and standards seem to change with the speed of hurried electrons. An excellent way to keep abreast of new cryptographic developments is to read the following Usenet news groups:

alt.privacy.clipper	Clipper chip news
alt.security	General security dialogues
alt.security.index	Index to alt.security
alt.security.pgp	Everything about PGP
alt.security.ripem	All about RIPEM
alt.society.civil-liberty	General civil liberties and privacy
comp.compression	Talk about compression algorithms
comp.org.cpsr.talk	CPSR related issues
comp.org.eff.news	News reports from EFF
comp.org.eff.talk	EFF related issues
comp.patents	Software patents, including RSA
comp.security.announce	Announcements of security holes
comp.society.privacy	General privacy issues
misc.legal.computing	Laws and computing

PART THREE

PGP:

Pretty Good
Privacy

What is PGP?

“ During the battle between Boris Yeltsin and the Russian Parliament last October [1993], with Russian freedom hanging in the balance, software author Philip Zimmermann received an electronic-mail message from Latvia. ‘If dictatorship takes over Russia,’ it read, ‘your PGP is widespread from Baltic to Far East now and will help democratic people if necessary. Thanks.’ ”

~ *Wall Street Journal*

~

PGP (also called “Pretty Good Privacy”) is an easy-to-use, highly secure computer program that encrypts (scrambles) and decrypts (unscrambles) data. For example, PGP can encrypt “André” so that it reads:

```
ª+Õ>$&C¿1,pÆî¢w}Iî≤ù¤tï>_føÉçWÛ?:^HpáÀ^GÉ^B1FF/Q
```

Your computer can decrypt this garble back into “André” if you use PGP. More technically, PGP software gives the user a choice. She can use single-key cryptography (useful for encrypting computer files that only she will read) or public-key cryptography (ideal for encrypting e-mail and files that other people will read).

Novices are sometimes fooled by the expression “Pretty Good Privacy.” There are two basic types of encryption: one that guards our privacy from our mother-in-law and the other that protects our privacy from highly sophisticated snoops. PGP is definitely of the latter variety. William M. Bulkeley wrote in the *Wall Street Journal*:

> *Admired by freedom lovers and criminals alike, PGP is one more thing: uncrackable, or as close to it as secret code has ever been. Even U.S. government snoopers can't break it.*

Even allowing for a little hyperbole, PGP is strong stuff. The “Pretty Good Privacy” name reflects the humor of PGP's creator.

PGP, a registered trademark of Philip Zimmermann, is the de facto world standard software for e-mail security. What does this mean in practice? It means that PGP is widely available, in many languages (including English, Esperanto, French, German, Italian, Lithuanian, Russian, Spanish, and Swedish) around the world. More importantly it is widely used, because computer users like it. By comparison, there are several competing crypto systems. One is called PEM, the Internet Privacy-Enhanced Mail standard. PEM may be an official standard, in theory, but, in practice, only a few people use it. I am reminded of the Susan Anthony dollar. Years ago, an American bureaucrat got the brilliant idea to mint a coin worth one dollar. After much cost and publicity, the coin was issued. Almost nobody wanted the coin (an official "standard"), which was easy to confuse with a quarter, and the Anthony dollar quickly vanished. Cyberspace will undoubtedly go through enormous changes in the next ten years. In particular, new encryption systems might emerge. But, if you want to send and receive private e-mail on the Internet today, PGP is the best buy in town.

Who Created PGP?

" They're [U.S. government officials] treating us like an enemy foreign population. "

~ American Philip Zimmermann

~

Philip Zimmermann, a computer consultant, was the original creator and remains the major driving force behind PGP. In 1990, Mr. Zimmermann secluded himself in his Boulder, Colorado computer room and started writing the PGP program. PGP was a big job. Zimmermann worked 12 hours per day for 6 months until he finished. Like many great projects, PGP was a labor of love. No one paid Zimmermann for this time. In fact, the project caused him and his family genuine financial hardships. PGP wiped out his life savings, and the PGP project caused Zimmermann to fall five months behind in his mortgage payments. When he finished the program in June 1991, Zimmermann wondered what to call his computer child. He was a fan of humorist Garrison Keillor's "Prairie Home Companion" radio show and decided to name his computer program after Ralph's Pretty Good Grocery — hence, Pretty Good Privacy.

In the summer of 1991, Zimmermann gave his PGP encryption program to friends. Apparently, someone placed PGP on the Internet. Someone downloaded the program and liked it. Someone else downloaded the program and liked it. Before long, people all over the world were downloading and using PGP. The program spread like crazy through the computer subculture. Within months, Bulletin Board Systems and Internet sites around the world made PGP available to their users. Top-quality "encryption for the masses" (in the words of Zimmermann) was finally available as "freeware." With the spread of PGP, Phil Zimmermann became a global folk hero to pro-privacy people.

What motivated Zimmermann to sacrifice his time for free? We live in a me-only corporate world where people expect to get paid (one way or the other) for saying hello to each other. We reside in a cut-throat legalistic society where people try to find ways to patent the air we breathe and the words we speak. Zimmermann is a refreshing exception to the rule. He is an idealist who believes in the power of decent, well-informed people. In the 1980's, he became concerned about the nuclear-arms race and was arrested for his anti-nuclear war protests. In 1990, Zimmermann's long time suspicions about the government were accentuated when he learned that the FBI (Federal Bureau of Investigation) and the NSA (National Security Agency) wanted to pass a law that would ban certain types of encryption. While this issue was being debated, Zimmermann decided to create PGP "to inoculate the body politic" from government spying. Philip Zimmermann's creation of PGP reminds one immediately of Thomas Jefferson, the Father of American Cryptography, who noted:

> "Every government degenerates when trusted to the rulers of the people alone. The people themselves therefore are its only safe depositories."

Zimmermann created PGP to allow the people themselves, us, to safeguard democracy. I should point out that Zimmermann did not invent any of the encryption techniques used in PGP. RSA, IDEA, and digital signatures were invented by others. Zimmermann wrote a program that incorporated the ideas and inventions of others.

Zimmermann is, by no means, the only force behind PGP. Other programmers around the globe have worked on subsequent PGP versions and shells. (A shell is a program that accepts commands from the user and runs other programs. For instance, there are shells that enable you to run PGP from menus on a screen. More about this later.) In addition, countless law-abiding people around the globe have spread the word about PGP.

Mr. Zimmermann earns his living by consulting people about cryptographic products. He is also seeking investors. He is working on a software package that would turn any multimedia PC (386 or above, with sound board and fast modem) into a secure telephone. He plans a free version of it to ensure wide distribution, perhaps establishing a standard protocol alternative to Clipper. At this time, the project has no funding, so it proceeds under the power of volunteer labor, as PGP did. Mr. Zimmermann hopes it will become as much of a standard as PGP has.

RESOURCE BOX

Philip Zimmermann

3021 11th Street
Boulder, Colorado 80304
303-541-0140
prz@acm.org

Philip Zimmermann's Statement to Congress

The following statement was made by Philip Zimmermann and is being published here with Mr. Zimmermann's support.

```
            Testimony of Philip Zimmermann to
            Subcommittee for Economic Policy,
                Trade, and the Environment
                US House of Representatives


    12 Oct 1993

    Mr. Chairman and members of the committee, my name is
    Philip Zimmermann, and I am a software engineer who
    specializes in cryptography and data security. I'm here
    to talk to you today about the need to change US export
    control policy for cryptographic software. I want to
    thank you for the opportunity to be here and commend
    you for your attention to this important issue.

    I am the author of PGP (Pretty Good Privacy), a pub-
    lic-key encryption software package for the protection
    of electronic mail. Since PGP was published domesti-
    cally as freeware in June of 1991, it has spread organ-
    ically all over the world and has since become the de
    facto worldwide standard for encryption of E-mail. The US
    Customs Service is investigating how PGP spread outside
    the US. Because I am a target of this ongoing criminal
```

continued

investigation, my lawyer has advised me not to answer any questions related to the investigation.

I. The information age is here.

Computers were developed in secret back in World War II mainly to break codes. Ordinary people did not have access to computers, because they were few in number and too expensive. Some people postulated that there would never be a need for more than half a dozen computers in the country. Governments formed their attitudes toward cryptographic technology during this period. And these attitudes persist today. Why would ordinary people need to have access to good cryptography?

Another problem with cryptography in those days was that cryptographic keys had to be distributed over secure channels so that both parties could send encrypted traffic over insecure channels. Governments solved that problem by dispatching key couriers with satchels handcuffed to their wrists. Governments could afford to send guys like these to their embassies overseas. But the great masses of ordinary people would never have access to practical cryptography if keys had to be distributed this way. No matter how cheap and powerful personal computers might someday become, you just can't send the keys electronically without the risk of interception. This widened the feasibility gap between Government and personal access to cryptography.

Today, we live in a new world that has had two major breakthroughs that have an impact on this state of affairs. The first is the coming of the personal computer and the information age. The second breakthrough is public-key cryptography.

With the first breakthrough comes cheap ubiquitous personal computers, modems, FAX machines, the Internet, E-mail, digital cellular phones, personal digital assistants (PDAs), wireless digital networks, ISDN, cable TV, and the data superhighway. This information revolution is catalyzing the emergence of a global economy.

But this renaissance in electronic digital communication brings with it a disturbing erosion of our privacy.

continued

In the past, if the Government wanted to violate the privacy of ordinary citizens, it had to expend a certain amount of effort to intercept and steam open and read paper mail, and listen to and possibly transcribe spoken telephone conversation. This is analogous to catching fish with a hook and a line, one fish at a time. Fortunately for freedom and democracy, this kind of labor-intensive monitoring is not practical on a large scale.

Today, electronic mail is gradually replacing conventional paper mail, and is soon to be the norm for everyone, not the novelty it is today. Unlike paper mail, E-mail messages are just too easy to intercept and scan for interesting keywords. This can be done easily, routinely, automatically, and undetectably on a grand scale. This is analogous to driftnet fishing — making a quantitative and qualitative Orwellian difference to the health of democracy.

The second breakthrough came in the late 1970s, with the mathematics of public key cryptography. This allows people to communicate securely and conveniently with people they've never met, with no prior exchange of keys over secure channels. No more special key couriers with black bags. This, coupled with the trappings of the information age, means the great masses of people can at last use cryptography. This new technology also provides digital signatures to authenticate transactions and messages, and allows for digital money, with all the implications that has for an electronic digital economy.

This convergence of technology — cheap ubiquitous PCs, modems, FAX, digital phones, information superhighways, et cetera — is all part of the information revolution. Encryption is just simple arithmetic to all this digital hardware. All these devices will be using encryption. The rest of the world uses it, and they laugh at the US because we are railing against nature, trying to stop it. Trying to stop this is like trying to legislate the tides and the weather. It's like the buggy whip manufacturers trying to stop the cars — even with the NSA on their side, it's still impossible. The information revolution is good for democracy — good for

continued

a free market and trade. It contributed to the fall of
the Soviet empire. They couldn't stop it either.

Soon, every off-the-shelf multimedia PC will become a
secure voice telephone, through the use of freely
available software. What does this mean for the
Government's Clipper chip and key escrow systems?

Like every new technology, this comes at some cost.
Cars pollute the air. Cryptography can help criminals
hide their activities. People in the law enforcement
and intelligence communities are going to look at this
only in their own terms. But even with these costs, we
still can't stop this from happening in a free market
global economy. Most people I talk to outside of
Government feel that the net result of providing privacy will be positive.

President Clinton is fond of saying that we should
"make change our friend". These sweeping technological
changes have big implications, but are unstoppable. Are
we going to make change our friend? Or are we going to
criminalize cryptography? Are we going to incarcerate
our honest, well-intentioned software engineers?

Law enforcement and intelligence interests in the
Government have attempted many times to suppress the
availability of strong domestic encryption technology.
The most recent examples are Senate Bill 266 which mandated back doors in crypto systems, the FBI Digital
Telephony bill, and the Clipper chip key escrow initiative. All of these have met with strong opposition
from industry and civil liberties groups. It is impossible to obtain real privacy in the information age
without good cryptography.

The Clinton Administration has made it a major policy
priority to help build the National Information
Infrastructure (NII). Yet, some elements of the
Government seems intent on deploying and entrenching a
communications infrastructure that would deny the citi-
zenry the ability to protect its privacy. This is unset-
tling because in a democracy, it is possible for bad
people to occasionally get elected — sometimes very bad
people. Normally, a well-functioning democracy has ways
to remove these people from power. But the wrong

continued

technology infrastructure could allow such a future government to watch every move anyone makes to oppose it. It could very well be the last government we ever elect.

When making public policy decisions about new technologies for the Government, I think one should ask oneself which technologies would best strengthen the hand of a police state. Then, do not allow the Government to deploy those technologies. This is simply a matter of good civic hygiene.

II. Export controls are outdated and are a threat to privacy and economic competitiveness.

The current export control regime makes no sense anymore, given advances in technology. There has been considerable debate about allowing the export of implementations of the full 56-bit Data Encryption Standard (DES). At a recent academic cryptography conference, Michael Wiener of Bell Northern Research in Ottawa presented a paper on how to crack the DES with a special machine. He has fully designed and tested a chip that guesses DES keys at high speed until it finds the right one. Although he has refrained from building the real chips so far, he can get these chips manufactured for $10.50 each, and can build 57000 of them into a special machine for $1 million that can try every DES key in 7 hours, averaging a solution in 3.5 hours. $1 million can be hidden in the budget of many companies. For $10 million, it takes 21 minutes to crack, and for $100 million, just two minutes. That's full 56-bit DES, cracked in just two minutes. I'm sure the NSA can do it in seconds, with their budget. This means that DES is now effectively dead for purposes of serious data security applications.

If Congress acts now to enable the export of full DES products, it will be a day late and a dollar short. If a Boeing executive who carries his notebook computer to the Paris airshow wants to use PGP to send email to his home office in Seattle, are we helping American competitiveness by arguing that he has even potentially committed a federal crime?

Knowledge of cryptography is becoming so widespread, that export controls are no longer effective at

continued

controlling the spread of this technology. People everywhere can and do write good cryptographic software, and we import it here but cannot export it, to the detriment of our indigenous software industry.

I wrote PGP from information in the open literature, putting it into a convenient package that everyone can use in a desktop or palmtop computer. Then I gave it away for free, for the good of our democracy. This could have popped up anywhere, and spread. Other people could have and would have done it. And are doing it. Again and again. All over the planet. This technology belongs to everybody.

III. People want their privacy very badly.

PGP has spread like a prairie fire, fanned by countless people who fervently want their privacy restored in the information age. Today, human rights organizations are using PGP to protect their people overseas. Amnesty International uses it. The human rights group in the American Association for the Advancement of Science uses it.

Some Americans don't understand why I should be this concerned about the power of Government. But talking to people in Eastern Europe, you don't have to explain it to them. They already get it — and they don't understand why we don't.

I want to read you a quote from some E-mail I got last week from someone in Latvia, on the day that Boris Yeltsin was going to war with his Parliament:

"Phil I wish you to know: let it never be, but if dictatorship takes over Russia your PGP is widespread from Baltic to Far East now and will help democratic people if necessary. Thanks."

Who's Using PGP?

Law-abiding people and corporations of all types use PGP. The common thread for all these PGP users is their need for data privacy. Let us look first at the corporate world. Suppose you are a corporate manager and must communicate with an employee, via e-mail, about some sensitive matter (for instance, poor job performance). Depending upon where your business is located, you might be legally required to protect the confidentiality of such communications. E-mail, as we have seen, can be notoriously non-confidential. PGP gives you the encryption power to obey the law!

Suppose you are an employee who must communicate restricted data files (for example, company trade secrets) over insecure telephone lines. If anybody intercepts these files, you might lose your job, or get arrested for giving these secrets to unauthorized people. PGP could protect your job and your reputation. One California accounting company scrambles its computer backup tapes with PGP, so that its clients do not have to worry about the tapes being read if they are lost or stolen. In short, it is often almost necessary to use encryption to stay within the spirit and the letter of the law these days.

The Electronic Frontier Foundation is one prominent group that uses PGP. Here is a message that they send to people, which could be a model for many other organizations (the PGP jargon will be explained in later sections):

```
This is the ASCII-armored PGP 2.6 public key
for the Electronic Frontier Foundation (EFF).
... Note that mail sent with this key will be
considered addressed to EFF in general, not
to a specific person, unless otherwise noted
in plaintext. To send personal information to
someone at EFF, for whatever reason, please
use that person's own key, or arrange some
other method of communication.

This key is provided principally for the
sending of sensitive legal information, and
the transmission of credit card numbers over
the net securely when becoming a member of
EFF. It takes us time and effort to decrypt,
so please don't use this key trivially. Thank
you. Please expect a delay, as the message
will have to be transferred to another system
for decryption (we do not keep our PGP or
secret key on the Internetted Unix systems
for security reasons).
```

Away from the corporate world, many people can use PGP to protect themselves. Perhaps you are Ross Perot running for president of the United States; maybe you are an Iowa abortion physician protecting your patients' medical records; or perchance you are a *Washington Post* journalist uncovering White House corruption. There are people who would love to intercept your records. PGP can help each of you. Daniel Salcedo, who works for the Human Rights Project of the American Association for the Advancement of Science (in Washington, D.C.), teaches activists in El Salvador and Guatemala to use PGP. As Salcedo told the *Wall Street Journal*, "In this business, lots of people have been killed." At this minute, many pro-democracy people around the world face torture and death at the hands of dictators who control telephone and computer networks. PGP can be more effective than guns at overthrowing these tyrants.

On a lighter note, I am reminded of a letter that I received from a college student:

> "I had a part-time job at a dry cleaner. One day I returned a diamond ring that I'd found in a man's coat pocket to his wife. Unfortunately, it was NOT her ring! It belonged to her husband's girlfriend. His wife was furious and divorced her husband over this incident. My boss told me: "Return jewelry ONLY to the person whose clothes you found it in, and NEVER return underwear that you find in pockets!" Until that moment, I thought my boss was a finicky woman. But she taught me the need for PGP."

Privacy, discretion, confidentiality, and prudence are hallmarks of civilization. Without them — if everyone spoke their minds openly at all times—few of us would be born, because sex would be rare. As for those people who *were* born, if they spoke openly at all times, they would live in a state of constant war.

How Safe is PGP? Will it Really Protect You?

Maybe your government or your mother-in-law can "break" PGP messages with supercomputers or sheer brilliance. I have no way of knowing the clandestine powers of these potential adversaries. However, three facts are certain.

Fact #1. Top-rate civilian cryptographers and computer experts have tried to break the PGP cryptosystem — without luck. PGP depends upon two algorithms for its security, RSA and IDEA (which I discussed earlier). RSA is used to encrypt PGP's keys, whereas IDEA is used to encrypt actual message texts.

How safe would you feel if you knew it would take 600 locksmiths several months to open the front door to your house — and if you could change your lock in five minutes? Personally, I would feel extremely safe. PGP appears to be at least that safe. In early 1994, Bellcore Communications Research Inc. announced that it had cracked the public-key RSA code, based on a 129-digit key. Bellcore accomplished this feat by using about 600 Internet volunteers around the globe, each of whom worked on a small part of the mathematical problem. This means that, if you used *that* 129-digit PGP key, the Bellcore army would be able to read your encrypted message. If you used *another* 129-digit key, it would take Bellcore about the same amount of time to crack that key as it did for them to crack the original key.

Some PGP (and other RSA system) users panicked when they read about Bellcore's success. Here is Phil Zimmermann's response:

> *It has been widely reported in the press that a famous RSA key, known as RSA-129, has been factored. This is an impressive achievement in factoring. Of the four principal workers on that project, three of them were involved with PGP development. RSA-129 is a 129-digit composite number that was factored into two primes, after 5000 MIP-years of computing effort by 600 people in 20 countries over eight months time using a couple thousand workstations. Many people have asked me if this means PGP is doomed because it uses RSA. PGP typically uses RSA keys that are about 307 digits long, far out of reach of these factoring techniques. I'm told that adding three digits to the length of a key causes the factoring workload to double. Three more digits added doubles it again. And so on. Now figure out what that means for adding 178 digits to bring up the key size to 307 digits. PGP is safe from these kinds of factoring attacks for a long time to come.*

In plain English, there is no need for alarm. Anyone who uses PGP's longest public keys (which I always recommend) can expect to stump the likes of Bellcore's 600-person army for months. Does anybody really want to spend all that time and money to read your e-mail? Especially when you can change your PGP key in five minutes? For all practical purposes, the Bellcore project has no impact on PGP users. Anybody requiring greater security should remember the two rules of ultimate secrecy: Never tell your secret to anybody, and never put a secret in writing.

Fact #2. Whomever proves that he or she can unravel PGP will earn quick fame in crypto circles. He or she will be applauded at banquets and will attract lots of grant money. More importantly:

Fact #3. PGP's programmers and users will broadcast this news world-wide on the Internet the minute it is verified as accurate.

Almost daily, someone posts an Internet notice such as "PGP Broken by Omaha Teenager." Take these claims with a grain of salt. The crypto world attracts its share of paranoids, provocateurs, and UFO aliens. To date, nobody has publicly *demonstrated* the skill to outsmart or outmuscle PGP.

Does PGP Provide Too Much Privacy?

Critics of PGP like to state that the package is too sophisticated and too secure for anybody but paranoids. They ridicule the idea that you and I need such a tool. These nay-sayers remind me of employers who dismiss potential employees for being "too educated." Do PGP's foes have too much sex, too much money, or too much status? Do they have too much privacy that they would like to give away? In any case, they have too little historical perspective.

While writing this book, I communicated with many PGP users and asked them why they use PGP. Bob Smart, who has written a front-end program for PGP, is mentioned in alt-security.pgp FAQs. You may come across him on the Internet. Mr. Smart sent me a letter that he has kindly permitted me to share with you:

> One of the major concerns that is often
> raised about ready access to encryption tech-
> nology is that it will somehow increase the
> level of privacy available to individuals
> beyond where it should reasonably be. I think
> this is an inaccurate analysis: PGP does not
> so much *increase* privacy as it does *restore* a
> balance that has recently been perturbed away
> from privacy.
>
> Until quite recently, most personal communi-
> cation was inherently private by virtue of
> the enormous volume of message traffic. It
> simply isn't feasible to sift through the mail
> on the off-chance that there might be "interesting"

material in some of the letters — and so a
certain anonymity has always been available.

With the advent of electronic communication,
and particularly e-mail, the situation is
very different: It is quite feasible to set a
computer to scan *all* the messages that pass
through some chosen mail path, "fishing" for
anything one deems interesting: references to
the CIA, mention of competitor companies or
their products, [or] words and phrases that
might signal a potential for blackmail or
fraud (for instance, a credit card number has
a distinctive and easily-recognized format —
one might scan all the passing messages for
such numbers).

Not only is it theoretically possible to monitor enormous streams of mail in this way,
it's downright cheap. A computer capable of
performing such a task can be had in chain
stores and swap meets all over the Western
world for under a thousand dollars. Anyone
can engage in this kind of activity, and it
is well within the bounds of feasibility to
set up many such monitoring stations to scan
many separate mail streams.

We are relatively safe from such intrusions
in the postal mails, since the process of
scanning letters and postcards is so labor-
intensive; electronic channels are much more
vulnerable to such monitoring in the first
place, and the public is for the most part
quite naive about the exposure. People who
would never write a company secret or a credit
card number on a postcard think nothing of
entrusting such information to e-mail...and
are often blissfully unaware of the number of
opportunities that are afforded for other
eyes to read the messages as they make their
way to the intended recipient.

PGP merely counteracts this erosion of privacy. If PGP were in widespread use, the balance of privacy would merely be driven back

```
to where it was before. Threats to privacy in
the modern world are unprecedented in human
history, owing to our unprecedented technolo-
gies for transferring, manipulating, and
searching vast oceans of data. PGP offers
nothing more radical than a return to the
expectations of privacy that our grandparents
took for granted (and that too many of us
take for granted in error today).
```

Well said, Bob!

Which Version of PGP You Should Get

PGP, like many computer programs, developed in steps. These began with Phil Zimmermann's first PGP release in June 1991. Versions 1.0 through 2.3a caused considerable legal confusion in the U.S. Some people condemned PGP as "Pretty Good Piracy" because, they claimed, it violated patent rights. Other people argued that since PGP was distributed for free (not sold), it did not violate anyone's rights. This heated debate stopped many universities and other institutions from using PGP.

On May 23, 1994, there were two *compatible* PGP versions in widespread use. ViaCrypt PGP version 2.4 was the fully licensed, commercial version for use within Canada and the U.S. Version 2.3a "freeware" was used throughout the rest of the world (where U.S. algorithm patents do not apply) — and by many people within the U.S. and Canada.

On May 24, 1994, version 2.6 appeared. I urge everyone to switch to PGP version 2.6 or higher at this time.

MIT PGP Version 2.6

On May 24, 1994, the Massachusetts Institute of Technology (MIT) began distributing MIT PGP version 2.6. This version — and its successor, version 2.6.2 — are "freeware" licensed (without charge)for restricted, noncommercial use in the United States and Canada. As I write this paragraph in September 1994, anyone can finally use PGP for e-mail security without worrying about infringing on anyone's patent rights! In PGP founder Philip Zimmermann's words, "This is a significant milestone in PGP's legal development."

There is a small price for this new freedom. MIT stated that, in order to protect RSA Data Security, Inc.'s intellectual property rights in public- key technology, MIT PGP versions 2.6 and 2.6.2 were designed so that the messages they create after September 1, 1994, will be unreadable by earlier versions of PGP — including ViaCrypt PGP version 2.4. MIT PGP versions 2.6 and 2.6.2 will, however, always be able to read messages *generated by* ViaCrypt PGP version 2.4.

Export of MIT PGP versions 2.6 and 2.6.2 is restricted by the U.S. government. Therefore, these versions are being released through a controlled File Transport Protocol (FTP) site maintained by MIT. This FTP site permits only people in the United States and Canada to access PGP. The MIT FTP site that carries PGP is net-dist.mit.edu, in the pub/PGP directory.

Phil Zimmermann, who worked on PGP version 2.6, assures us that "PGP 2.6 is as strong as earlier versions. It contains no back doors." He adds, "I urge all PGP users in the U.S. to upgrade to version 2.6, to help move toward eradication of earlier versions of PGP. This will improve the overall political and legal landscape surrounding PGP."

What will happen to worldwide compatibility? In the Summer of 1994, MIT promised to publish details on the simple format change so that earlier international versions of PGP might be independently upgraded by the Europeans. As of this writing, I don't know whether people outside the U.S. will develop a new version, or whether they will simply use the MIT PGP version(s).

(Update. *As this book goes to press, MIT PGP Version 2.6.2 has replaced Version 2.6 in America. Version 2.6.2i is the most recent global version. Version 3.0 is being written.*)

ViaCrypt PGP Version 2.7

ViaCrypt PGP Version 2.7 was released in July 1994, partly in response to the new MIT PGP format. ViaCrypt PGP 2.7 is fully licensed for private or commercial use in the U.S. and Canada. Version 2.7 is completely *compatible* with MIT PGP version 2.6. The ViaCrypt product incorporated a default setting to automatically change its output format to the new format on September

1, 1994. However, the user can at any time override the default setting and produce output in either the old format or the new format.

Finding PGP

While I was writing this book, both MIT PGP version 2.6.2 and ViaCrypt PGP 2.7 were introduced, and several future PGP products were announced. PGP is undergoing explosive growth now that it is completely legal in the U.S. and Canada. Who knows what new companies, distribution channels, and products might exist by the time you read this page? Therefore, the following advice about getting PGP may be superceded by new options in the near future.

How and where you can get PGP depends on where you live (i.e., in what country) and on your computer skills. As of this writing, there are three ways to find PGP software.

1. Contact ViaCrypt. ViaCrypt is an American company that distributes PGP products fully licensed for commercial use in the U.S. and Canada. Because of export laws, ViaCrypt can only supply PGP to the citizens of these two countries.

I recommend that all individuals (who are not computer experts) and businesses contact ViaCrypt. ViaCrypt PGP Version 2.7 is easy to install, has extra features not found in freeware versions, and comes with the latest documentation. In addition, if you get PGP from ViaCrypt, you can easily verify that nobody has tampered with your PGP! Unless you are a computer expert, these factors make a big difference. I dealt with ViaCrypt before the company knew I was writing this book; I found the ViaCrypt people helpful and efficient. Their current products include:

ViaCrypt PGP for Macintosh

ViaCrypt PGP for MS-DOS

ViaCrypt PGP for UNIX

RESOURCE BOX

ViaCrypt

2104 West Peoria Avenue
Phoenix, Arizona 85029
602-944-0773 (phone)
602-943-2601 (fax)
800-536-2664 (credit card orders only)
e-mail: viacrypt@acm.org

ViaCrypt PGP for WinCIM/CSNav (CompuServe)

ViaCrypt PGP for Windows

2. Use Archie and FTP. Computer experts, or at least computer enthusiasts willing to learn Internet lingo, can use the Internet to transfer PGP to their own computers.

Archie is a system that allows you to search indices of files available on public servers on the Internet. You can use Archie to find FTP sites around the world that make PGP freeware available. Historically, this is how most people in the U.S. found PGP before ViaCrypt existed. FTP sites are still the source of PGP for most people from Sweden to South Africa. MIT Version 2.6.2 is available to U.S. citizens through FTP. Information is available via FTP from net-dist.mit.edu (in the /pub/PGP directory).

To understand Internet jargon, you can read books such as Ed Krol's popular *The Whole Internet User's Guide & Catalog*, O'Reilly & Associates.

RESOURCE BOX
O'Reilly & Associates, Inc.
103 Morris Street, Suite A Sebastopol, California 95472 800-998-9938

3. Dial your local bulletin board system. Thousands of BBSs around the world distribute perfectly legal computer freeware. Historically, many people have downloaded PGP versions from these BBSs. To learn more about BBSs, and to find lists of BBSs in your area, you can read *Boardwatch Magazine*.

When you are exploring the BBS world, be sure to visit the Electronic Frontier Foundation's BBS. Its data phone number is 202-861-1224.

Important Note: If you get a copy of the current freeware version of PGP, be sure that your version has the *PGP User's Guide*

RESOURCE BOX
Boardwatch Magazine
7586 West Jewell Avenue, Suite 200 Lakewood, Colorado 80230 303-973-6038 (Editorial) 303-973-4222 (BBS) 800-933-6038 (Subscriptions) e-mail: jack.rickard@boardwatch.com

included in the compressed file. Under no circumstances should PGP ever be distributed without the user documentation. Any version of PGP found in a release package with no manual should be avoided. Someone may have tampered with the software — and even if the software is OK, no one should use PGP without understanding some of the security concepts that are explained in its manual. Also, no one should use or distribute PGP without reading the legal issues explained in the manual.

Registering with a Public Key Server

Once you start using PGP, you will generate a public key for yourself. Other people will use that key to send you encrypted material. How does someone find your key? The most direct way is for you to e-mail the key to her. This is analogous to giving her your telephone number. A second method is for you to list your key in a public key server. This is analogous to listing your telephone number in your city phone book.

Public key servers exist around the world. Unlike telephone books, public key servers are run by volunteers. These servers allow you to list your key and to look up other people's keys. You only have to send your key to one server; that key server will automatically send your key to all other known servers.

Because these servers are run by volunteers, they tend to come and go. As of this writing, here are a few existing key servers:

pgp-public-keys@demon.co.uk

pgp-public-keys@dsi.unimi.it

pgp-public-keys@ext221.sra.co.jp

pgp-public-keys@io.com

pgp-public-keys@kub.nl

pgp-public-keys@pgp.ox.ac.uk

I list these servers only for purposes of demonstration, so that you will know what these addresses mean if you run across one. Note from the addresses ("uk"= United Kingdom, "jp"= Japan, etc.) that, if you list your public key in the United States, your PGP key will be distributed automatically around the world. This server network is one graphic example of PGP's global reach. In order to find the Internet address for current public key servers, go to the **alt.security.pgp** UseNet news group.

How do you use a key server? Once you find its e-mail address, send it a message with the word HELP on the *subject* line. You will receive a response similar to this:

From: PGP Key Service <pgp-public-keys@kub.nl>
Errors-To: teun.nijssen@kub.nl
Subject: Your command, HELP

Key server software written by Michael Graff <explorer@iastate.edu>

For questions or comments regarding this key server site, contact
teun.nijssen@kub.nl

Current version: 1.1.1.1 1994/06/20 03:09:59

NOTE!
This service has been set up to help transfer public keys between PGP users.
It does NOT attempt to guarantee that a key is a valid key; use the signatures
on a key for that kind of security. This service can be discontinued at any
time without prior notification.
Direct questions and comments to <teun.nijssen@kub.nl>
PGP Public Keyservers
There are PGP public key servers which allow one to exchange public keys
running through the Internet and UUCP mail systems.

NOTE!
This service is here only to help transfer public keys between PGP users. It
does NOT attempt to guarantee that a key is a valid key;
use the signatures on a key for that kind of security.
Each keyserver processes requests in the form of mail messages.
The commands for the server are entered on the Subject: line.

> To: pgp-public-keys@kub.nl
> From: johndoe@some.site.edu
> Subject: help

Sending your key to ONE server is enough. After it processes your key, it will
forward your add request to other servers automagically.

For example, to add your key to the keyserver, or to update your key if it is
already there, send a message similar to the following to any server:

To: pgp-public-keys@kub.nl
From: johndoe@some.site.edu
Subject: add

——-BEGIN PGP PUBLIC KEY BLOCK——-
Version: 2.3A

<blah blah blah>

——-END PGP PUBLIC KEY BLOCK——-

continued

COMPROMISED KEYS: Create a Key Revocation Certificate (read the PGP docs on how to do that) and mail your key to the server once again, with the ADD command.
Valid commands are:

Command	Message body contains
ADD	Your PGP public key (key to add is body of msg)
INDEX	List all PGP keys the server knows about (-kv)
VERBOSE INDEX	List all PGP keys, verbose format (-kvv)
GET	Get the whole public keyring (split)
GET userid	Get just that one key
MGET regexp	Get all keys which match /regexp/
LAST days	Get the keys updated in the last `days' days

Examples for the MGET command:

MGET teun	Gets all keys which have "teun" in them
MGET iastate	All keys which contain "iastate"
MGET 12345678 I 90ABCDEF	Those two keyid's

Just try not to use ``MGET .*'' — use ``GET'' instead.

Check the Usenet newsgroup alt.security.pgp for updates to the list of active key servers

Should you list your public key with one of these key servers? At present, only a small percentage of PGP users do so. There are two reasons for this. First, many PGP users do not know about these servers. Second, many PGP users communicate only with friends and business associates whom they know well; they see no advantage to publicly listing their key(s). Similarly, many people have unlisted telephones. In San Francisco, for example, roughly one-third of the telephone numbers are unlisted.

On the other hand, listing your key in a public server can help protect you. Suppose you post messages on the Internet, and you want readers to be sure that it was, in fact, you who wrote these messages. You can PGP-sign your letters, and strangers will be able to verify your signature by checking your publicly listed key.

Stable Large Email Database (SLED)

SLED (Stable Large Email Database) is a formalized version of the public key servers, plus a lot more. It is an on-line directory where you can list your Internet e-mail address(es) and/or PGP public key(s). Also, you can use SLED to search for the e-mail addresses and/or PGP public keys of your friends, business associates, etc. SLED provides an extremely flexible search mechanism. Unlike a conventional telephone directory, SLED allows you to search for someone based on his nicknames, past employers, past projects, organization affiliations, school background, previous e-mail addresses, and a variety of other information. Unlike regular phone directories, all information is current. Users can update their material whenever they want. Unlike public key servers, SLED has only authenticated listings for real people with real e-mail addresses.

Support For PGP Data Encryption

SLED is a public repository for PGP keys. SLED public keys are signed by SLED with the signature indicating that the user's authenticity has been verified by receipt of a matching "bank check." The storage and signing of public keys is an optional feature of SLED. You can join and use SLED without knowing PGP.

SLED uses ViaCrypt PGP. As of this writing, SLED offers discount coupons to members who want to purchase ViaCrypt PGP.

Privacy Protection and Controlling Your Personal Data

The people who run SLED say that SLED is designed to provide users with privacy and control over their personal data. Users are protected from commercial junk mailers, head hunters, and other data collectors (SLED managers say) in the following ways:

◆ They require user permission to add listings to the directory.

◆ They do not sell or trade mailing lists.

◆ They do not send mass e-mail solicitations to their users. They maintain a list of users who wish to receive ongoing information regarding SLED services.

◆ The system's search mechanism makes it difficult for outside entities to create mailing lists from the database.

◆ The system's search mechanism limits released information to:

   1. User name

   2. User e-mail addresses

3. PGP public key (if provided)

4. Verification of matching search words

The system does not provide a user's entire profile to searchers. Only matching information is displayed.

- ◆ The system does not include telephone numbers or home/business addresses in a user profile. If another user desires such information, they can e-mail the user to request it.

- ◆ All users must agree to an Acceptable Use Policy.

For More Information on SLED

You can receive pages of details if you send e-mail to Larry Drebes at:

> `ldrebes@drebes.com`

or

> `drebes@sled.com`

or

> `sled@drebes.com`

Finding the Latest PGP News

There are two easy ways to keep in touch with the rapidly growing PGP world. If you are a registered ViaCrypt user, you will automatically receive updates about any new versions or features. These notices may be enough for you, if you view PGP as merely a practical tool.

If you are a PGP enthusiast and want to know everything going on in the PGP world — from the latest ftp site to the most recent legislative battle — there is a UseNet newsgroup exactly for you. It is called alt.security.pgp. Here is a sample screen from this newsgroup:

```
alt.security.pgp (47T 131A 0K 0H R)    h=help

  1 +    Hypothetical: If you knew your computer was t  Christopher Creutz
  2 + 4  Why not to talk to police?                     Christopher Creutz
  3 + 23 RSADSI Warning                                 David Sternlight
  4 + 2  Temporary Defense to the Clearsig Menace       Guy Berliner
                                                             continued
```

```
 5 +     The Latest Sternlight War (Was: Re: RSADSI Wa     Louis Emmet Mahone
 6 + 19  NSA Had Hand in DES (was Re: pgp -c or crypt?  Guy Berliner
 7 +     the Electronic Curmudgeon                         Rodney Lewis
 8 +     Let's not panic                                   John Dehaven
 9 +     What's a Sternlight?                              Glen Roberts
10 +     Problems? Yeah.                                    James Salsman
11 +     key add error                                     John S.
12 +     Possible dangerous feature of PGP (multiple r  pcattin@iiic.ethz.
13 +     Microsoft Natural Keyboard                        John Sampson
14 +     Possible dangerous featur                         John Dehaven
15 + 2   HELP! PGP261S.ZIP                                 robert.rothenburg@
16 + 2   legal crypto signatures                           Bob Bales

Alt-Z FOR HELP I ANSI-BBS I FDX I 9600 N81 I LOG CLOSED I TERMINAL I ON-LINE
```

When you start reading **alt.security.pgp**, pay special attention to any FAQ (Frequently Asked Questions) postings. This newsgroup has several regular contributors who help educate PGP novices, and update PGP experts, by distributing FAQs that ask and answer questions about PGP. This is the best place to find the locations of public key servers, and other information that changes frequently. You can simply download these FAQs to your computer. Two individuals whose FAQs have helped me are Ed Edstrom and Michael Johnson. Edstrom is a software engineer who wants fellow computer users to use PGP. Johnson is a privacy enthusiast who gave me permission to tell you:

```
I run a computer bulletin board system that
contains encryption and privacy software,
called the Colorado Catacombs BBS. Set your
modem to 8 data bits, 1 stop bit, and no par-
ity, and call at the highest speed your modem
supports (up to 28,800 bps) at 303-772-1062.
(Denver, Colorado callers can also call
938-9654).

I am the inventor of the Diamond Encryption
Algorithm. I support the EFF.
```

Edstrom and Johnson, like many helpful people in cyberspace, are volunteers. They do a lot of work to educate us, without receiving a dime for their efforts. When you encounter such folks, please thank them.

PART FOUR

Using PGP
on the
PC

Quick Start For Manual Haters

Let us start this user manual part of the book realistically. Many of us dislike computer manuals (or microwave oven manuals for that matter). We have a software diskette in our hands, and we want to get started *now!* We don't want a humorless writer telling us to read 100 pages before we can see results. Computers have fast processors, and many computer users have fast minds. We expect manuals to be fast.

Fortunately, PGP is an easy program to learn. With a little effort, you will be able to protect your data files and e-mail from snoops. If you already know how to operate a few software packages, you will probably get a good feeling for PGP within an hour. After playing with PGP for a weekend, you might feel confident that you are a security expert — perhaps overly confident. In any case, I'll bet you have fun.

Here are a few public secrets about how to skip the dry stuff and jump to the juicy action sections.

1. If you want to use PGP for anything other than cluttering your desk, read these sections:

2. .If you want to encrypt and decrypt files for your use only, also read this section:

3. If you want to understand public keys, so that you can encrypt and decrypt secret e-mail letters to and from someone else, read these sections:

4. If you want to find out how to have more fun, read the remaining sections. I recommend that you save the "Setting Configuration Parameters" section until last. This contains technical material that you may never need.

For Curious Readers Only: PGP is designed for people who want computer security. There are clever people who might want to intercept your e-mail and your computer files. Thus, all humor aside, I urge you to study PGP's subtle safeguards carefully before you start sending your public key into the outside world. I also advise that you read the final section, "Security Considerations (For Paranoids Only)," even if you are not paranoid!

Installing PGP On Your PC

PGP is easy to install. If you want to drive a car, you have to locate the gas pedal, the brake pedal, and the steering wheel. Similarly, in order to install PGP, you have to know how to find the DOS prompt and how to move between one *directory* and another. It also helps to know what a computer *reboot* means. Your computer manual should cover these fundamental topics.

ViaCrypt PGP version 2.7 is distributed on both 3-½" and 5-¼" diskettes. Here is how to install the program from those disks. (If you are using PGP version 2.6, I'll assume that you are already computer-savvy, and know how to open a directory and transfer the PGP files to that directory.)

Pick the ViaCrypt disk that is the right size for your computer system and insert the disk into your A: drive. (If you want to use the B: drive, just substitute B: for A: in the directions that follow.)

Type:

> **A:** [press the Enter key]

This will set your computer to read the A: drive.

Type:

> **Install** [press the Enter key]

Using PGP on the PC

The following message will appear on your screen:

```
                    ViaCrypt PGP for MS-DOS

Installing ViaCrypt PGP for MS-DOS from A: to  C:\VPGP
═══════════════════════════════════════════════════════

| Thank you for purchasing ViaCrypt PGP for MS-DOS                 |
| |ViaCrypt PGP will be installed in the directory shown above.    |

| If the directory does not currently exist, it will be           |
| created.  If you wish to install ViaCrypt PGP into a             |
| different directory, enter it in the space above.               |
|                                                                 |
|  Press RETURN to continue                                       |

1993- 1994 by ViaCrypt, a division of Lemcom Systems, Inc.
```

Unless you specify otherwise, ViaCrypt will create a directory called "VPGP" on your hard disk and transfer the PGP program to that directory. If you prefer, you can edit the "C:\VPGP" line to create a directory called "Private", "Secret", or anything you want. I rename the directory to "PGP" because I have used previous PGP versions and that directory name is hardwired into my brain.

After you make your decision, press the Enter key.

If the directory name you choose *does not* already exist, the PGP install program will create the directory automatically. If it *does* exist, the install program will prompt you for confirmation. (If you are upgrading from ViaCrypt 2.4, reinstalling to an existing directory will update your program, your help files, and ViaCrypt PGP's configuration file [config.txt]. It will leave your current key rings intact.)

At this point, the install program will begin transferring the PGP information from the floppy disk to your hard disk. When this process is complete, you will see:

```
                    ViaCrypt PGP for MS-DOS
Installing ViaCrypt PGP for MS-DOS from A: to  C:\VPGP
═══════════════════════════════════════════════════════

| Your AUTOEXEC.BAT is about to be updated to add ViaCrypt PGP     |
| to your search path.  Your existing AUTOEXEC.BAT file will       |
```

continued

```
|                                                                      |
| be saved as AUTOEXEC.OLD                                             |
|======================================================================|
| Update your AUTOEXEC.BAT?                                            |
|Yes | No |                                                            |

1993- 1994 by ViaCrypt, a division of Lemcom Systems, Inc.
```

Are you using ViaCrypt for the first time? If so, select "Yes." Or are you upgrading ViaCrypt? If so, select "No."

Next, the install program will ask you this:

```
                    ViaCrypt PGP for MS-DOS

Installing ViaCrypt PGP for MS-DOS from A: to  C:\VPGP
========================================================================
| Your machine will now re-boot so that the updates to your          |
| AUTOEXEC.BAT will take affect.                                      |
========================================================================
| Reboot your Computer System ?                                      |
|Yes | No |                                                          |


    1993- 1994 by ViaCrypt, a division of Lemcom Systems, Inc.
```

If you select "Yes," the install program will reboot (restart) your computer. If you select "No," the install program will ask you:

```
                    ViaCrypt PGP for MS-DOS

Installing ViaCrypt PGP for MS-DOS from A: to  C:\VPGP
========================================================================
| Change To Application Directory?                                   |
|Yes | No |                                                          |
========================================================================

    1993- 1994 by ViaCrypt, a division of Lemcom Systems, Inc.
```

If you select "Yes," you will be ready to use PGP. If you select "No," you will return to the DOS prompt.

Select and enter:

`Yes`

Congratulations! You have successfully installed PGP, and you are now ready to learn PGP.

Setting Your Time Zone

PGP is used in many time zones around the United States and around the world. PGP (like many other programs) dates certain files by using a variable called "TZ" to indicate your time zone. ViaCrypt makes it easy for you to set this time-zone variable.

Type:

`SETTZ`

You will see:

```
SETTZ — Utility to correctly initialize the TZ environment variable.
Select your time zone:

l    1.  Hawaii Time Zone,        UTC - 11   hours          l
l    2.  Alaska Time Zone,        UTC - 10   hours          l
l    3.  Pacific Time Zone,       UTC - 8    hours          l
l    4.  Mountain Time Zone,      UTC - 7    hours          l
l    5.  Central Time Zone,       UTC - 6    hours          l
l    6.  Eastern Time Zone,       UTC - 5    hours          l
l    7.  Atlantic Time Zone,      UTC - 4    hours          l
l    8.  Quit, making no changes                            l

l    Enter your choice (1 - 8) :                            l
```

Enter your choice, and PGP will ask you:

`Does your locality observe Daylight Saving`
`Time [y/n]?`

Just about everyone can answer yes to this question. Enter your choice.

SETTZ will update your AUTOEXEC.BAT file to add a "SET TZ=" line. It will also make a backup copy of your original AUTOEXEC.BAT file called AUTOEXEC.TZ.

After you reboot your computer, PGP will be able to date your PGP materials with the proper time zone.

Using PGP on the PC

Escaping Panic If You Get Lost

If you get lost and need on-line help, here are three commands that might save you.

cls clears the screen of unwanted junk
pgp -h gives you a summary of PGP commands
pgp -k gives you a summary of key-management commands

Selecting Which PGP Crypto To Use

PGP offers two distinct kinds of cryptography ("crypto"). These choices are *conventional crypto* (also known as *single-key)* and *public-key crypto* (also known as *double-key).* With conventional crypto, you *encrypt* (scramble) and *decrypt* (unscramble) a message with the same key. With public-key crypto, you encrypt (scramble) a message with a public key and decrypt (unscramble) the same message with a secret key.

Conventional crypto is the faster and easier of the two cryptos to master. It is ideal when you want to encrypt and decrypt messages (or files) that only you will read. For example, you might encrypt your intimate diary, your stock portfolio, or your romantic epistles. Public-key crypto is superior when you need to encrypt memos, documents, or files for someone else to read on his or her computer. For instance, you might use public key crypto to mail business plans, tax records, or legal contracts to a colleague.

With either PGP crypto, you can encrypt any file on your computer. It makes no difference to PGP whether that file was created by a word processor, a spreadsheet, a database manager, a graphics package, a utility, or an electronic game. PGP crypto performs two functions: 1) It scrambles the contents of your file, and 2) it "compresses" (shrinks the size of) your file. To illustrate the latter, I used PGP's conventional crypto to encrypt the "PGP.EXE" file (the file that runs PGP). The original file is 298,677 bytes in size. The encrypted file takes up 116,333 bytes. This impressive compression factor suggests why many people encrypt even nonconfidential files in order to free extra storage space on their disk.

Using PGP'S Conventional Cryptography

The next two sections explain how to encrypt and decrypt files using PGP's conventional cryptography.

Encrypting with Conventional Cryptography

Conventional crypto is PGP's secure, easy-to-use way to encrypt files that only you will decrypt and read in the future.

The general form of this command is:

```
pgp -c textfile
```

You can remember this command, c, as in **C**onventional. Note that the "-" character before "c" is the "minus" sign on your keyboard. Be sure to leave a space between the "pgp" and the "-" character.

Here is a sample letter, which I have stored in a file called "DEMO.TXT" in the standard place, C:\PGP\:

```
Peachpit Reader
123 Bright Street
Cyberspace 01234

Dear Peachpit Reader:

Bravo! You've discovered this book, and you
are in the midst of an exciting journey.

Peachpit Press has many more adventures for
you. It offers you a diverse set of computer
books that combine technical expertise with
humor and a social conscience.

Please contact Peachpit today and ask for its
beautiful catalog. Be sure to say hello from
me.

See You in the Future,

André Bacard
```

Encrypt this letter with PGP conventional crypto.

Type:

```
pgp -c demo.txt
```

or

```
pgp -c Demo.txt
```

or

```
pgp -c c:\pgp\demo.txt
```

Press the Enter key.

Note that PGP assumes that the file DEMO.TXT is in the \PGP directory, unless you state otherwise. I could have stored the letter on a floppy disk and specified A:\DEMO.TXT or A:\LETTERS\DEMO.TXT.

PGP will produce a message similar to this on your screen:

```
[C:\PGP]
>pgp -c demo.txt
ViaCrypt PGP 2.7 - Pretty Good Privacy for everyone.
U. S. Patent Nos. 4,200,770, 4,218,582, 4,405,829 and 4,424,414
licensed exclusively by Public Key Partners.
U. S. Patent No. 5,214,703 licensed by Ascom Tech AG.
Zip compression by Mark Adler and Jean-loup Gailly, used with permission.
(c) 1990-1994 Philip Zimmermann
(except for DigiSig+ Cryptographic Engine and IDEA Cipher).
(c) 1993-1994 DigiSig+ Cryptographic Engine by ViaCrypt,
a division of Lemcom Systems, Inc.  21 June 94
ViaCrypt PGP is export restricted.  Refer to ViaCrypt PGP software license.
Current time: 1994/10/02 18:11 GMT
You need a pass phrase to encrypt the file.
Enter pass phrase:
```

(Note: *In order to avoid needless repetition, the patent and legal material will not be reproduced in future sample PGP screens.*)

For the pass phrase, pick something easy to remember.

Type:

```
123abc
```

PGP will prompt you to re-enter the same pass phrase again to insure that you do not make a typographical error. After you re-key your pass phrase, the following message will appear:

```
[C:\PGP]
ViaCrypt PGP 2.7 - Pretty Good Privacy for everyone.
Enter same pass phrase again: Just a moment....
Ciphertext file: demo.pgp
```

Using PGP on the PC

You're finished! You have successfully encrypted a file! It's that easy. PGP has encrypted the Peachpit letter, using the pass phrase 123abc, and has put the new file in C:\PGP\DEMO.PGP. Note that PGP automatically adds the ".PGP" extension to the file, to remind you that the new file contains a cipher-text. Note also that PGP automatically stores the encrypted ("ciphertext") file in the same directory as the unencrypted ("plaintext") file.

If you use your word processor to peek at this DEMO.PGP file, you will see an unintelligible mess of symbols. This is exactly the goal of crypto!

For curious readers only: You may wonder why PGP asks for a "pass phrase" instead of a "password." When asked for a "password", most people choose a short word or string of characters such as their name or "123abc". These passwords are easy for amateurs — much less professional snoops — to guess. PGP hopes that this "pass phrase" prompt will encourage you to pick at least a series of words. In this manual, I use short pass phrases for conve-nience. Away from this manual, I use complicated pass phrases.

Decrypting with Conventional Cryptography

It is easy to decrypt (unscramble) any conventionally PGP-encrypted file if you remember the pass phrase. The general form of the decryption com-mand is:

```
pgp ciphertextfile
```

Note that the normal "-" is missing in this command!

Let us decrypt the above letter about Peachpit Press. Type:

```
pgp demo.pgp
```

or

```
pgp c:\demo.pgp
```

or

```
pgp demo
```

Note that PGP will look for the ".pgp" extension, even if you do not type the extension.

The following message will appear on your screen:

```
[C:\PGP]
ViaCrypt PGP 2.7 - Pretty Good Privacy for everyone.
File is conventionally encrypted.
You need a pass phrase to decrypt this file.
Enter pass phrase:
```

Type:

> **123abc**

You will see:

```
[C:\PGP]
ViaCrypt PGP 2.7 - Pretty Good Privacy for everyone.
Enter pass phrase: Just a moment....Pass phrase appears good. .
Plaintext filename: demo
```

Note that PGP stores your decrypted material in the file DEMO — *not* in the original file DEMO.TXT. At this point, you can use your word processor to verify that DEMO and DEMO.TXT contain the identical material!

For the sake of illustration, suppose that you already had a file called DEMO (without an extension) before you instructed PGP to process your encrypted file "DEMO.PGP".

PGP would generate this message:

```
[C:\PGP]
ViaCrypt PGP 2.7 - Pretty Good Privacy for everyone.
Enter pass phrase: Just a moment....Pass phrase appears good. .
Plaintext filename: demo
Output file 'demo' already exists.  Overwrite (y/N)?
```

You could put this decrypted data into a new file of your choice by typing:

> **n**

PGP would then instruct you as follows:

```
[C:\PGP]
ViaCrypt PGP 2.7 - Pretty Good Privacy for everyone.
Enter new file name:
```

You could enter any file name — well, it's best to pick a name that you haven't already used for something else — and send this file to the directory or disk of your choice. Here is an example. Type:

```
c:\pgp\peachpit
```

If you use your word processor to examine DEMO.TXT and PEACHPIT, you will discover that they are identical. PGP does work!

Using PGP's Public Key Cryptography

(Warning: *Responsible people do not send PGP messages to friends in countries, companies, or government agencies that are hypersensitive about crypto, unless they have explicit permission to do so!*)

Creating and Organizing PGP Keys

Generating your public and secret keys

The first step in using PGP's public-key cryptography system is to generate your public key. When you instruct PGP to create a public key for you, PGP will automatically produce a second, secret key that is mathematically connected to your public key. PGP can invent an astronomically huge number of different key pairs. You can feel confident that your key pair will be unique.

Let us begin by using the PGP command to generate your keys. The general form of this command is:

```
pgp -kg
```

You can remember this command, kg, as in **K**ey **G**enerate.

Type:

```
pgp -kg
```

Note that here again the "-" character before kg is the "minus" sign on your keyboard. Be sure to leave a blank space between "pgp" and the "-" character.

The following message will appear on your screen:

```
[C:\PGP]
ViaCrypt PGP 2.7 - Pretty Good Privacy for everyone.
Pick your RSA key size:
    1)    512 bits-    Low commercial grade, fast but less secure
    2)    768 bits-    High commercial grade, medium speed, good security
    3)    1024 bits-   "Military" grade, slow, highest security
Choose 1, 2, or 3, or enter desired number of bits:
```

For learning purposes, it is best to select the 512-bit option because this is the fastest option. The creation of RSA keys is complex and time-consuming, even for a computer. I have watched a personal computer with a 286 chip take 30 minutes to calculate a 1024-bit key. When the time comes for you to generate a public key to distribute to your friends and the public, I recommend that you generate a 1024-bit key. It is well worth waiting a few minutes to give yourself the highest level of security.

Type:

    1

The following message will jump onto your screen (usually messages are displayed, but this one has a kangaroo in its lineage):

```
[C:\PGP]
ViaCrypt PGP 2.7 - Pretty Good Privacy for everyone.
Generating an RSA key with a 512-bit modulus.
You need a user ID for your public key.  The desired form for this user ID is
your name, followed by your E-mail address enclosed in <angle brackets>, if
you have an E-mail address.
For example:  John Q. Smith <12345.6789@compuserve.com>
Enter a user ID for your public key:
```

Your user ID (also spelled "userid" in PGP jargon) allows other people to store, identify, and access your public key in their computers. Your user ID labels your PGP public key much the way your name pinpoints your telephone number in the white pages of your telephone directory.

For most purposes, it is prudent to use both your full name and your e-mail address. This way nobody will confuse you, Jane Cheddar <jcheddar@mail.com>, with any of a thousand other people who call themselves Jane.

For some purposes, you may want to create a user ID that gives information other than your real name and address. You might be a business and want your user ID to promote a product. Or you might be responding to a personal ad and want to keep your real identity secret for now.

Choosing your user ID can be lots of fun. You can use spaces and punctuation. Note also that user IDs are not case sensitive: they do not distinguish between uppercase and lowercase letters, so PGP will read *Ted* and *ted* as the same name. To keep your user ID aesthetically pleasing, I recommend that you limit its total length to fewer than 40 total characters. Here are a few acceptable choices:

```
Peachpit Press <Phone 510-548-4393>
President Bill Clinton
Joe's Deli *** Best Pizza in Town ***
Single Mom <Seeks Florida Scuba Diver>
Cyberspace, Inc.
```

For illustration purposes this time enter:

```
André <e-mail address>
```

The screen will say:

```
[C:\PGP]
ViaCrypt PGP 2.7 - Pretty Good Privacy for everyone.
You need a pass phrase to protect your RSA secret key.
Your pass phrase can be any sentence or phrase and may have many words,
spaces, punctuation, or any other printable characters.
Enter pass phrase:
```

The trick is to pick a phrase that other people are unlikely to guess, but that you can remember. One example is "My pink elephant weighs one pound!" A second method is to choose your pass phrase in a foreign language. A third method is to select a paragraph from your favorite book and fabricate your pass phrase by stringing together the first letters from each of the words. This way you will not have to remember your pass code — but beware: You will have to remember where you put the book! The longer your pass code, the harder it is for someone else to guess it.

Never use your name, your Social Security number, your telephone number, or common words such as "code," "secret," or "sex." An amazing number of people use these words for computer pass codes. You should also be aware that professional snoops (and amateur ones too!) crack pass phrases using computerized dictionaries that scan thousands of single words in seconds.

(Caution: *Do not forget or misplace your pass phrase. PGP has no "back doors" or weaknesses that allow you to pay a computer expert to come to your office and recover your lost phrase. PGP grants you total freedom to accept responsibility for your acts.*)

Because you are learning, pick an easy pass phrase. Type:

`hispasscode`

Note that this phrase uses no spaces between the words. If you use spaces (for example, "his pass code"), you must remember and enter the spaces in the same way to unlock your key.

The screen now prompts you to:

```
[C:\PGP]
ViaCrypt PGP 2.7 - Pretty Good Privacy for everyone.
Enter same pass phrase again:
```

This double-check is vital for your safety. It insures that you do not lose valuable documents because of typographical errors. Yes, this double-check can be an irksome repetition, but the consequences of an error make the extra time spent on re-entry worthwhile! Notice that PGP does not "echo" (show your keystrokes) when you type your pass phrase. This is a second safety precaution to stop anyone from looking over your shoulder and memorizing your pass phrase.

Type hispasscode again and press the Enter key. The screen switches to:

```
[C:\PGP]
ViaCrypt PGP 2.7 - Pretty Good Privacy for everyone.
Note that key generation is a lengthy process.
We need to generate 608 random bits.  This is done by measuring the time
intervals between your keystrokes.  Please enter some random text on your
keyboard until you hear the beep:
 608
```

These random bits are generated in order to create your RSA keys. Once the random bits are created, PGP places this RANDom SEED material in a file called C:\PGP\RANDSEED.BIN. You can ignore this file if you see it in your PGP directory.

Start typing keystrokes. After you hear the beep, you will see something like the following on your screen:

```
[C:\PGP]
ViaCrypt PGP 2.7 - Pretty Good Privacy for everyone.
   0 * -Enough, thank you.
    ++++!...............................................++++!EK
Key generation completed.
```

(For Curious Readers Only: *As you sit watching your screen while PGP generates your keys, you may wonder what the stream of characters means. The following table lists these characters and their meaning.*)

Character	Meaning
.	Number tested is not a prime
+	Number tested may be a prime
!	Number tested is a prime
E	Trying an exponent
K	Generating components of the key

When you see the "E" flash onto your screen, you will know that your computer has just about completed generating your keys.

Congratulations! You have just generated your first PGP public and secret keys.

For purposes of this manual, you will be using a second public key. This is a good time for you to repeat the above lesson. Please generate a 512-bit public key with the following data:

User ID: **Susan <phone number>**

Pass Phrase: **herpasscode**

Where PGP stores your public and secret keys

Use your word processor to look at the directory where you have installed your PGP software package. For most users, this will be the C: hard drive. You will discover a number of files. The list of files may vary a little, depending on which version of PGP you are using and on where you got that version.

Here is a sample directory:

```
Directory of C:\PGP
.        <DIR>                        05-17-94      4:53p
..       <DIR>                        05-17-94      4:53p
AUTOEXEC.BAT             91           08-01-94      9:59p
CONFIG      TXT       6,382           06-21-94      1:34p
KEYS        ASC       2,391           02-07-94      4:43p
PGP         EXE     298,677           06-21-94      1:01p
PGP         HLP       3,833           06-21-94      1:53p
PGPSIG      ASC       2,502           06-21-94      2:42p
PUBRING     PGP       2,117           10-08-94     11:42a
RANDSEED    BIN          24           10-09-94      3:44p
SECRING     PGP         836           10-08-94     11:43a
SETTZ       EXE      16,858           06-21-94      5:26p
```

Pay special attention to the files PUBRING.PGP and SECRING.PGP in this list. These two files are essential for your computer security! PGP automatically stores the public keys that you generate, plus the public keys that you collect from other people, on a PUBlic key ring. This file is appropriately named PUBRING.PGP. Similarly, your secret keys are stored on a SECret key ring, which is aptly called SECRING.PGP.

(Note: *You may instruct PGP to store your keys in files other than PUBRING.PGP and SECRING.PGP. If you select this option, be sure to remember the names of your files and to treat them safely.*)

Can you read the PUBRING.PGP and SECRING.PGP files with your word processor? No, you cannot. These PGP files are not text files. If they were, anybody could read and steal your secret keys. If you peeked at these files with WordPerfect 5.1, you would see wierd symbols that looked like hieroglyphics. Here is a sample screen:

```
File: C:\PGP\PUBRING.PGP Revised: 10-08-94 11:42a
eyä⌠«_fϊ
Δx^A'∩
B¡k$Ÿ^⌡
›{Æ?ñ&4le^\Θ_D¥+¬eLÇ ſpμ⌐»4è_*3ïδCúŸ»jò–à√cëó...âΩ'"∞^A@ë
â^Yñ~(


8æ⌠∞p°^X.ª4GVE@PŸ^D{√a^HÃºeÃ⌠Å2»%^UΣZ,⌡π^NDwg^X^g∞±=
X<æ∞Ã^HW z
```

continued

```
æ"À|f"ƒ]èF_^K@»ŒVv≤ƒ±
í5Vöjûnû«èÜè°îÄ^^:É^VÆ_∂ªø&Γ"|kδμ˩én!^BÅ9%iïHûl...·»R^Yw›/Θ`^H-^K06
φ-^^êπ<tí"EhGñ


ÿW∂Q"_hU«)_^\Åøyâ=(1,RÃë^Qh^Vö¬agμºêRñOÇRnß^X?ΘGŸΓñf∞^A@¥"ViaC
rypt <70304.41@


o}δ*^N^^·Σ>
ÿr,sí|ü^C^TâPóα^Qμ_τÉ·^X3^F[a∫¿"vΩ¬ôg


l^^¥!∫^TK'
√)M'-t;;û«)Z^TUÑ}
Look: 1 Next Doc; 2 Prev Doc: 0
```

Do not worry, these strange files make perfect sense to PGP.

(Very Important: *Always back up your PUBRING.PGP and SECRING.PGP files onto a floppy disk after you generate, add, or alter any keys! Store these backup files in a location that is physically separate from your computer. This can protect your irreplaceable keys in case of a computer crash, a fire, a theft, or some other disaster.*)

Viewing your public key ring

Now is a good time to inspect your public key ring. Think of your PGP key ring as similar to the key ring (or key chain) that you keep in your pocket or in your purse. You probably fasten a house, a car, and an office key to your chain. Most of us do not label our keys: rather, we recognize our keys by their shapes, colors, and sizes.

So far, we have manufactured two PGP keys, one for **André** and one for **Susan**. Let us see how PGP marks these keys in its key ring. The general form of the command we want is:

```
pgp -kv[v] [userid] [keyring]
```

You can remember this command, **kv**, as in **K**ey **V**iew. The material inside the brackets is optional. Note that brackets are *not* typed in an actual command. Nonprogrammers often panic when they see this command. It brings back nightmares about algebra class or tax forms. Don't worry. Be happy. Phil Zimmermann knew what he was doing when he designed this command.

To learn the key view command, you should work through a few examples. Start with the simplest case, which will enable you to see all of the keys in your key ring. (Be sure you've made one for Susan.)

Go to the DOS prompt and type:

```
pgp -kv
```

A message similar to the following will appear on your screen:

```
[C:\PGP]
ViaCrypt PGP 2.7 - Pretty Good Privacy for everyone.
Key ring: 'c:\pgp\pubring.pgp'

Type   bits/keyID      Date         User ID
pub    512/EAAA9367    1994/07/27   Susan    <phone number>
pub    512/1455A57D    1994/07/27   André    <e-mail address>
2 matching keys found.
```

I said "similar" because the numbers and the letters will vary for every person who generates keys.

Note what the PGP key ring tells you about each key. André's key is stored in file PUBRING.PGP, it has 512 bits, and it was created on July 27, 1994. PGP also labels André's key with a key ID, 1455A57D. This key ID has eight characters. Previous versions of PGP used six characters. Because PGP has attracted so many new users, two extra characters were added — to reduce the likelihood of duplicate key IDs.

Let's progress, step by step, through the optional parts of the above command. Type:

```
pgp -kvv
```

Note the second "v". This command will list all of the signatures attached to the keys on your key ring. At this stage of this manual, we do not have any signatures. Therefore, PGP will generate the same screen as above.

Type:

```
pgp -kv Susan
```

or

```
pgp -kv Sus
```

or

```
pgp -kv "Susan"
```

These entries illustrate the [**userid**] option. This instructs PGP to show you only the key for a particular user — in this case, Susan. Note that PGP will search for user ID fragments, such as "**sus**". This can be helpful if the user ID is long and you are rushed for time. In the last entry, you will see that I have enclosed **Susan** in quotation marks. Why? Suppose you have two keys, one for Susan Jones and one for Susan Smith. It is important to put "**Susan Jones**" in quotation marks, so that PGP does not scan for the first Susan on your ring and return Susan Smith's key.

Let's move on to the [**keyring**] option. Many people keep copies of their house keys under a welcome mat. Similarly, many PGP users store backup key rings on floppy disks, both for safety and for easy transport. The [**keyring**] option tells PGP where to find your key ring, if it is not in the standard C:\PGP\PUBRING.PGP file. Here are a few samples.

Suppose I go to the DOS prompt, type, and enter:

```
pgp -kv b:\pubring.pgp
```
or
```
pgp -kv b:\secring.pgp
```
or
```
pgp -kv b:\mykeys.pgp
```

All three commands will go to my B: disk drive and return the requested key ring to my screen. In the second example, note that you can list your secret keys just as you can catalog your public keys. The third example illustrates that you can name or rename your key chain to "mykeys" — or to whatever you wish, within the bounds of DOS file-naming rules.

To avoid repetition, I'll refrain from explaining this [**keyring**] option again with every remaining PGP command for which it is appropriate.

Looking at your public key

By now you are probably eager to see your public key, this magical key that you can use to shield your privacy.

You can copy (or extract) any key from your public or secret key ring. This process allows you to look at your key and, if you want, to distribute your key(s) to other people. *Warning*: Never give your *secret* key(s) to anyone else! To do so is the equivalent of passing out duplicate keys to your bank safe-deposit box.

When you copy (or extract) a key, the original key stays on its key ring. It is not erased! If the key has signatures, those signatures are copied along with the key.

The general form of this command is:

```
pgp -kx[a] userid keyfile [keyring]
```

You can remember this command, **kx**, as in **K**ey e**X**tract.

Let's look at an example. Type:

```
pgp -kx André
```

The following message will appear on your screen:

```
[C:\PGP]
ViaCrypt PGP 2.7 - Pretty Good Privacy for everyone.
Extracting from key ring: 'c:\pgp\pubring.pgp', userid "andré".
Key for user ID: André <e-mail address>
512-bit key, Key ID 1455A57D, created 1994/07/27
Extract the above key into which file?
```

You can send this key to any file on your hard drive or on a floppy disk. For simplicity, enter:

```
mykey
```

The screen will read:

```
[C:\PGP]
ViaCrypt PGP 2.7 - Pretty Good Privacy for everyone.
Extract the above key into which file? mykey
Key extracted to file 'mykey.pgp'.
```

Note that PGP automatically adds the ".PGP" extension, unless you specify otherwise. You could have entered "**MYKEY.LIS**" or whatever other extension you use to help organize your computer files.

You could accomplish the same task from the original command line by entering either:

```
pgp -kx "André" Mykey
```

or

```
pgp -kx "André <e-mail address>" Mykey.
```

These alternatives offer two new lessons. First, notice the quotation marks around the user ID. These quotes are necessary so that PGP can distinguish between "**André Mykey**" (a two-word name that you might choose for a key) and "**André**" **Mykey** (a key named "André" and a key ring named "Mykey").

Second, suppose you enter:

pgp -kx "André" Mykey

The screen will read:

```
[C:\PGP]
ViaCrypt PGP 2.7 - Pretty Good Privacy for everyone.
Key extracted to file 'mykey.pgp'.
```

If you immediately type and enter:

pgp -kx "André <e-mail address>" Mykey

You will receive this message:

```
[C:\PGP]
ViaCrypt PGP 2.7 - Pretty Good Privacy for everyone.
Key ID 1455A57D is already included in key ring 'mykey.pgp'.
Keyring extract error.
For a usage summary, type:  pgp -h
```

This error message simply means that you cannot extract the same key into one file more than once. You could eliminate this problem either by deleting the file MYKEY.PGP (using the DOS command line or your favorite application), or by picking another file name, such as MYKEY.LIS.

Good job! Your public key is now stored in file MYKEY.PGP. This file contains incomprehensible symbols that have meaning to PGP but not to mere people. You can give MYKEY.PGP to a friend without giving him or her any other keys that might be on your public key ring. However, you must transport this file on a disk, not via electronic mail. (See the next paragraph.)

Many people prefer to transmit their public keys with electronic mail because e–mail is so fast and inexpensive. In order to prepare your public key for e-mail, you must amend the **kx** command. In practice, the following is the only version of this command that I use. Enter:

pgp -kxa "André" Mykey

Note the addition of the **a**, as in **ASCII**. (See the section on ASCII files.) This "a" instructs PGP to create an ASCII version of your public key that can be printed on a typewriter or transmitted by e-mail.

Your screen will now read:

```
[C:\PGP]
ViaCrypt PGP 2.7 - Pretty Good Privacy for everyone.
Transport armor file: mykey.asc
Key extracted to file 'mykey.asc'.
```

This is exactly what you want. If you use your word processor to read file MYKEY.ASC, you will discover something like this:

```
——-BEGIN PGP PUBLIC KEY BLOCK——-

Version: 2.7
mQA9Ai35DRoAAAEBgMdRJRQQml4h9OdQtGrAINUvGfXvCGyZnyHIuNBrFO
FJxhKL2papfaGrmX8QAFEbQZbWUgPG15bmFtZUB3ZWxsLnNmLmNhLnVzPg
=j1/2

——-END PGP PUBLIC KEY BLOCK——-
```

This is André's public key. The public key includes:

1. The " — -BEGIN PGP PUBLIC KEY BLOCK — -" line
2. The version line
3. All the scrambled characters
4. The " — -END PGP PUBLIC KEY BLOCK — -"

This is important! Suppose you received the above PGP public key in your e–mail. You would have to make a file of this *complete* key in order for PGP to process your key. Some novices think that the key consists only of the scrambled characters in the center, so they are never able to get keys to work.

Most 512-bit keys are of roughly the same length. Perhaps you have seen public keys that are 10 times the length of André's key. Keys with 1024 bits tend to be longer than 512-bit keys. Also, some individuals ask a half-dozen or more people to sign their public key. These signatures add extra characters to a public key.

Using PGP on the PC

To send this key via e-mail, you simply transmit file MYKEY.ASC the same way that you send any other letter, message, or text file. (See the section on decryption to learn how to process an incoming e-mail key.) If you prefer, you can also send this public key on a disk through "snail mail" (regular mail).

Many people see their public key for the first time and cry, "Oh my God! Do I have to type or remember this long key?" Fortunately, no. PGP does all the work for you.

Adding a key to your key ring

PGP exists to help you communicate with your relatives, friends, and colleagues. This two-way correspondence is possible if, and only if, you have their public keys on your key ring and they have *your* public key on *their* key rings.

The first challenge you face in this section is to summon a new public key from the outside world. You cannot add Susan or André's key to your ring, because these keys are already present.

Look at the files that came with your PGP program. Your version should have a file called KEY.ASC or KEYS.ASC. (If you don't have one of these files, just follow along with this text.) This file includes, at the very least, the public key for PGP's creator, Philip Zimmermann. I use the commercial version of PGP, ViaCrypt version 2.7. Take a look at what is included in my KEYS.ASC file.

The general form of this command is:

```
pgp -ka keyfile.
```

You can remember this command, **ka,** as in **K**ey **A**dd.

Type:

```
pgp -ka keys.asc
```

At this point, the following message appears on my screen:

```
[C:\PGP]
ViaCrypt PGP 2.7 - Pretty Good Privacy for everyone.
Looking for new keys...
pub    1024/C7A966DD    1993/05/21    Philip R. Zimmermann <prz@acm.org>
pub     512/67ECF13D    1993/07/29    David A. Barnhart <CIS:70275,1360>
pub    1024/CB768501    1993/10/13    ViaCrypt <Phone (602) 944-0773>

Checking signatures...
pub    1024/C7A966DD    1993/05/21    Philip R. Zimmermann <prz@acm.org>
sig!        67ECF13D    1993/07/30    David A. Barnhart <CIS:70275,1360>
```

continued

```
pub       512/67ECF13D   1993/07/29    David A. Barnhart <CIS:70275,1360>
sig!          C7A966DD    1993/10/25    Philip R. Zimmermann <prz@acm.org>
sig!          CB768501    1993/10/25    ViaCrypt <Phone (602) 944-0773>
pub      1024/CB768501    1993/10/13    ViaCrypt <Phone (602) 944-0773>
sig!          C7A966DD    1993/10/25    Philip R. Zimmermann <prz@acm.org>
sig!          CB768501    1993/10/25    ViaCrypt <Phone (602) 944-0773>

Keyfile contains:
3 new key(s)
One or more of the new keys are not fully certified.
Do you want to certify any of these keys yourself (y/N)?
```

The section on key certification is still ahead of you. Therefore, type:

n

The public keys belonging to ViaCrypt, Philip R. Zimmermann, and David A. Barnhart have just been added to our key ring alongside Susan and André's keys.

To verify this, type:

pgp -kv

PGP will display a screen like the following:

```
[C:\PGP]
ViaCrypt PGP 2.7 - Pretty Good Privacy for everyone.
Key ring: 'c:\pgp\pubring.pgp'

Type     bits/keyID       Date          User ID
pub     1024/C7A966DD    1993/05/21    Philip R. Zimmermann <prz@acm.org>
pub      512/67ECF13D    1993/07/29    David A. Barnhart <CIS:70275,1360>
pub     1024/CB768501    1993/10/13    ViaCrypt <Phone (602) 944-0773>
                                        ViaCrypt <70304.41@compuserve.com>
                                        ViaCrypt <viacrypt@acm.org>
                                        ViaCrypt <FAX (602) 943-2601>
pub      512/EAAA9367    1994/07/27    Susan <phone number>
pub      512/1455A57D    1994/07/27    André <e-mail address>
5 matching keys found.
```

You can now copy (extract) these new keys and distribute them to whomever you wish. Note the importance of this. Phil Zimmermann's public key is available to everyone in the PGP world. This makes it almost impossible for someone to create a phony public key and pretend to be Phil. Whomever gets the phony key will know it is phony when he or she compares it with the key that comes with PGP.

PGP has the ability to detect whether or not a file contains keys. For example, one of the files included in your PGP software is CONFIG.TXT; this file has nothing to do with keys.

Type:

```
pgp -ka config.txt
```

The following message will appear on your screen:

```
[C:\PGP]
ViaCrypt PGP 2.7 - Pretty Good Privacy for everyone.
No keys found in 'config.txt'.
Keyring add error.
For a usage summary, type:  pgp -h
```

You may also receive the previous message if someone sends his or her public key to you incorrectly. This often happens with novices.

Removing a key or user ID from your key ring

There are several reasons why you might want to remove a key from your key ring. Perhaps you have quit corresponding with Susan, or maybe Susan has changed her public key. Also, your pubring might be overly crowded with practice keys that you have made while learning PGP!

The general form of this command is:

```
pgp -kr userid
```

You can remember this command, **kr**, as in **K**ey **R**emove.

You do not want to remove the keys that you already have on your key ring, because you will continue using them. So, for practice, you can create a new key called "Trash" and then remove it.

Use the instructions under "Generating Your Public and Secret Keys," to add a key named "Trash" to your key ring. Then type:

```
pgp -kr Trash
```

The following message will appear on your screen:

```
[C:\PGP]
ViaCrypt PGP 2.7 - Pretty Good Privacy for everyone.
Removing from key ring: 'c:\pgp\pubring.pgp', userid "trash".
Key for user ID: Trash <city dump>
1024-bit key, Key ID D4A96RDD, created 1993/08/11
Are you sure you want this key removed (y/N)?
```

Type:

        y

PGP will now notify you:

```
[C:\PGP]
ViaCrypt PGP 2.7 - Pretty Good Privacy for everyone.
Key removed from key ring.
```

Congratulations! You have successfully removed a key.

Viewing the "fingerprint" of a public key

PGP is designed to protect your computer privacy and security. Therefore, PGP helps you determine whether or not any public key is legitimate or the work of an impostor. Suppose Susan is your accountant, and she mails you the following letter:

        Hello John,

        Please mail me your tax records for last
        year. I'm enclosing my PGP public key, so
        that only I can read your files.

        Cordially,
        Susan

How do you know that the public key enclosed in Susan's letter belongs to Susan? Perchance Sam Scam, who runs her e-mail service, has intercepted her letter to you, substituted a fraudulent public key for hers, and rerouted her letter to you. When you respond to Susan, Sam Scam could log all your tax records, then reforward your letter to Susan using her real public key. Scam could keep both of you under surveillance for a long time without you knowing.

Here is one way to verify Susan's key, using the telephone — assuming that you can recognize her voice. You will ask her to corroborate her public key's *fingerprint*, after first checking it on your computer. The general command for viewing fingerprints is:

```
pgp -kvc userid
```

You can remember this command, **kvc**, as in **K**ey **V**iew and **C**onfirm.

Type:

```
pgp -kvc Susan
```

A message similar to this will appear on your screen:

```
[C:\PGP]
ViaCrypt PGP 2.7 - Pretty Good Privacy for everyone.
Key ring: 'c:\pgp\pubring.pgp', looking for user ID "susan".
Type bits/keyID          Date          User ID
pub     512/EAAA9367     1994/07/27    Susan <phone number>
Key fingerprint =  17 D5 C2 0B B5 D0 6F 26  2A BA 10 4D 76 F6 C1 CA
1 matching key found.
```

When Susan is on the telephone, ask her to read you the fingerprint that her own computer gives for her public key. Compare this with what your computer tells you. If both fingerprints are identical, you have a proper key. If the fingerprints are different, a third person may be playing games with your lives.

Selecting keys via key ID

So far, you have looked at public keys by accessing the user ID (for instance, Susan), or a fragment of the user ID (for example, Sus). This is the most common approach, because we normally think of a certain person and want that person's key.

But suppose that you use two public keys — perhaps you use one for your colleagues and the other for your friends. Each of your public keys might have the same user ID; however, they will have different key IDs. PGP provides a way for you to access the exact key that you want — namely, you can select a particular key ID rather than a user ID.

For example, Susan's key ID on my machine is EAAA9367. (Remember that her key ID will be different on your machine!) The general command for selecting keys via key ID is:

```
pgp -kv 0xkeyID
```

Note that the "0" is the number zero.

Type:

```
pgp -kv 0xEAAA
```

or

```
pgp -kv 0xeaaa9367
```

(Of course, the characters you type after the "x" should correspond to Susan's key ID that corresponds to Susan in *your machine*, not mine!)

A message similar to this will appear on your screen:

```
[C:\PGP]
ViaCrypt PGP 2.7 - Pretty Good Privacy for everyone.
Key ring: 'c:\pgp\pubring.pgp', looking for user ID "0xEAAA".
Type bits/keyID        Date          User ID
pub    512/EAAA9367    1994/07/27    Susan <phone number>
1 matching key found.
```

Signing a public key

PGP provides another important security check: It allows you to *sign* other people's public keys — and, if you wish, to sign your own keys.

Previously, we added keys for ViaCrypt, David Barnhart, and Phil Zimmermann to our key ring. Suppose that I have never met or talked with David Barnhart. How do I know that the public key associated with his name on my key ring actually belongs to Barnhart?

Look at the key ring displaying the Barnhart key. (See the previous section, "Viewing Your Public key ring.") After his key, you will see the following line:

```
sig!  A966DD  1993/10/25   Philip R.Zimmermann <prz@acm.org>
```

The "sig!" line means that Barnhart's key was signed by Phil Zimmermann. I have met Phil, and I know that he signs keys only if he is sure of the owner's identity. Furthermore, I have Phil's public key on my key ring, so I can use PGP to verify that Phil's signature is valid. The bottom line is this: Phil says that David's key is authentic. Therefore, unless I hear strong evidence to the contrary, I can trust that David Barnhart's key belongs to David Barnhart.

The general form of the key-signing command is:

```
pgp -ks her_userid -u your_userid [keyring]
```

You can remember this command, **ks**, as in **K**ey **S**ign.

Note that you will replace the placeholder *"her_userid"* with the actual userid for the person whose key you are signing. You will replace *"your_userid"* with your own userid.

In this case, type:

```
pgp -ks Susan -u André
```

The following message will appear on your screen:

```
[C:\PGP]
ViaCrypt PGP 2.7 - Pretty Good Privacy for everyone.
Looking for key for user 'susan':
Key for user ID: Susan <phone number>
512-bit key, Key ID EAAA9367, created 1994/07/27
READ CAREFULLY:  Based on your own direct first-hand knowledge, are
you absolutely certain that you are prepared to solemnly certify that
the above public key actually belongs to the user specified by the
above user ID (y/N)?
```

Type:

```
y
```

A new screen will appear:

```
[C:\PGP]
ViaCrypt PGP 2.7 - Pretty Good Privacy for everyone.
You need a pass phrase to unlock your RSA secret key.
Key for user ID "André <e-mail address>"
Enter pass phrase:
```

Type the pass phrase that you earlier assigned to your secret key:

```
hispasscode
```

A screen like the following will appear:

```
[C:\PGP]
ViaCrypt PGP 2.7 - Pretty Good Privacy for everyone.
Enter pass phrase: Pass phrase is good.  Just a moment....
Key signature certificate added.
```

Many PGP users also sign their *own* keys. Commands of the form:

```
pgp -ks Susan -u Susan
```

or

pgp -ks André -u André

will accomplish this task.

Viewing the signatures on your public key ring

PGP permits you to list all of your public keys, along with any accompanying signatures. This is helpful if you receive PGP mail from someone whom you cannot remember. If you look at his or her signatures, you might recall who referred you to this person and why.

The general command for this is a variant of the command you have already learned for viewing keys. Type:

pgp -kvv *userid*

You can remember this command, **kvv**, as in **K**eys, **V**iew, and **V**erify.

Type:

pgp -kvv Susan

The following message will appear on your screen:

```
[C:\PGP]
ViaCrypt PGP 2.7 - Pretty Good Privacy for everyone.
Key ring: 'c:\pgp\pubring.pgp', looking for user ID "susan".
Type bits/keyID          Date          User ID
pub     512/EAAA9367     1994/07/27    Susan <phone number>
sig            1455A57D                André <e-mail address>
1 matching key found.
```

This PGP memorandum tells you that Susan's key was "sig" (signed) by André.

For a list of *all* the signatures on your key ring, omit the user ID in this command. Type:

pgp -kvv

Every signature on your key ring will appear on your screen.

```
[C:\PGP]
ViaCrypt PGP 2.7 - Pretty Good Privacy for everyone.
Key ring: 'c:\pgp\pubring.pgp'
Type      bits/keyID    Date         User ID
pub    1024/C7A966DD   1993/05/21   Philip R. Zimmermann <prz@acm.org>
sig         67ECF13D                David A. Barnhart <CIS:70275,1360>
sig         8DE722D9                (Unknown signator, can't be checked)
sig         865AA7F3                (Unknown signator, can't be checked)
sig         FF67F70B                (Unknown signator, can't be checked)
pub     512/67ECF13D   1993/07/29   David A. Barnhart <CIS:70275,1360>
sig         C7A966DD                Philip R. Zimmermann <prz@acm.org>
sig         CB768501                ViaCrypt <Phone (602) 944-0773>
pub    1024/CB768501   1993/10/13   ViaCrypt <Phone (602) 944-0773>
sig         C7A966DD                Philip R. Zimmermann <prz@acm.org>
sig         CB768501                ViaCrypt <Phone (602) 944-0773>
                                    ViaCrypt <70304.41@compuserve.com>
                                    ViaCrypt <viacrypt@acm.org>
                                    ViaCrypt <FAX (602) 943-2601>
pub     512/EAAA9367   1994/07/27   Susan <phone number>
sig         1455A57D                 André <e-mail address>
pub     512/1455A57D   1994/07/27   André <e-mail address>
5 matching keys found.
```

Removing signatures from a public key

There are times when you might want to remove signatures from your public key. Call it Spring cleaning. Maybe your best friend has six signatures on her key; you have no need for these signatures! Every key and signature on your ring slows down PGP. Computers are fast, but why clog them unnecessarily with unwanted data? Some PGP users have hundreds of signatures on their rings, belonging to keys that they never use.

The general form of the signature-removal command is:

```
pgp -krs userid [keyring]
```

You can remember this command, **krs**, as in **K**ey **R**emove **S**ignatures.

At this point, Susan's public key is signed by André. Let us take away André's signature. Type:

```
pgp -krs Susan
```

The following message will appear on your screen:

```
[C:\PGP]
ViaCrypt PGP 2.7 - Pretty Good Privacy for everyone.
Removing signatures from userid 'susan' in key ring 'c:\pgp\pubring.pgp'
Key for user ID: Susan <phone number>
512-bit key, Key ID EAAA9367, created 1994/07/27
Key has 1 signature(s):
sig          1455A57D     André <e-mail address>
Remove this signature (y/N)?
```

Type:

```
y
```

You will see the confirmation:

```
[C:\PGP]
ViaCrypt PGP 2.7 - Pretty Good Privacy for everyone.
1 key signature(s) removed.
```

You can verify that this signature has been removed by viewing your key ring with the **pgp -kvv** command.

Checking the certifications on your key ring

PGP encourages you to "certify" each key that you add to your key ring. Furthermore, PGP permits you to check those certifications any time you wish.

The general form of this command is:

```
pgp -kc userid
```

You can remember this command, **kc**, as in **K**ey **C**ertifications.

Type:

```
pgp -kc André
```

A message like this will appear on your screen:

```
[C:\PGP]
ViaCrypt PGP 2.7 - Pretty Good Privacy for everyone.
Key ring: 'C:\PGP\pubring.pgp', looking for user ID "andré".
Type      bits/keyID    Date          User ID
pub       512/1455A57D  1994/07/27    André <e-mail address>
```

This screen verifies that the user ID "André" is on your public key ring. You will get more information about "André" and all public keys, if you simply type:

`pgp -kc`

Here is a typical response screen:

```
[C:\PGP]
ViaCrypt PGP 2.7 - Pretty Good Privacy for everyone.
KeyID       Trust        Validity     User ID
C7A966DD    undefined    undefined    Philip R. Zimmermann <prz@acm.org>
            undefined                 David A. Barnhart <CIS:70275,1360>
            undefined                 (KeyID: 8DE722D9)
            undefined                 (KeyID: 865AA7F3)
            undefined                 (KeyID: FF67F70B)
67ECF13D    undefined    undefined    David A. Barnhart <CIS:70275,1360>
            undefined                 Philip R. Zimmermann <prz@acm.org>
            undefined                 ViaCrypt <Phone (602) 944-0773>
CB768501    undefined    undefined    ViaCrypt <Phone (602) 944-0773>
            undefined                 Philip R. Zimmermann <prz@acm.org>
            undefined                 ViaCrypt <Phone (602) 944-0773>
                         undefined    ViaCrypt <70304.41@compuserve.com>
                         undefined    ViaCrypt <viacrypt@acm.org>
                         undefined    ViaCrypt <FAX (602) 943-2601>
* EAAA9367 ultimate  complete  Susan <phone number>
* 1455A57D ultimate  complete  André <e-mail address>
```

This chart shows that the person who owns this public key ring has *ultimate* trust in Susan's ability to certify keys and has *complete* trust in the validity of Susan's public key. Notice the *undefined* description alongside Philip Zimmermann. The owner of this public key ring has not certified his level of trust in Philip Zimmermann or in the validity of Zimmermann's public key.

Editing your trust for a user ID

PGP allows you to modify the certifications. Maybe you had a shallow trust in someone when you first corresponded with him, but three months later, you have positive confidence in him.

The general form of this command is:

`pgp -ke userid`

You can remember this command, **ke**, as in **K**ey **E**ditor.

Now you will change your trust rating for Philip Zimmermann's key. Type:

`pgp -ke Philip`

Your screen will show something like this:

```
[C:\PGP]
ViaCrypt PGP 2.7 - Pretty Good Privacy for everyone.
No secret key available.  Editing public key trust parameter.
Key for user ID: Philip R. Zimmermann <prz@acm.org>
1024-bit key, Key ID C7A966DD, created 1993/05/21
This key/userID association is not certified.
  Questionable certification from:
  David A. Barnhart <CIS:70275,1360>
  Questionable certification from:
  (KeyID: 8DE722D9)
  Questionable certification from:
  (KeyID: 865AA7F3)
  Questionable certification from:
  (KeyID: FF67F70B)
Current trust for this key's owner is: undefined
Make a determination in your own mind whether this key actually
belongs to the person whom you think it belongs to, based on available
evidence.  If you think it does, then based on your estimate of
that person's integrity and competence in key management, answer
the following question:
Would you trust "Philip R. Zimmermann <prz@acm.org>"
to act as an introducer and certify other people's public keys to you?
(1=I don't know. 2=No. 3=Usually. 4=Yes, always.) ?
```

You can answer however you wish by entering the appropriate number.

It is credible, but difficult to prove one way or the other, that PGP boosts personal responsibility. Every PGP user knows that other users are constantly evaluating his or her trustworthiness. If this process spurs a few people towards greater accountability, all of us benefit.

Editing your user ID or pass phrase

PGP makes it easy for you to edit your user ID or your pass phrase. Perhaps you want to change your userid from "John Doe <123 Huckleberry Street>" to "John Doe <345 Blueberry Lane>", or maybe you want to want to add the nickname "Debbie" to your user ID "Deborah". Or you might want to change your pass phrase to one that is easier to remember.

(Important: *You can only edit user IDs that you have created, and for which you have a pass phrase. Otherwise, anybody could edit your user ID on his or her key ring.*)

You use the same general command that you used to edit trust certifications:

```
pgp -ke userid
```

Again, you can remember this command, **ke**, as in **K**ey **E**ditor. (Note that the command to edit *your own* user ID or pass phrase has the exact same form as the command to edit your trust in some *other* user ID.)

Let us add the nickname "Suzie" to Susan's user ID. Type:

pgp -ke Susan

The following message will appear on your screen:

```
[C:\PGP]
ViaCrypt PGP 2.7 - Pretty Good Privacy for everyone.
Editing userid "susan" in key ring: 'C:\PGP\pubring.pgp'.
Key for user ID: Susan <phone number>
512-bit key, Key ID EAAA9367, created 1994/07/27
You need a pass phrase to unlock your RSA secret key.
Key for user ID "susan"
Enter pass phrase:
```

Type:

herpasscode

Your screen will read:

```
[C:\PGP]
ViaCrypt PGP 2.7 - Pretty Good Privacy for everyone.
Current user ID: Susan <phone number>
Do you want to add a new user ID (y/N)?
```

Type:

y

Your screen will read:

```
[C:\PGP]
ViaCrypt PGP 2.7 - Pretty Good Privacy for everyone.
Enter the new user ID:
    Type:
    Suzie
    The screen will read:
[C:\PGP]
ViaCrypt PGP 2.7 - Pretty Good Privacy for everyone.
Make this user ID the primary user ID for this key (y/N)?
```

Type:

n

Your screen will read:

```
[C:\PGP]
ViaCrypt PGP 2.7 - Pretty Good Privacy for everyone.
Do you want to change your pass phrase (y/N)?
```

Type:

n

Your screen will read:

```
[C:\PGP]
ViaCrypt PGP 2.7 - Pretty Good Privacy for everyone.
Secret key ring updated...
Public key ring updated.
```

If you view your key ring at this stage, you will notice something like this:

```
[C:\PGP]
ViaCrypt PGP 2.7 - Pretty Good Privacy for everyone.
Type       bits/keyID   Date         User ID
pub    512/EAAA9367     1994/07/27   Susan <phone number>
Suzie
```

Suppose that, once this change is made, Susan sends her public key to Global Travel Agency. The Global Travel Agency employees could access Susan's public key by typing either **Susan** or **Suzie**. If we had selected Suzie as the "primary" user ID, this nickname would be at the top of the list on the above screen.

Disabling/re-enabling a key on your public key ring

PGP allows you to disable a public key. Suppose you have a public key with the user ID "Philip Zimmermann," and that you no longer want to send PGP messages to Philip Zimmermann. Whatever your reason for making this change, you can keep Philip Zimmermann on your keyring while assigning the key a disabled or inactive status.

The general form of this command is:

```
pgp -kd userid
```

You can remember this command, **kd**, as in **K**ey **D**isable.

Type:

```
pgp -kd Philip
```

PGP will ask you:

```
[C:\PGP]
ViaCrypt PGP 2.7 - Pretty Good Privacy for everyone.
Key for user ID: Philip R. Zimmermann <prz@acm.org>
1024-bit key, Key ID C7A966DD, created 1993/05/21
Disable this key (Y/N)?
```

Type:

```
y
```

The public key has now been disabled. You can verify this if you check your public key ring. The expression "pub@" will precede the Philip Zimmermann user ID, as demonstrated below:

```
[C:\PGP]
ViaCrypt PGP 2.7 - Pretty Good Privacy for everyone.
Key ring: 'c:\pgp\pubring.pgp'
Type        bits/keyID      Date          User ID
pub@ 1024/C7A966DD    1993/05/21        Philip R. Zimmermann <prz@acm.org>
```

You can no longer use this key to encrypt messages.

Suppose circumstances have changed, and you desire to re-enable (reactivate) Philip's public key. Type:

```
pgp -kd Philip
```

PGP will ask you:

```
[C:\PGP]
ViaCrypt PGP 2.7 - Pretty Good Privacy for everyone.
Key for user ID: Philip R. Zimmermann <prz@acm.org>
1024-bit key, Key ID C7A966DD, created 1993/05/21
Key is disabled.
Key is already disabled.
Do you want to enable this key again (y/N)?
```

Type:

    y

You have restored the Philip Zimmermann public key user ID to active status, as demonstrated in this screen (review the section on viewing your public key ring):

```
[C:\PGP]
ViaCrypt PGP 2.7 - Pretty Good Privacy for everyone.
Key ring: 'c:\pgp\pubring.pgp'
Type      bits/keyID   Date        User ID
pub    1024/C7A966DD   1993/05/21  Philip R. Zimmermann <prz@acm.org>
pub     512/67ECF13D   1993/07/29  David A. Barnhart <CIS:70275,1360>
pub    1024/CB768501   1993/10/13  ViaCrypt <Phone (602) 944-0773>
                                   ViaCrypt <70304.41@compuserve.com>
                                   ViaCrypt <viacrypt@acm.org>
                                   ViaCrypt <FAX (602) 943-2601>
pub     512/EAAA9367   1994/07/27  Susan <phone number>
                                   suzie
pub     512/1455A57D   1994/07/27  André <e-mail address>
5 matching keys found.
```

Creating a key compromise certificate

PGP provides a command to help you cope with disaster. Suppose that you are foolish enough to write your pass phrase on a piece of paper, and that your corporate competitor reads your pass phrase. Even worse, imagine that he sneaks onto your computer and makes a copy of your secret key.

This puts you in big trouble! You must tell everyone who has your public key to quit using it. (This could be virtually impossible.) To solve this problem, PGP allows you to issue a *key compromise* or *key revocation* certificate. This certificate bears your signature, made with the identical key that you are revoking.

After you create this certificate, send it to everyone possible and request them to add your key compromise to their public key chains. If, in the future, they try to encrypt a message using your revoked key, PGP will stop them from doing so. Along with this key revocation certificate, you can send everyone your new, secure public key that you will have created for yourself (this time, without keeping a paper record of your new pass phrase!).

The general form of the key-revocation command is:

    `pgp -kd ` *userid*

You can remember this command, **kd**, as in **K**ey **D**isable.

Note that the command to revoke *your own* user ID is exactly the same command used to *disable someone else's* user ID. PGP decides which of the two operations to perform by looking to see if the userid is in your secret key ring.

To revoke this new key, type:

```
pgp -kd Fred
```

For the sake of this demonstration, I created a new key pair for user ID **Fred** so that I would not destroy other keys, such as Susan and André, that will prove useful in the future. For simplicity (not security), I used the pass phrase **fredpass** for user ID Fred. You can now add the same key to your own public key ring if you want to perform the following steps.

PGP will query you:

```
[C:\PGP]
ViaCrypt PGP 2.7 - Pretty Good Privacy for everyone.
Key for user ID: fred
512-bit key, Key ID 4FF0138D, created 1994/10/08
Do you want to permanently revoke your public key
by issuing a secret key compromise certificate
for "fred" (y/N)?
```

Type:

```
y
```

You will see:

```
[C:\PGP]
ViaCrypt PGP 2.7 - Pretty Good Privacy for everyone.
You need a pass phrase to unlock your RSA secret key.
Key for user ID "Fred"
Enter pass phrase:
```

Type:

```
fredpass
```

The following will appear:

```
[C:\PGP]
ViaCrypt PGP 2.7 - Pretty Good Privacy for everyone.
Enter pass phrase: Pass phrase is good.  Just a moment....
Key compromise certificate created.
```

If you look at your key ring, you will see "*** KEY REVOKED ***" along-side the User ID Fred:

```
[C:\PGP]
ViaCrypt PGP 2.7 - Pretty Good Privacy for everyone.
Key ring: 'c:\pgp\pubring.pgp'
Type        bits/keyID    Date         User ID
pub        512/4FF0138D   1994/10/08   *** KEY REVOKED ***
                                       fred
pub       1024/C7A966DD   1993/05/21   Philip R. Zimmermann <prz@acm.org>
pub        512/67ECF13D   1993/07/29   David A. Barnhart <CIS:70275,1360>
pub       1024/CB768501   1993/10/13   ViaCrypt <Phone (602) 944-0773>
                                       ViaCrypt <70304.41@compuserve.com>
                                       ViaCrypt <viacrypt@acm.org>
                                       ViaCrypt <FAX (602) 943-2601>
pub        512/EAAA9367   1994/07/27   Susan <phone number>
                                       suzie
pub        512/1455A57D   1994/07/27   André <e-mail address>
6 matching keys found.
```

Using PGP on the PC

Encrypting with PGP's Public Key Cryptography

This section explores the various options available to encrypt messages to one or more people.

Encrypting a message to one person

PGP's public key (double-key) crypto is designed so that you can send a private message to one or more recipients that only they can read. You encrypt the message using the recipient's public key, while they decrypt it using their secret key.

In the next two sections, you will create encrypted files that you can hand-deliver or ship on computer disks — but not e-mail — to your friends or colleagues. Disk exchanges have several advantages over e-mail. With a disk, you can deliver huge files (for example, spreadsheets larger than one million bytes); whereas most Internet e-mail systems reject files larger than 50,000 bytes. One disk can carry hundreds of different files, whereas it is very tedious to e-mail 100 files! Encryption to disk lets you exchange complex graphics files that are ruined when converted into ASCII format for e-mail. In addition, disk transfers are more private than e-mail. You can easily slip someone a disk over a cup of coffee, while computers can monitor when — and to whom — you send e-mail. The people who operate your e-mail system can observe that you send or receive PGP messages; in some companies or countries, this could focus unwanted attention towards you.

Now you're ready to put PGP to work and encrypt a message that only Susan can read.

The general form of the encryption command is:

```
pgp -e textfile her_userid
```

You can remember this command, **e**, as in **E**ncrypt.

Type:

```
pgp -e Demo.txt Susan
```

PGP will now encrypt the Peachpit Letter (which I have put in ASCII form in file "Demo.txt"), using Susan's public key. The following message will appear on your screen:

```
[C:\PGP]
ViaCrypt PGP 2.7 - Pretty Good Privacy for everyone.
Recipients' public key(s) will be used to encrypt.
Key for user ID: Susan <phone number>
512-bit key, Key ID EAAA9367, created 1994/07/27
Also known as: suzie
Ciphertext file: demo.pgp
```

Note that PGP stores the encrypted files as DEMO.PGP. Remember that *only* Susan will be able to decrypt this message. Even though you encrypted the file, you cannot read it! Therefore, be sure to keep the file containing your *plaintext* message to Susan — if you want to remember what you sent to her.

Encrypting a message to several people

PGP allows you to simultaneously encrypt a message for several different people. The general form of this command is:

```
pgp -e textfile userid1 userid2 userid3
```

Let us see an example. Type:

`pgp -e Demo.txt Susan André`

The following message will appear on your screen:

```
[C:\PGP]
ViaCrypt PGP 2.7 - Pretty Good Privacy for everyone.
Recipients' public key(s) will be used to encrypt.
Key for user ID: Susan <phone number>
512-bit key, Key ID EAAA9367, created 1994/07/27
Also known as: suzie
Key for user ID: André <e-mail address>
512-bit key, Key ID 1455A57D, created 1994/07/27
Ciphertext file: demo.pgp
```

The new encrypted message, stored as DEMO.PGP, can be read by Susan and/or André independently of each other. PGP does not inform those recipients who can decrypt a message (in this case, Susan and André) which other people can also decrypt the same message.

Note that this PGP command is an excellent way for you to supply yourself with an encrypted copy of your outgoing mail. Simply add your user ID to the other user IDs. For example, if we assume that "You" is a user ID on your secret key ring, you could type:

`pgp -e Demo.txt Susan André You`

Making an ASCII file for e-mail

One popular way to send encrypted messages from one person to another is by using electronic mail. E-mail is often picky. Many e-mail systems only accept messages that are made of ASCII text. You must, therefore, be able to convert your encrypted files into ASCII format.

Robin Williams gives us the following definition of ASCII in her very useful book, *Jargon: An Informal Dictionary of Computer Terms.*

> *ASCII (pronounced "askee") stands for American Standard Code for Information Interchange. It's a standardized coding system used by almost all computers and printers for letters, numerals, punctuation marks, and invisible characters such as Return, Tab, Control, etc. The fact that almost everyone agrees on ASCII makes it relatively easy to exchange information between different programs, different operating systems, and*

Using PGP on the PC

even different computers. ...

In ASCII, each character has a number which the computer or printer uses to represent that character. For instance, a capital A is number 65 in the code. Although there are 256 possible characters in the code, ASCII standardizes only 128 characters, and the first 32 of these are "control characters," which are supposed to be used to control the computer and don't appear on the screen. That leaves only enough code numbers for all the capital and lowercase letters, the digits, and the most common punctuation marks.

Another ASCII limitation is that the code doesn't include any information about the way the text should look (its format). ASCII only tells you which characters the text contains. If you save a formatted document as ASCII, you will lose all the font formatting, such as the typeface changes, the italics, the bolds, and even the special characters... .

PGP, as we shall see, easily converts your encrypted files into ASCII format *(ASCII armor* in PGP jargon).

Check your word processor's manual to learn how to convert a normal (formatted) file into an ASCII file. Remember that because ASCII files lack special features such as italics, the meaning of your message might be altered. It is best to anticipate and eliminate possible problems in advance. For example, I was careful to avoid special characters in the Peachpit Press demonstration letter.

Encrypting a message for e-mail

In previous sections, you learned how to encrypt messages to transfer onto computer disks (but not e-mail) and give to your friends or colleagues. You learned that PGP automatically gives these ciphertext files a ".PGP" extension.

Electronic mail is often more practical than disk transactions. E-mail can be sent around the world in seconds for pennies, whereas it may take days and dollars to ship disks via Federal Express or other carriers. The Internet e-mail system operates 24 hours every day, whereas conventional postal services work perhaps eight-hour days. In addition, you can send e-mail to many recipients by pushing a couple of keys, whereas disks must be individually sealed and shipped. To maintain e-mail privacy, you can use anonymous remailers, as discussed in Part I.

To encrypt a file for e-mail transmission, you must use PGP's ASCII armor. The general form of this ASCII encryption command is:

pgp -ea textfile recipient_userid

You can remember this command, **ea**, as in **E**ncrypt in **A**scii.

Type:

pgp -ea Demo.txt Susan

The following message will appear on your screen:

```
[C:\PGP]
ViaCrypt PGP 2.7 - Pretty Good Privacy for everyone.
Transport armor file: demo.asc
```

Note that PGP adds the ".ASC" extension to remind you that this file is available for e-mail transmission.

Here is what the Peachpit letter looks like encrypted in ASCII armor:

```
----BEGIN PGP MESSAGE----

Version: 2.7

hEwCusDTduqqk2cBAf96Y/T+m2f86EAxOrKUpHeWl8CjQhZ33ZxLsN6+Yd
4FKXNKcJDtKbpVkYfEFTR15UA5tVR/fdAKVOIVW+pgAAApXj6jOQNok9HQ
7QSXLkpe9xRen9Kpm+DGHAjhPHbOAnYQMJDYHujkUuhKoZZ1Lpw9Etf1St
XZx7rfE0DQP1LEOa+jFRDZWxuszkZFjRrNzgtiPO8HC5rxHmjAR3Tg1Sxp
YGkr4MF0vXHT5imPEYH6eKXjXOuDgMZP1HVxq9nYCNszHw3X6WlAMyKWTm
2QEZUICmrH1ZAL8U4pYoJT2kgv9FRYHsenxykSSkMTWvIyLCu+az7fBJUD
BQf9Yqexu4CyDn7/3dJy56m2G1EsTk5dqeifW+h8wYtY9sxTeJpxCCj+gD
YD4Wp2vb7PjIbM+G824eb82DjcvOK283h56FWPAsDlpPw9cRKm1/JQU3Nr
ZDBXgkOwlRFAgdYjyyRi31+2kpD333cmVNwBqV7HVE1TYT3XitTxmBZt0m
bZkKnX6euCG6PQ0PS47IPBmjA7qzMnKcIjamvzOsqOugOY+v78YM3FIqux
20YEDdJP4imS9QAilDZdKX5xRYNla/szpxpkHE+CvuxqKoxN1FJD5Bp+7m
3mreLju9lTJOFycstZ755VEauMsPOK/OF6+fqa0Y0IWY9GLMfKMjlOKBWO
5XyklnFzCHxowjrw24NFWcGyrnhgY0PI47wk2ssGtqG4YPdHasmmCGlb7r
```

continued

```
dVwSepAq4lnZBpP0x+G1LBkd0EG9WYA1nQQt23IYLlmvlt0khHkZSbDeqf
QfYTeSCdrnMGNi+RqWE+UI3RI9bqPghD+06xr+tZE4j3ajpanMlGxlO+bs
ShlTprVJRhnfc7YyoabSUvX7qr8U/PqjegRODvAyfK3sJ2HYdP39Y8WY5w
2jnQRuAuczKhI6HR

=dAYR

——-END PGP MESSAGE——-
```

Observe that this ASCII file clearly announces to Susan that she has a PGP message. Without the " — -BEGIN PGP MESSAGE — -" and " — -END PGP MESSAGE — -" headers, Susan might suppose that all the garbled characters between the headers are simply the result of an e-mail transmission error, and delete your message.

For Paranoid Readers Only: Some PGP boosters regard these headers as a security weakness. Suppose you reside under a dictatorship which, intolerant of your privacy, has outlawed encryption. If you acquired these headers in your e-mail, and they were discovered, you could be arrested. For this reason, computer experts are trying to develop a "stealth" PGP that eliminates the headers, while letting you know that you have a PGP message. The dilemma these experts face is easy to perceive.

Adding a comment line to ViaCrypt PGP's output

ViaCrypt PGP version 2.7 added a nice new feature that works in conjunction with the **-a** command. Suppose you want to add a cleartext comment to the encrypted ASCII letter that you send to Susan. There are two ways to accomplish this:

        A. Add "**+comment=*comment***" on the command line,

or

        B. Add "**comment=*comment***" to your CONFIG.TXT file

In either case, you would substitute your actual comment for the "*comment*" placeholder.

I'll demonstrate the first method. (to change your CONFIG.TXT file, see "Setting Configuration Parameters") Suppose you want to say "Hello Susan" at the top of your encrypted letter to Susan. You would type:

        pgp -ea +comment="Hello Susan" demo.txt Susan

ViaCrypt PGP version 2.7 will generate a message similar to the following:

```
----BEGIN PGP MESSAGE----

Version: 2.7

Comment: Hello Susan

hEwCusDTduqqk2cBAgDDAWOqHLHtzsS+QthY3IZOFRmKhy9/JA5GAy1C9O
Om7/5f3bqq3/F+j6eSNKtGWbVKazHWXmVg+/Lnkw5766xWpgAAApWB47OV
G8Qqh0HTWVQu+GMYFXgyW6R6vaRu8Fz8GOLmOxc8XREnhq0aG/Isw4+xju
WyzKO22evErRO5Ka1KJjyS2QZGkYtC9uIdJzkejJB7DiYr9clo6l9xv8TQ
vHjZR3DgjM8gDlOgof8kXE7rdqkxwhlRngKyUqj8EkEKPwOTEENQcr+h8A
HjrxC1F4q5d99eYiF5FkgS1oxjxyg6MkHDemAkkhNrTUCWQTehpS4dnQ6x
02JCxDx8oAhlzChh8zSoMMmkKV4pMiG6DZdtWME7j1iRbtWzjz8fqVPa9S
1bbyrv48M6xiYUIBbDe3f3p6tWQ/NpSRxl+jKxjdd6IaYIq8GZWL48fbL2
TGxcVhOuBoSvdc5UzsRstUkUasbk6pzfbEXNtpwJN0VillnbkIiRhNAAPE
INOnbKsZT5ngxem19iTdVoEQc53iulITsWTUBtnVXu1qi7rGAt7uvZi9Ci
8RUaQl1SuWJErkdQ2CkEX8fLOzmuCyc7oV2cCe/0mNWm3fGtej7Bh6eXOf
BUEziHjwN58CDhBlvAyaLEmBkGAmGaZH9nix752j3TcGjcOJlNOYPk6nLY
5QxIn+xjX/PY9CnR810iM3Nx1ueBHJV5kAtFwwygP4RFQFUXMVPQQCFsMk
pVS5rTrklAb8Cg/Ugk0T6Jm9nNBLCalYjcvnJ2scKQ+p8FmUcEpcqWmg5J
xAeKiNMEGtxPHDNwmCBevIIXrL3clnU2i2MnidWvGDovLg+A3soPRoV5FA
6ZDyaMLabm1DjSMsnbVsTdWyHhGAERuSXj19ga0Ph4T0YnL6oZkwHCdYQG
pyHnqnIS/60goVi/GytActPkEv0aLdOLzNCORzsyQBm2KRLCpDM/+VGaX3
DT9OCk

=ph1h

----END PGP MESSAGE----
```

Note that the characters in this encrypted message differ from the characters that appeared in the previous example, in which we encrypted the identical file to Susan. PGP does not produce the same results twice. That is part of its power!

Signing a message with your secret key

PGP lets you sign disk files so that the person who receives your file can verify that you sent it. Suppose Susan is running for president of Computer Professionals for Social Responsibility, and she wants to mail a disk containing a copy of her platform and resumé to 10 fellow members — each of whom has Susan's PGP public key on his or her key ring. Suppose, further, that Susan is sending public information that does not require encryption. Susan could use PGP to sign each copy of the file, which is called "PLATFORM".

The general form of the command Susan wants is:

```
pgp -s textfile [-u signer's userid]
```

You can remember this command, **s**, as in **S**ign.

If you have created a file called "PLATFORM" and placed it in your \PGP\ directory, you can try this by typing:

```
pgp -s Platform -u Susan
```

The following message will appear on your screen:

```
[C:\PGP]
ViaCrypt PGP 2.7 - Pretty Good Privacy for everyone.
A secret key is required to make a signature.
You need a pass phrase to unlock your RSA secret key.
Key for user ID "Susan <phone number>"
Enter pass phrase:
```

Type:

```
herpasscode
```

PGP will respond:

```
[C:\PGP]
ViaCrypt PGP 2.7 - Pretty Good Privacy for everyone.
Key for user ID: Susan <phone number>
512-bit key, Key ID EAAA9367, created 1994/07/27
Just a moment...
Signature file: platform.pgp
```

(Important: *Although the resulting file has a ".PGP" extension, this file is not encrypted. It is merely signed, and people can still read it.*)

Note that Susan used her *secret* key to sign PLATFORM. When the other Computer Professionals for Social Responsibility members process Susan's PLATFORM.PGP file (see the section on Decrypting for how to process a signed file), their PGP programs will search for Susan's *public* key and then generate this message:

```
[C:\PGP]
ViaCrypt PGP 2.7 - Pretty Good Privacy for everyone.
File has signature. Public key is required to check signature.
Good signature from user "Susan <phone number>".
Signature made 1994/06/26  18:33 GMT
```

This message confirms Susan did indeed sign PLATFORM.

Notice the *time stamp* (18:33 GMT), which tells you that Susan signed her file at 18:33 (or 6:33 PM) Greenwich Meridian Time. GMT is the standard time used in England and *is* the conventional international basis for setting standard time elsewhere. I advise against taking this time stamp too seriously. The time stamp is accurate only if Susan had her computer's clock set properly when she installed PGP — and if her computer clock is working properly. Many computer users ignore their time clocks.

Encrypt "for her eyes only"

PGP offers you a clever function that Phil Zimmermann humorously named "For Her Eyes Only". Suppose you are a U.S. Senator who wants to discuss a confidential vote with your colleague, and you know that her secretary has access to her computer. This case presents a common danger: Your colleague might decrypt your message and accidentally leave the decrypted file on her computer for anyone to read. Worse yet, your colleague might put your decrypted message into a file and later use it to blackmail you!

PGP offers a partial solution to this problem. The general form of the command you want is:

```
pgp -em textfile her_userid
```

You can remember this command, **em**, as in **E**ncrypt and **M**ore.

Type:

```
pgp -em Demo.txt Susan
```

(Important: *This "more" function only works for text files, so be sure that DEMO.TXT is in ASCII text format.*)

PGP will inform you:

```
[C:\PGP]
ViaCrypt PGP 2.7 - Pretty Good Privacy for everyone.
Recipients' public key(s) will be used to encrypt.
Key for user ID: Susan <phone number>
512-bit key, Key ID EAAA9367, created 1994/07/27
Ciphertext file: demo.pgp
```

Jump ahead of yourself a bit and decrypt the file. This will show you how "For Her Eyes Only" works. Type:

   pgp demo.pgp

Notice that this decryption command lacks the "-" character that you have used for previous commands. PGP will advise you:

```
[C:\PGP]
ViaCrypt PGP 2.7 - Pretty Good Privacy for everyone.
File is encrypted.  Secret key is required to read it.
Key for user ID: Susan <phone number>
512-bit key, Key ID EAAA9367, created 1994/07/27
You need a pass phrase to unlock your RSA secret key.
Enter pass phrase:
```

Type:

   herpasscode

The following message will appear on your screen:

```
[C:\PGP]
ViaCrypt PGP 2.7 - Pretty Good Privacy for everyone.

This message is marked "For your eyes only". Display now (Y/N)?
```

Type:

   y

When you enter "y", the files will appear on your screen. If the file has more lines than your screen, you will receive a message something like this:

```
[C:\PGP]
ViaCrypt PGP 2.7 - Pretty Good Privacy for everyone.
More —90% — Hit space for next screen,
Enter for new line, 'Q' to quit —
```

Enter whatever key is appropriate.

Why is this "For Her Eyes Only" command so clever? Because the message appears *only* on the recipient's screen — no plaintext file is generated. The only file that Susan has from you, DEMO.PGP, is encrypted. Unless Susan is indiscreet enough to read your message while someone is looking over her shoulder, your message is only between the two of you.

For Paranoid Readers Only: This "For Her Eyes Only" option is *not* very secure. If Susan is a sophisticated computer user, there are ways for her to generate a plaintext file to use against herself or you. (In the spirit of magician David Copperfield, I feel it is counterproductive to reveal the tricks that Susan might use.) The -**m** option is really a warning from you to the person decrypting your file not to make a plaintext file.

Encrypt and wipe textfile

PGP helps you solve another security problem. Suppose you encrypt a file to Susan. What do you do with the plaintext that remains on your own computer? When you use your word processor or DOS to "delete" a file, the file does not vanish from your computer! It's as if you throw a piece of paper into a trash can, rather than into a paper-shredder. Your software simply puts a sign on your disk saying that it is OK to write over that same disk space. And many people have both the software and the expertise required to read the secret files that you thought were gone!

If you want, however, ViaCrypt PGP version 2.7 can "wipe" away your plaintext file by covering that file's space on the disk with pseudo-random data. (Earlier versions of PGP used zeros to overwrite the input file.) The general form of this command is:

```
pgp -ew textfile her_userid
```

You can remember this command, **ew**, as in **E**ncrypt and **W**ipe.

For this example, you can create any file you are willing to immediately destroy. Let us call this file "PEST."

Then type:

```
pgp -ew Pest Susan
```

The following message will appear on your screen:

```
[C:\PGP]
ViaCrypt PGP 2.7 - Pretty Good Privacy for everyone.

Cipher file: pest.pgp
File pest wiped and deleted.
```

PGP created the ciphertext file PEST.PGP, and immediately thereafter deleted and "wiped" the plaintext file PEST.

Note that this wiping procedure requires caution. If you make a mistake — for example, you encrypt your message to the wrong person — you cannot retrieve your original file and correct your error!

Encrypt and convert to local text convention

PGP lets you encrypt a file that, when decrypted by the recipient, will automatically fit the recipient's text-line conventions. Perhaps you have received e-mail or files that are troublesome to read because the incoming lines have carriage returns in strange places.

Why does this happen? Sadly but truly, different computer operating systems treat lines of ASCII text differently. MS-DOS terminates all lines of ASCII text with a carriage return and a linefeed. UNIX ends all lines of ASCII text with just a linefeed. Macintosh uses just a carriage return.

PGP, as a courtesy to your reader, helps solve this problem. The general form of the desired command is:

```
pgp -et message.txt  her_userid
```

You can remember this command, **et**, as in **E**ncrypt and **T**ext. Note that this option, like the **"-m"** option, works only if your plaintext file is in ASCII form.

Type:

```
pgp -et demo.txt Susan
```

PGP will notify you that it created the ciphertext file DEMO.PGP. However, if input file DEMO.TXT is not in ASCII text format, PGP will automatically turn off the **"t"** option and you will receive the following notice:

```
[C:\PGP]
ViaCrypt PGP 2.7 - Pretty Good Privacy for everyone.

Warning: 'demo.txt' is not a pure text file.
File will be treated as binary data.
```

This means that you will be unable to transmit this binary file made from binary data via e-mail.

Combining encryption options

I have discussed various encryption options. In alphabetical order, they are: **a** (ascii armor), **e** (encrypt), **m** (more or "For Her Eyes Only"), **s** (sign), **t** (text align), and **w** (wipe). These options can be combined within a single command — a practice that sometimes creates easy words to remember.

Here are a few examples:

```
pgp -eat     Document     Susan
pgp -meat    Document     André
pgp -seat    Document     Susan -u André
pgp -sew     Document     André
pgp -steam   "Document"   Susan -u André
```

Which one command is the best for overall usage? None! They all do different things. I am particularly fond of:

```
pgp -sea
```

This command is easy to remember, and it automatically prepares files for e-mail. Even if I store the file on disk rather than e-mail it, nothing is lost.

I do *not* use the **"-w"** option because it is too easy for me to destroy something irreplaceable. I *do* use a special program, unrelated to PGP, to safely and completely erase my obsolete files.

Decrypting with PGP's Public Key Crypto

In this section, you'll learn The various ways of decrypting files with public key crypto.

Basic public key decryption

You have learned many ways to encrypt public key files. But suppose you *receive* a file called "URGENT.PGP" on a disk. (I will discuss e-mail shortly.)

You have no way of knowing whether this file contains an encrypted message, a public key, a signature, or all of the above.

Fortunately, PGP will tell you what is in the file. Better yet, you only need to remember one basic command! The general form of this command is:

```
pgp ciphertext [-o plaintext_file]
```

Note that this command lacks the "-" character.

Following are three examples that illustrate the decryption of encrypted messages, public keys, and signatures.

Example 1. Suppose you receive a file called "URGENT.PGP," which — unbeknownst to you — contains a regular encrypted message.

The ".PGP" extension suggests that it is a PGP-encrypted file, so you decide to try and decrypt it. Type:

```
pgp urgent.pgp
```

or

```
pgp urgent
```

Note that PGP assumes that the *ciphertext* file has the ".PGP" extension, unless you specify a different extension.

PGP will prompt you for your pass phrase:

```
[C:\PGP]
ViaCrypt PGP 2.7 - Pretty Good Privacy for everyone.

File is encrypted.  Secret key is required to read it.
Key for user ID: André <e-mail address>
512-bit key, Key ID 1455A57D, created 1994/07/27

You need a pass phrase to unlock your RSA secret key.
Enter pass phrase:
```

After you enter the correct pass phrase, PGP will state:

```
[C:\PGP]
ViaCrypt PGP 2.7 - Pretty Good Privacy for everyone.
Plaintext filename: urgent
```

Congratulations! You have decrypted your first message. You can read this file with your word processor.

Example 2. Suppose you receive a file called "ANDRE.ASC," which —
unbeknownst to you — contains André's public key.

To test this file, type:

```
pgp andré.asc
```

PGP will prompt you:

```
[C:\PGP]
ViaCrypt PGP 2.7 - Pretty Good Privacy for everyone.

File contains key(s).  Contents follow...
Type bits/keyID    Date      User ID
pub   512/1455A57D 1994/07/27 André <e-mail address>
1 matching key found.

Do you want to add this keyfile to keyring 'C:\PGP\pubring.pgp' (y/N)?
```

Since the key is already in your key ring, enter:

```
n
```

Example 3. Suppose you receive a file called "SIGNED.PGP," which —
unbeknownst to you — contains a signed file.

Type:

```
pgp signed.pgp
```

or

```
pgp signed
```

PGP will request your pass phrase, and then offer you information similar to this:

```
[C:\PGP]
ViaCrypt PGP 2.7 - Pretty Good Privacy for everyone.

File has signature. Public key is required to check signature.
Good signature from user "André <e-mail address>"
Signature made 1994/06/27 16:31 GMT
```

Where to put the decrypted files?

You can put decrypted files anywhere you want by using the **[–o plain-
textfile]** option in the basic decryption command. Suppose you want to

decrypt a file called "URGENT.PGP". Here are sample commands that you could use to name and store the resulting file:

```
pgp urgent.pgp -o result

pgp urgent -o c:\pgp\result

pgp urgent -o a:\tom

pgp urgent.pgp -o c:\business\tom
```

(Hint: *You might want to put sensitive files onto floppy disks, which you can physically hide. It is risky to leave these files on your hard disk, which is easy for a snoop to hunt through.*)

Decrypting e-mail

PGP makes it easy to decrypt files. However, when you collect your e-mail, you may receive many encrypted messages that incorporate e-mail headers. Which part of this e-mail do you make into a file to feed PGP? In this section, I shall solve that riddle.

Here is a sample piece of e-mail that includes a PGP message:

```
Date: Wed, 29 Jun 1994 08:29:26 -0700

From: André Bacard <abacard>

Message-Id: <199406291529.IAA29777>

To: abacard

Subject: PGP Book Sample


----BEGIN PGP MESSAGE----

Version: 2.7

hDwC6UwcOMUVkoEBAYCESa1YELzwhkKrjHcZZyVb09Xx7WI0Ywn8zu6Tk+
UjTAO6DeGhPJf6JLzZHmk0bRSmAAAC7SxTfVUjjgErvWYcfflXh6EbdrFo
su3jJ15n0+97hIS04TNK6+1t4m0zdQ88bsbdlwJVsZA4v+7gzL27WvACFH
7PiwBLi3BwtXeYW1HVBPkVLXjk6P4JThtv8xaSvDpZmpbKBm0/zcX/8m1G
QgtzUUFNoTC1ULMoIFZ0uqcjTJlDzQ3YMoKfy5fxhH2X4KK2RHdyzXrcdJ
```

continued

```
6du/BnO0nvtKGW+eDUw2zgFAb7mbr4/VAEfcQ8QBIysMoNQ2gm/ZHDr489
aeB7drgC1YcMdgFDUBkCeDji6RrV3PqSXkWE3y5isyIcQrRqSIVdWBsfxf
KZgWjvLalw4jtn4HhxaQW4URB/Kq5ot6cOepEgXeDy2Oveg0dIsJRkq0Mo
6M59JmlRfhumzoUXzW1WAne5yi0Jj5v/vKuIGPSTuyIdLVYO3nPY9a8+HN
4FkILNvitMeHLeWL/lSIQfYBRcBLWEfKuMqvw4YfxhHKLIeu0RF0C+kqQA
5nSKGmxNnJViFq5rMkr9ezBHBdQjGwVdVEBC1RfQWHnUve4WSvxgdDjCfn
kVn6GUwpUXoWLGvOxDFEhyOosGdtyFvIrvyLEkjlQSXQRbNHhFlAE91RN/
GOJURLqLT3ScGs6qR5oQNSNDAuQiCdRiy6tpW79qy4hVozjmd+Fz5OUwix
bY+48OwfVWNvZZGKWQ8ULbHUMNp2ZqQeVcQzYERadeO+fYRc7xr5yTleij
CY/ZuIy7RfiIVZEz6AiqQ2cPKst0AWYo7hcEPlG1C1BCCkM9pi+52bf2nb
1Jk+/RqjYSs3/Ku4x7/lrFNaI9tyPBTr3Kh+U7CFRuk8y7eupnXrvucT9s
W+Q5+LGJQVL8kWbqRGIJ/bikzDI5cCq/zIr/30jTJ7dhfwPvPdoKku7fpl
x1tgeBIMWhQBza3SVoVePjHAPeIoW/hFpX7RNJmqiLsCLrcWoHNLSjamVp
3vrR59q6cLEBtCcefhtyP4/FxhAN143Vs16SxGP0yPK

=qav2

——-END PGP MESSAGE——-
```

To make a file suitable for decryption, you must include the following material:

The "——BEGIN PGP MESSAGE——" line

The Version line

All the scrambled characters

The "——END PGP MESSAGE——" line

You might also want to include the e-mail header material for your records; that is your option.

For the sake of illustration, assume you saved this material in a file called "MAIL." Since your e–mail appeared on your screen, this new file contains control characters associated with your computer. To purge these characters, use your word processor to convert MAIL to an ASCII file (call it "MAIL.ASC").

You are just about ready to read your mail. Type:

pgp mail.asc -o legible

to decrypt your PGP message and place the result in a file called "LEGIBLE."

(Note: *PGP will search through the file MAIL.ASC looking for PGP material, which it will decrypt and place in the file LEGIBLE. PGP will not put non-PGP material (for example, your e-mail headers) into the plaintext file that it creates!*)

Using PGP on the PC

You are finished! Pat yourself on the shoulder.

With a little practice, it becomes second nature to process PGP mail. Sometimes I receive 10 PGP messages at a time. It is time-consuming to redo these steps 10 times. Therefore, I have written a WordPerfect program (a *macro)* that sorts my mail for me. If you get lots of mail, you might program your word processor or create *batch files* to help process your mail.

Decrypting for your screen only

This command is similar to "For Her Eyes Only" encryption (see the section, "Encrypt For Her Eyes Only") Suppose you need to decrypt a file and look at it on your screen, but you do not want to create a plaintext file. Or maybe you are in a hurry and want to simply read a file before running out the door.

The general form of this command is:

```
pgp -m ciphertext
```

You can remember this option, **m**, as in **M**ore. Note that, unlike the basic decryption command, this one requires the old "-" again.

To test this option, write yourself a short note and encrypt it into a file called MIRROR.PGP.

Then type:

```
pgp -m mirror.pgp
```

After PGP prompts you for your pass phrase, PGP will display the plaintext file on your screen.

(Note: *You might discover a few lines of garbage (random symbols) at the top of your screen. These symbols reflect control characters in your word processor. If you converted your short note into an ASCII file before you encrypted it, PGP would not generate this garbage.*)

Recovering the original filename

PGP has a few "sneaky" commands — sneaky because they can catch people off guard. This section discusses one such command. Suppose you receive a PGP e-mail message, which you then convert into an ASCII file called MAIL.ASC for PGP to decrypt. Perhaps you want to know what file name the *sender* used for the message that he sent you. In a moment, you will see why this information might interest you.

The general form of this command is:

```
pgp -p ciphertextfile
```

You can remember this command, **p**, as in **P**laintext.

Type:

```
pgp -p mail.asc
```

PGP will give you a message something like this:

```
[C:\PGP]
ViaCrypt PGP 2.7 - Pretty Good Privacy for everyone.
Plaintext filename: jerk
```

This will tell you that whoever sent you a letter made either a Freudian slip, an indiscretion, or a typographical error when he named your file "JERK."

(Note: *Since recipients of your PGP-encrypted messages can use this -p option, it is important to choose file names tactfully!*)

Advanced Digital Signatures

This section explores the very popular *clearsig* messages, as well as more exotic PGP signatures, and useful .bat files.

Clear signing a plaintext message

PGP permits you to sign public keys, documents, and files in various ways. So far, you have practiced basic signing of public keys and files. In this and subsequent sections, you will learn how to use other forms of digital signatures.

Suppose you write a *nonconfidential* letter to someone — a letter that you want to secure with your digital signature but do *not* want to encrypt. Furthermore, suppose that you would like to e–mail this letter.

PGP has a useful solution for your needs. As a model, use the next letter — which I have saved in an ASCII file called CFP94.TXT.

```
Dear Susan,

Thanks for your excellent remarks at the Fourth
Conference on Computers, Freedom and Privacy
(CFP '94)!
```

```
See You in the Future,
```

```
André
```

The general ViaCrypt version 2.7 form of this command is:

```
pgp -sat plaintextfile -u your_userid
```

Earlier PGP versions used this command:

```
pgp -sat +clearsig=on plaintextfile -u your_userid
```

Note that the new word is *clearsig*, not *clearsign*. However, because these two words are so similar, and because the second word is more intuitive than the first, PGP users often employ the two words interchangeably. We are already familiar with the "**s**," "**t**," and "**a**" options.

You can have André sign this letter. Type:

```
pgp -sat cfp94.txt -u andré
```

After ViaCrypt PGP 2.7 prompts you for André's pass phrase — and you respond — PGP will put the signed letter in a new file.

Your screen will show:

```
[C:\PGP]
ViaCrypt PGP 2.7 - Pretty Good Privacy for everyone.
Clear signature file: cfp94.asc
```

Here is what the clear signature file looks like:

```
---BEGIN PGP SIGNED MESSAGE---

Dear Susan,

Thanks for your excellent remarks at the Fourth Conference
on Computers, Freedom and Privacy (CFP '94)!

See You in the Future,

André
```

continued

```
——-BEGIN PGP SIGNATURE——-

Version: 2.7

iQBFAgUBLhBiuqLuAgn5V1btAQGN8gF/ZFHx+Pqsp2uASY6T6/IS80qgdg
9k+8AiR3Yw0Zg8uo8mmkXEiOw4W/pswBzt8bIY

=K1a9

——-END PGP SIGNATURE——-
```

Susan can check that this signature belongs to André by decrypting the file, as follows. She would type:

pgp cfp94.asc

If the signature is good, PGP will say so:

```
[C:\PGP]
ViaCrypt PGP 2.7 - Pretty Good Privacy for everyone.
File has signature.  Public key is required to check signature. .
Good signature from user "André <e-mail address>".
Signature made 1994/10/09 14:55 GMT
Plaintext filename: cfp94
```

Suppose someone intercepts André's letter and changes it to read as follows:

```
——-BEGIN PGP SIGNED MESSAGE——-

Dear Susan,

Thanks for your LOUSY remarks at the Fourth Conference on
Computers, Freedom and Privacy (CFP '94)!

See You in the Future,

André>
```
continued

```
—-BEGIN PGP SIGNATURE—-

Version: 2.7

iQBVAwUBLpgEU64pWv8UVaV9AQGFHQH/brcfJR/veiHPeHDntXv4fuXLlc
Yocbb8LIjeJ8gn/6LB0eyjGFGNekyoS9GLuVIewb6xKkedG7JPja/wLYIN

=GEog

—-END PGP SIGNATURE—-
```

When Susan checks the signature on this letter, PGP will report:

```
[C:\PGP]
ViaCrypt PGP 2.7 - Pretty Good Privacy for everyone.
WARNING: Bad signature, doesn't match file contents!
Bad signature from user "André <e-mail address>".
Signature made 1994/10/09 14:55 GMT
Plaintext filename: cfp94
```

PGP's clear text signature is one of my favorite features, because of PGP's power to detect and signal *most* unauthorized editing of my messages. I often use this command before I post a message on UseNet or other network conferences.

How secure are clear signed messages?

Clear signed *(clearsig,* if you prefer) messages are *not as secure* as other PGP signatures! Clear signed messages have two security weaknesses.

Weakness #1. PGP can give a *false indication of intentional tampering.* This uncommon false reading can happen if you send a clearsig message through an e-mail system that performs character set conversions, or one that adds or strips spaces from the ends of lines. PGP programmers have known about this glitch for some time. Another encryption system, PEM (Internet Privacy Enhanced Mail), has the same weakness.

Solution #1a. You can eliminate Weakness #1 by sending your clearsig message via disk rather than e-mail.

Solution #1b. If PGP gives you a "Bad Signature" message, you can directly contact the person who digitally signed the message and verify his actual message.

Weakness #2. PGP may occasionally tell you that a clearsig message has a "good signature" even if the message has been fraudulently altered. In September 1994, a few **alt.security.pgp** readers publicized a simple, clever trick to fool PGP users. It is counterproductive for me to reveal the details of this trick, but to protect myself against it, I observe Solution #2.

Solution #2. When you instruct PGP to check the signature on a clear signed message, PGP will output a plaintext file. This output file is *more reliable* than the input file.

Consider the following example of a tampered letter sent to Susan:

```
---BEGIN PGP SIGNED MESSAGE---

I have tampered with this letter.

Dear Susan,

Thanks for your excellent remarks at the Fourth
Conference on Computers, Freedom and Privacy
(CFP '94)!

See You in the Future,

André

---BEGIN PGP SIGNATURE---

Version: 2.7

iQBVAwUBLpgEU64pWv8UVaV9AQGFHQH/brcfJR/veiHPeHDntXv4fu
XLlcYocbb8LIjeJ8gn/6LB0eyjGFGNekyoS9GLuVIewb6xKkedG7JP
ja/wLYINEg==>

=GEog>

---END PGP SIGNATURE---
```

When PGP processes this letter, it will declare:

```
[C:\PGP]
ViaCrypt PGP 2.7 - Pretty Good Privacy for everyone.
File has signature.  Public key is required to check signature. .
Good signature from user "André <e-mail address>".
Signature made 1994/10/09 14:55 GMT
Plaintext filename: cfp94
```

Note that PGP says the signature is good. Technically, this statement is accurate: the *signature* is good. But the *letter* has been doctored!

If you use your word processor to read PGP's output (plaintext file CFP94), you will see the *untampered* text:

```
Dear Susan,

Thanks for your excellent remarks at the Fourth
Conference onComputers, Freedom and Privacy
(CFP '94)!>

See You in the Future,

André
```

In conclusion: Clearsig messages, if used properly, provide a useful, casual form of security. Like paper documents, photographs, or tape recordings, however, they can be doctored. To put this security risk into perspective, remember that whoever has the power to intercept your e-mail can do much more harm than fool around with your clearsig messages!

Useful batch files

Batch (.BAT) *files* are a powerful DOS tool that experts love, but novices dread. Basically, batch files allow users to easily perform repetitive jobs. It is beyond the scope of this manual to study batch files in depth, but I want to give a few examples that I find useful. You might want to adapt these to your needs.

I have created a text file called ANDRE.BAT which I use with ViaCrypt PGP version 2.7. It resides in my \PGP\ directory, and contains the following single line of text:

```
pgp -sat %1 -u "André Bacard"
```

(Before version 2.7 came along, I used the following ANDRE.BAT, which will work with version 2.7 as well as earlier versions):

```
pgp -sat +clearsig=on %1 -u "André Bacard"
```

The "%1" is a placeholder for the name of the plaintext file (in ASCII format) that is to be signed. Suppose I want to sign the letter that we have used in this section. I type:

```
andré cfp94.txt
```

PGP automatically goes to my CFP94.TXT file, asks for my pass phrase, and signs the letter. The advantage of running this batch file is that I do not have to remember and type the awkward command string.

The second batch file, which I call SIGN.BAT, is more complex. I write all my e-mail letters in a directory called C:\PCLITE (it is named after the ProComm Lite software that I use for e-mail). Sometimes I want to PGP-sign five letters in succession. It is tedious to type the command five times and to type my pass phrase five times. Therefore, I employ the following SIGN.BAT file:

```
@echo off

:PGPLOOP

if "%1" == "" goto LOOPEND

pgp -sat c:\pclite\%1 -u "André Bacard"

shift

goto PGPLOOP

:LOOPEND

SET PGPPASS=UUUUUUUUUUUUUUUUUUUUUUUUUUUUUUUUUUUUU

SET PGPPASS=************************************

SET PGPPASS=antidisestablishmentarianism+222222222

SET PGPPASS=

echo All Documents Are Signed!
```

Suppose you want to sign five letters, called LET1, LET2, LET3, LET4, and LET5 type:

```
set pgppass=mysecretpassphrase

sign let1 let2 let3 let4 let5
```

PGP signs all five letters, puts the signed letters in the C:\PCLITE directory with their new .ASC extensions, resets my PGP pass phrase (so that there is no interceptible record of my real pass phrase), and announces: "All Documents Are Signed!"

(Important Notice: *Use the set pgppass=yoursecretpassphrase trick with caution! Anybody can intercept your pass phrase if he has access to your computer. By typing set in your PGP program, he will generate a screen such as the following:*)

```
[C:\PGP]
>set
COMSPEC=C:\DOS\COMMAND.COM
TZ=PST8PDT
PROMPT=[$p]$_$g
PATH=C:\WP51\;C:\PGP
PGPPATH=C:\PGP
PGP=yoursecretpasscode
```

The last line in the above screen seriously compromises your security! That is why my batch file ends by resetting the pass phrase variable from my *real* pass phrase to a dummy phrase.

While I'm talking about batch files, I have slightly adjusted the previous SIGN.BAT to decrypt *batches* of incoming PGP mail. Here is a look at UNSEAL.BAT:

```
@echo off
:PGPLOOP
if "%1" == "" goto LOOPEND
pgp c:\pclite\%1 -u "André Bacard"
shift
goto PGPLOOP
:LOOPEND
SET PGPPASS=UUUUUUUUUUUUUUUUUUUUUUUUUUUUUUUUUUUUUU
SET PGPPASS=************************************
SET PGPPASS=antidisestablishmentarianism+222222222
SET PGPPASS=
echo All Documents Are Unsealed!
```

With a little tinkering, you can adjust these batch files to your own computer's setup, and make them as fancy as you wish.

Separating signatures from messages

When you write your signature in the non-computer world, you normally sign a piece of paper at the bottom of a letter or other document. Your signature stays on that piece of paper. Similarly, all of the PGP signatures that you have used so far are physically attached to documents.

Sometimes it is useful to have signatures that are physically separated from any document. For example, suppose you collect a million signatures to get a voter initiative placed on the California ballot. You want to be able to give the million signatures to the Registrar of Voters without also having to lug around a million copies of the 10-page voter initiative! On a smaller scale, you might want 10 people in your company to sign that they have read a memo, and you might want to keep these signatures physically separate from the memo itself.

PGP allows you to make a signature certificate that is separate from the document that you are signing. The general form of this command is:

pgp -sb *textfile* **[-u** *your_userid***]**

You can remember this command, **sb**, as in **S**igning and **B**reaking the signature apart from the document.

Suppose Susan wants to testify that she has read the memo that is stored in file CFP94.TXT. She would type:

pgp -sb cfp94.txt -u susan

After Susan gives PGP her pass phrase, PGP will say:

```
[C:\PGP]
ViaCrypt PGP 2.7 - Pretty Good Privacy for everyone.
Signature file: cfp94.sig
```

Susan could send this signature file to you along with the original memo. You could verify that Susan's signature was indeed hers by entering:

pgp cfp94.sig

PGP will respond:

```
[C:\PGP]
ViaCrypt PGP 2.7 - Pretty Good Privacy for everyone.
File has signature.  Public key is required to check signature.
File 'cfp94.sig' has signature, but with no text.
Please enter filename of material that signature applies to:
```

Type:

      `cfp94.txt`

PGP will answer:

```
[C:\PGP]
ViaCrypt PGP 2.7 - Pretty Good Privacy for everyone.
Good signature from user "Susan <phone number>".
Signature made 1994/10/09 16:44 GMT
Signature and text are separate.  No output file produced.
```

The signature certificate has another valuable application that can help every software user. How can you be sure that the software you are using has not been sabotaged with a virus, or otherwise altered? If your software manufacturer distributes a PGP signature certificate along with the software, PGP users can verify that the software is tamper-free. ViaCrypt PGP version 2.7 provides this security in the PGPSIG.ASC file. (For full details on this security check, see the section "Ensuring That Your Computer Is Virus — and Hacker-Free" towards the end of this book.)

Suppose you want to check that your PGP.EXE file (the PGP executable program) is tamper-free. ViaCrypt has signed this file, and you can verify its digital signature. Type:

      `pgp pgpsig.asc`

PGP will indicate:

```
[C:\PGP]
ViaCrypt PGP 2.7 - Pretty Good Privacy for everyone.
File has signature.  Public key is required to check signature.
File 'pgpsig.$00' has signature, but with no text.
Please enter filename of material that signature applies to:
```

Type:

```
pgp.exe
```

Finally, PGP will respond:

```
[C:\PGP]
ViaCrypt PGP 2.7 - Pretty Good Privacy for everyone.
Good signature from user "ViaCrypt <Phone (602) 944-0773>".
Signature made 1994/06/21 20:23 GMT
WARNING: Because this public key is not certified with a trusted
signature, it is not known with high confidence that this public key
actually belongs to: "ViaCrypt <Phone (602) 944-0773>".
Signature and text are separate. No output file produced.
```

You could get the same result by typing:

```
pgp pgpsig.asc pgp.exe
```

This will generate a screen almost identical to the last one:

```
[C:\PGP]
ViaCrypt PGP 2.7 - Pretty Good Privacy for everyone.
File has signature. Public key is required to check signature.
File 'pgpsig.$00' has signature, but with no text.
Text is assumed to be in file 'pgp.exe'.
Good signature from user "ViaCrypt <Phone (602) 944-0773>".
Signature made 1994/06/21 20:23 GMT
WARNING: Because this public key is not certified with a trusted
signature, it is not known with high confidence that this public key
actually belongs to: "ViaCrypt <Phone (602) 944-0773>".
Signature and text are separate. No output file produced.
```

If you see the above output, you can feel more confident that your copy of ViaCrypt PGP version 2.7 has not been tampered with.

Detaching a signature certificate

PGP offers a command that lets you create signature certificates separate from files even if those files were *not* signed in the way demonstrated in the last section. The general form of this command is:

```
pgp -b ciphertext
```

To illustrate this command, I encrypted the input file CFP94.TXT and signed it using André's key. The resulting file is called CFP94.PGP. If Susan received this file and wanted to verify it, she would type:

```
pgp -b cfp94.pgp
```

After Susan provides her pass phrase, PGP will tell her:

```
[C:\PGP]
ViaCrypt PGP 2.7 - Pretty Good Privacy for everyone.
File has signature.  Public key is required to check signature. .
Good signature from user "André <e-mail address>".
Signature made 1994/10/09 16:51 GMT
Writing signature certificate to 'cfp94.sig'
```

Leaving a signature intact after decryption

PGP normally removes signatures when a file is decrypted and its contents are stored in a plaintext file. However, sometimes you might like to keep the signature attached to the plaintext file. Suppose you keep a record of all your sales correspondence. It is much easier to scan these letters if they are stored in plaintext. But then how do you know when these letters were signed? Do you have proof that they *were* signed? Or suppose that you want to send a copy of a signed document to a third party. PGP provides answers.

The general form of the "decrypt with signature" command is:

```
pgp -d ciphertextfile
```

For this section, I have again encrypted CFP94.TXT and signed it with André's key. The resulting file is called CFP94.PGP. If Susan received this file and wanted to decrypt it with the signature intact, she would type:

```
pgp -d cfp94.pgp
```

After PGP processes Susan's pass phrase, it will report:

```
[C:\PGP]
ViaCrypt PGP 2.7 - Pretty Good Privacy for everyone.
This file has a signature, which will be left in place.
Plaintext filename: cfp94
Output file 'cfp94' may contain more ciphertext or signature.
```

Why the last line of output? Because the option "**-d**" only searches for André's signature on CFP94.PGP. It could be that the input file CFP94.TXT was *itself* an encrypted file, with a signature from someone else.

If you examine CFP94 with your word processor, you will see something like this:

ëU^C^E.É^T√«)Z^TUÑ}^A^A⌡h^An'8yεÇσnπ∏∫U.&uδ^OV'ïç]_$m¿oS*NxÖ^Nî
{;7è ͣ^T» ͣq ^AÇ›π^Rm6E :!¥â¡ ͦπ%_b cfp94.txtDear Susan,
Thanks for your excellent remarks at the Fourth Conference on
Computers, Freedom and Privacy (CFP '94)!
See You in the Future,
André

The strange symbols that precede the letter represent André's signature.

Bravo! You have now conquered all of PGP's commands.

Setting Configuration Parameters

Software packages typically have *default values* that they use unless you specify otherwise. For example, your word processor may automatically print documents in single-spaced, Courier, 12-point type, unless you instruct it to switch to double-spaced, Arial, 14-point.

ViaCrypt PGP version 2.7 (and previous versions of PGP) has default values of its own, which are also called *parameters.* For example, PGP does not *echo* (show on the screen) your pass phrase, unless you instruct PGP to do so. It is quite possible that you will never need or want to change any of these default values. However, in this section, I'll explain some options that you have. (A few more, very technical, options can be found in your ViaCrypt documentation.)

(Note: *The default settings given in the following CONFIG.TXT section are for PGP Version 2.7. Other PGP versions may have different default settings!*)

Examining and Editing Your CONFIG.TXT File

Your PGP program comes with a file called CONFIG.TXT, which contains the configuration options that you may select. You can use your word processor to examine and change this file.

The CONFIG.TXT is too unwieldy to print in full. However, here are two little pieces of the ViaCrypt PGP 2.7 CONFIG.TXT file:

```
# Sample config.txt file for ViaCrypt PGP 2.7
# Blank lines are ignored, as is anything following a '#'.
# Keywords are not case-sensitive.
# Whatever appears in here can be overridden on the command line,
# by specifying (for example) "+armor=on".
# MyName is substring of default user ID for secret key to make   signatures.
# If not set, PGP will use the first key on your secret  keyring  (the last
# key you created) if you don't specify the user with -u
# MyName = "John Q. Public"
```

This first sample piece of the CONFIG.TXT file contains a series of lines that each begin with the "#" character. These lines explain the "rules of the game" — in other words, how to alter the CONFIG.TXT options that follow. Don't be scared by these lines. They are awkward because they are written by programmers for programmers. Nonprogrammers, like myself, must reread these instructions several times, and then they make perfect sense.

Here is a second piece of CONFIG.TXT:

```
# The following commented-out settings are *not* the defaults.
# Uncomment (remove the leading "#" character) them to get the
# non-default behavior indicated.
# showpass = on      # Echo password when user types it
```

Now let's get practical. Suppose you find it difficult to type your pass phrase when you cannot see what you have already typed. Suppose further that you use your computer at home, and that nobody looks over your shoulder. You might want PGP to echo (to show on the screen) your password as you type it.

In the previous sample, you will see the line "# showpass = on". If you properly edit out the "#" character and properly save your new CONFIG.TXT, then "showpass = on" will become the new default value. From then on, your pass phrase will always show on the screen as you type it. You can also switch on many other options by simply removing the "#" before them.

(Important Notice: *Use extreme caution when editing your CONFIG.TXT file! The editing process you should use depends on which version of DOS you are using. So check your manual carefully. Having learned the hard way, I always make a backup copy of my working CONFIG.TXT file before I start playing around with options.*)

There is a second way to override the default for one time only. For example, you can turn the echo on as follows. Type:

```
pgp -sat +showpass=on demo.txt -u André
```

When you add "+showpass=on" to the basic "pgp..." command, it instructs PGP to echo the pass code for this one command only.

Similarly, you can select many other options by removing their leading "#" characters in CONFIG.TXT, or by adding a line to CONFIG.TXT, or by adding a "+" statement to the command line. A few of these PGP options are pragmatic, whereas others are esoteric. For the sake of completeness, I shall list more options than you may ever need.

Adding a Comment Line to ViaCrypt PGP's Output

ViaCrypt PGP version 2.7 added a nice new feature that works in conjunction with the **-a** command. Suppose you want to add a cleartext comment to the encrypted ASCII letter that you send to Susan. There are two ways to accomplish this:

```
A. Add "+comment=comment" on the command line
```

or

```
B. Add "comment=comment" to your CONFIG.TXT file
```

I illustrated the first method in an earlier section that had the same name as this one.

Alternative Locations for Pubring, Secring, or Randseed

ViaCrypt PGP 2.7 allows you to specify a location for your key rings and random number seed file other than the one defined by the PGPPATH environment variable:

1. To change the location of your public keyring, simply add a line to your CONFIG.TXT file specifying the full path and file name you want to use:

```
pubring=full_path_and_filename
```

This is useful if you want to keep a company or a departmental keyring on a LAN's server.

2. To change the location of your secret keyring, simply add a line to your CONFIG.TXT file specifying the full path and file name you want to use:

```
secring=full_path_and_filename
```

This is useful if you want to keep your secret keyring on a floppy disk instead of on your hard drive.

3. To change the location of your random number seed file, simply add a line to your CONFIG.TXT file specifying the full path and file name you want to use:

```
randseed=full_path_and_filename
```

ARMOR (ASCII Armor Output)

`Default setting: ARMOR=off`

The ARMOR parameter tells PGP whether or not to automatically create ciphertext or keys in the ASCII file format. **ARMOR=on** is equivalent to the **–a** command. ASCII output files are suitable for e-mail, and they are named with the .ASC extension.

If you use PGP primarily for e-mail, you might want to switch this setting to **ARMOR=on.**

ARMORLINES (Size of ASCII Armor Multipart Files)

`Default setting: ARMORLINES=720`

The ARMORLINES parameter tells PGP what size "chunks" to use when breaking up large ASCII files for e-mail transmission. This is important because most Internet mailers prohibit files larger than 50,000 bytes.

Suppose you want to e-mail a document that is 200,000 bytes. PGP will break up this document into several file chunks and will name these chunks with the suffixes ".AS1", ".AS2", ".AS3", etc. Each chunk will contain 50,000 or fewer bytes (that is, 720 or fewer lines of text).

You can change this default value. For example, FidoNet e-mail files usually have an upper limit of about 32,000 bytes (or 450 lines). If you use FidoNet, you might set ARMORLINES=450.

BAKRING (File Name for Backup Secret Key Ring)

`Default setting: BAKRING=""`

The BAKRING parameter tells PGP where to check the validity of your public key against a backup copy of your secret keyring.

Your PGP security ultimately depends on your own ultimately-trusted public key or keys. ViaCrypt PGP has a way to check that nobody has tampered with your own public key. To make this check, PGP must compare your public key against a *safe* backup copy of your secret key. A safe place to put this backup copy is on a write-protected floppy disk. A secret key contains all the data on your public key, plus some secret data.

Suppose you set BAKRING="a:\secring.pgp". When you use the -kc command, PGP will check your whole public keyring.

If BAKRING="", PGP will not check your own key against any backup copy.

CERT_DEPTH (How Deep May Introducers Be Nested)

Default setting: CERT_DEPTH=4

The CERT_DEPTH parameter tells PGP how many levels deep you may nest introducers to certify other introducers to certify public keys on your public key ring. (Does this remind you of a philosophy or a law class?) For example, if **CERT_DEPTH=1**, there may be only one layer of introducers below your ultimately-trusted key. If that were the case, you would be required to directly certify the public keys of all trusted introducers on your keyring. If you set **CERT_DEPTH=0**, you could have no introducers at all, and you would have to directly certify each and every key on your public keyring in order to use it. The minimum CERT_DEPTH=0, the maximum CERT_DEPTH=8.

CHARSET (Local Character Set for Text Files)

Default setting: CHARSET=NOCONV

The CHARSET parameter tells PGP which local character set your machine uses. This is important because PGP processes messages in many non-English languages with non-ASCII character sets.

The choices are NOCONV (no conversion), LATIN1 (ISO 8859-1 Latin Alphabet 1), KOI8 (used by most Russian Unix systems), ALT_CODES (used by Russian MS-DOS systems), ASCII, and CP850 (used by most western European languages on MS-DOS PCs).

LATIN1 is the internal representation used by ViaCrypt PGP. So, if you select LATIN1, no conversion is done. ViaCrypt PGP also treats KOI8 as LATIN1, even though it is a completely different character set (Russian), because trying to convert KOI8 to either LATIN1 or CP850 would be futile anyway. This means that setting CHARSET to **NOCONV**, **LATIN1**, or **KOI8** are all equivalent to ViaCrypt PGP.

If you use MS-DOS and exchange messages in western European languages, set **CHARSET="CP850"**. This will make ViaCrypt PGP convert incoming text messages from LATIN1 to CP850 after decryption. If you use the **-t** (textmode) option, ViaCrypt PGP will convert your CP850 text to LATIN1 before encrypting it.

CLEARSIG (Cleartext Signed Messages)

`Default setting: CLEARSIG=on`

The CLEARSIG parameter tells PGP whether you want to sign cleartext messages *without* encrypting them. Previous PGP versions had CLEARSIG=off as the default. ViaCrypt realized that cleartext signatures are becoming very popular, and changed this default.

You can force ViaCrypt PGP to go back to the earlier convention if you change this setting to **CLEARSIG=off**.

The **CLEARSIG=on** message type is similar to the MIC_CLEAR message generated by Internet Privacy Enhanced Mail (PEM).

COMPATIBILITY (Of PGP Versions)

`Default setting: PKCS_COMPAT=1`

The PKCS_COMPAT=1 parameter tells ViaCrypt PGP 2.7 which encrypted output format to use. Until September 1, 1994, Viacrypt PGP 2.7 generated output that was readable by ViaCrypt version 2.4 by ViaCrypt version 2.7, and by MIT PGP 2.6.

After September 1, 1994, ViaCrypt PGP 2.7 by default generated output that was readable only by ViaCrypt Version 2.7 and by MIT PGP 2.6.

The PKCS_COMPAT=2 parameter instructs ViaCrypt PGP version 2.7 to generate output that is understandable by all versions of ViaCrypt PGP (2.4 and 2.7) as well as by MIT PGP 2.6. This might be useful if you have a friend who has made the mistake of keeping the older version.

The PKCS_COMPAT=3 parameter instructs ViaCrypt PGP version 2.7 to generate output that is understandable by version 2.7 and by MIT PGP 2.6, but *not* by ViaCrypt PGP 2.4. (This setting was different from PKCS_COMPAT=1 because it did not wait until September 1, 1994 to generate this kind of output. However, this option is moot, because — unless your computer's time clock is *way* off, or you have somehow traveled backwards in time — you are reading this manual after September 1, 1994.

COMPLETES_NEEDED (Number of Trusted Introducers)

`Default setting: COMPLETES_NEEDED=1`

The COMPLETES_NEEDED parameter tells PGP the minimum number of completely trusted introducers that you require in order to fully certify a public key for your public key ring. If you "completely trust" one person, I see no need to change this setting.

COMPRESS (Enable Compression)

`Default setting: COMPRESS=on`

The COMPRESS parameter tells PGP to enable or disable data compression before encryptng. Just about everyone wants to have smaller files. Therefore, unless you are an expert trying to debug PGP — and it's already perfect! Right? — this option has little value.

INTERACTIVE (Ask for Confirmation for Key Adds)

`Default setting: INTERACTIVE=off.`

The INTERACTIVE parameter tells PGP how to add a key file, which itself contains multiple keys, to your key ring. **INTERACTIVE=on** tells PGP to ask for confirmation for each key before adding it to your key ring. **INTER-ACTIVE=off** instructs PGP *not* to ask for confirmation for each key.

KEEPBINARY (Keep Binary Ciphertext Files After Decrypting)

`Default setting: KEEPBINARY=off`

The KEEPBINARY parameter tells PGP whether or not to keep the intermediate ".PGP" file during decryption.

When PGP reads an ".ASC" file, it converts the ASCII file back into a ".PGP" (binary) file before decrypting IT. **KEEPBINARY=off** instructs PGP to automatically delete this ".PGP" file. **KEEPBINARY=on** tells PGP to save this intermediate file.

You can always decrypt the "ASC" file again, so there is not much need to keep an intermediate file.

LANGUAGE (Foreign Language Selector)

`Default setting: LANGUAGE="en"`

The LANGUAGE parameter tells PGP which language to use when displaying messages such as "Please enter your pass phrase." ViaCrypt PGP is written in English; however, PGP is available in many languages. If you have a European PGP version, you might change this option to, say, Spanish or German.

MARGINALS_NEEDED (Number of Marginally Trusted Introducers Needed)

Default setting: MARGINALS_NEEDED=2

The MARGINALS_NEEDED parameter tells PGP the minimum number of marginally trusted introducers required to fully certify a public key on your public key ring. This gives you a way of fine-tuning PGP's skepticism.

MYNAME (User ID for Making Signatures)

Default setting: MYNAME=""

The MYNAME parameter tells PGP which user ID to use by default when making signatures. If MYNAME is not redefined to "André" or some other user ID, *the most recent secret key* that you installed on your secret key ring will be used to make signatures. Whenever you use the **-u** option, you automatically override this setting.

SHOWPASS (Echo Pass Phrase to User)

Default setting: SHOWPASS=off

The SHOWPASS parameter tells PGP that you either want to see your pass phrase as you type it, or do *not* want to see it. Selecting **SHOWPASS=off** means that nobody can look over your shoulder and steal your pass phrase. If this is not a problem, **SHOWPASS=on** might make it easier for you to type.

TEXTMODE (Assuming Plaintext is a Text File)

Default setting: TEXTMODE=off

The TEXTMODE parameter tells PGP whether or not to assume that an input file is a text file. If TEXTMODE=on (which is equivalent to the **-t** command), PGP assumes that the input file is a text file, not a binary file, and converts the text to "canonical text" before encrypting it. Canonical, or standard, text has a carriage return and a line feed at the end of each line of text.

PGP automatically turns this mode off if it detects that an input file contains binary data.

TMP (Directory Path Name for Temporary Files)

`Default setting: TMP=""`

The TMP parameter tells PGP which directory to use for PGP's temporary scratch files. The best place to put scratch files is on a RAM disk, if you have one. That speeds up the program, and it increases security. If "TMP=" is not defined, the temporary files go in the current directory.

VERBOSE (Quiet, Normal, or Verbose Messages)

`Default setting: VERBOSE=1`

The VERBOSE parameter tells PGP how much message material to give you. Your choices are VERBOSE=0, VERBOSE=1, or VERBOSE=2.

0   Displays messages only if there is a problem.

1   Normal default setting. Displays a reasonable amount of detail in diagnostic or advisory messages.

2   Displays maximum information, usually to help diagnose problems in PGP. But we have already established that PGP is perfect. Right?

Security Considerations (For Paranoids Only)

❝ *Most human beings have an almost infinite capacity for taking things for granted.* **❞**

~ Aldous Huxley, *Themes and Variations*

By learning and *using PGP correctly*, you have greatly increased your computer security, compared with your perilous pre-encryption days. Nonetheless, complacency can be a costly luxury. Some people feel so self-assured once their front door has three locks that they forget that their kitchen window is open. There is no such thing as "absolute" security in the computer world or in any slice of life. Here are a few security matters to consider.

Has Anyone Tampered with Your PGP?

If you use ViaCrypt PGP version 2.7, it is easy for you to answer this question. Once you have installed version 2.7, you will find a file called PGP-SIG.ASC. Simply read PGPSIG.ASC and follow the instructions. Here are the contents of that file:

```
----BEGIN PGP MESSAGE----

Version: 2.4

iQCVAgUALgdMLWhHpCDLdoUBAQEX5AP/YD4fUmvmU4NhF6dzlXjWp8LhyA
4mrzpq7zPTjgv9okOu+r7+sS4jmX4P4ZMCMoA0rGqX75Ymg5TQFEM+RzDH
i2GUEtyu3lzGrqes2E4TSFeEGyw665EAuax3L0bItkWzL25vvxfzrlAXX/
bTcTAfXOXQWZGfjSE+QGp1DlUFYEw=

=5XE2

----END PGP MESSAGE----
```

The first nine lines of this file contain the digital signature of ViaCrypt PGP version 2.7 for MS-DOS. You can verify this signature. First, you need to add ViaCrypt's public key to your key ring. You can do so by typing:

pgp -ka keys.asc

This will add ViaCrypt's public key — and several others — to your public key ring. Next, you should verify the fingerprint of ViaCrypt's public key. Type:

pgp -kvc viacrypt

You should see the following display:

```
[C:\PGP]
ViaCrypt PGP 2.7 - Pretty Good Privacy for everyone.
Key ring: 'pubring.pgp', looking for user ID "viacrypt".
Type bits/keyID    Date      User ID
pub  1024/CB768501 1993/10/13 ViaCrypt <Phone (602) 944-0773>
  Key fingerprint = EC A9 0D F1 87 F7 8A 75  91 3B 1C 6A 8B 9A 8B 2F
     ViaCrypt <70304.41@compuserve.com>
     ViaCrypt <viacrypt@acm.org>
     ViaCrypt <FAX (602) 943-2601>
1 matching key found.
```

Compare the 16 octets that you see to the right of "Key fingerprint = " on your own screen with those shown above. They should match exactly.

Now that you have a known, verified copy of ViaCrypt's public key on your key ring, you can safely verify the digital signature attached to the PGP.EXE file. Type:

pgp pgpsig.asc

You should see:

```
[C:\PGP]
ViaCrypt PGP 2.7 - Pretty Good Privacy for everyone.
File has signature.  Public key is required to check signature.
File 'pgpsig.$00' has signature, but with no text.
Please enter filename of material that signature applies to: .
```

Type:

pgp.exe

Finally, you should see:

```
[C:\PGP]
ViaCrypt PGP 2.7 - Pretty Good Privacy for everyone.
Good signature from user "ViaCrypt <Phone (602) 944-0773>".
Signature made 1994/06/21 20:23 GMT
Signature and text are separate.  No output file produced.
```

If you see the above output, then you can be assured that your copy of ViaCrypt PGP 2.7 for MS-DOS has not been tampered with.

Ensuring That Your Computer Is Virus- and Hacker-Free

PGP has no built-in defense against viruses that can destroy computer programs in general and PGP in particular. The computer world contains some very clever people. Perhaps someone can develop or has developed, a PGP virus that can capture your pass phrase, secret key, or deciphered messages, and forward these goodies to him or her when you are using your e-mail system. Stranger things have happened.

Maybe someone else has created a PGP imitation that seems to work like PGP, but subtly breaks your security. Phony ATM machines have been installed in Europe and the United States to capture users' secret codes and then steal their money!

Fortunately, you can protect yourself against these threats. You can use a commercial anti-virus program to check your computer files regularly. You can also periodically check that your PGP program has not been tampered with. (See the previous section.)

Are You Telling Your Friends Too Much?

" *If you want privacy, choose your friends carefully. A high-tech snoop cannot compete with a wagging tongue.* **"**

~ An Anonymous Wit

~

The weakest link in any security system is the least secure person. Many people like to boast how clever they are. It is a safe bet that more than one PGP user has bragged over a glass of wine that his pass phrase is "I'm the smartest dude alive" or whatever. If you know anybody going through a divorce, you realize that people can remember "inconsequential" remarks for a long time.

If you want to keep your pass phrase secret, do not tell it to anybody, ever! Similarly, do not tell people where you keep your backup secret keys, or any other details that can be used against you in the future.

Where Are Your "Deleted" Files?

As discussed above under "Encrypt and Wipe Textfile," most operating systems, such as MS-DOS, do *not* really "delete" files. If you tell your computer to "delete" the file LETTER.TXT, it simply marks the disk space where LETTER.TXT is stored. This mark says that it is OK to store a new file — say, FINANCE.TXT — in the same location. Anybody with the proper software can read the LETTER.TXT file that you mistakenly think is gone.

As also discussed in the section above, ViaCrypt PGP Version 2.7 has a "wipe" function that covers the LETTER.TXT with pseudo-random characters. This security is clearly better than none. However, it is still possible for people with sophisticated equipment to read the magnetic data underneath PGP's pseudo-random characters. If you are *very* security-conscious, you might want to keep all your plaintext files on floppy disks, which you can peri-odically melt or otherwise destroy.

Is Anyone Fooling with Your Public Key?

It is possible that the person who runs your e-mail system regularly reads your e-mail. If he is so inclined, he might be happy to come across your pub-lic key. He could generate a *phony* public key with your correct name and e-mail address. He could then forward this phony key to your correspondents, and read their encrypted mail to you.

If you suspect this problem, I recommend that you immediately switch e-mail systems — unless you want to play an elaborate trick to catch the snoop red-handed. Such tricks are beyond the scope of this book. If the snoop is your employer, you might want to send your public key to its intended recipients inside an encrypted message, or deliver it to them on disk.

Is Someone Listening to Your Keystrokes?

Computers transmit radio signals. For example, a 50 MHz (MegaHertz) computer operates at a frequency of 50 MHz. One MegaHertz means the elec-tric current is cycling through at a frequency of one million times per second. Somebody with the proper equipment (translated: "lots of money") can sit in a high-tech van outside your office and intercept those signals — which reveal all of your keystrokes. This electromagnetic attack would make your computer an open book.

Such attacks can be stopped by shielding your computer and cabling, so that your system does not emit signals. "Tempest" is the name for this shield-ing technology, and you can purchase "Tempest" systems.

Is a Traffic Cop Watching You?

Suppose a snoop studies your telephone bills and sees that you have called the residential number (123)456-7890 five times every week for the last year. The snoop does not have to know anything about those calls to tell that the person at the number is important to you. If you are rich, a snoop inclined toward kidnapping people might consider grabbing the person at (123)456-7890 for a ransom.

This is the essence of "traffic analysis": namely, a snoop can tell a lot about you by watching whom you send e-mail to, and who sends e-mail to you. One defense against traffic analysis is to use anonymous remailers, as described in the section by that name, earlier in this book.

Are You on a Party Line?

In the "good ol' days," almost everyone had telephone *party lines*. Neighbors could (and often did) discreetly pick up their receiver and catch up on the local gossip. Today, many people plug into multi-user computer systems — especially at work. It is amazing to me that people use these systems to discuss confidential business, and social, matters. Personally, I run PGP only on my personal computer which is under my physical control. I would not think of using a multi-party system — which, to me, would be like whispering into an open microphone.

What is the Cost of Paranoia?

Tyrants everywhere love paranoia, because it paralyzes people. Paranoia is an expensive emotional, social, and political dead-end. Advocates of democracy value *awareness*, because it activates people. I believe that PGP contributes to democratic awareness.

PART FIVE

BIBLIOGRAPHY

Bibliography

Adler, Stephen J. "Debatable Device: Privacy, Technology Collide in a Dispute Over an Intimate Test." *The Wall Street Journal,* February 3, 1993, page A12. Explores the mind-boggling case of an American citizen who was forced to submit to a penile plethysmograph in order to keep his job.

Bacard, André. "Privacy in the Computer Age." *The Humanist,* January-February, 1993. Supplies examples of privacy problems that should concern every citizen.

Bacard, André. "The Cash-Free Nightmare: The Cryptography Solution." Baltimore, Maryland: *The Oxford Club Communique,* April 1994. This article discusses the pros and cons of a cash-free society, and how to protect your privacy.

Bailey, Ronald. "Code Blues." *Reason,* May 1994, p. 36. Discusses PGP and the government effort to control encryption.

Baker, Stewart A. "Don't Worry. Be Happy. Why Clipper is Good for You." *WIRED,* June 1994, p. 100. Stewart Baker, chief counsel for the National Security Agency, defends the Clipper Chip.

Bamford, James. *The Puzzle Palace: Inside The National Security Agency, America's Most Secret Intelligence Organization.* New York: Penguin Books, 1982. Explores the NSA, which is responsible for U.S. cryptographic policy.

Barlow, John Perry. *Decrypting The Puzzle Palace.* Washington, D.C.: Electronic Frontier Foundation, 1992. Explores the role of the NSA (National Security Agency), the government agency that controls American encryption policy.

Barr, Stephen. "IRS Employees Disciplined for Computer Abuse: Some Created Bogus Refunds — Others 'Browsed' Through Records." *San Francisco Chronicle,* August 3, 1993, front page [reprinted from WASHINGTON POST]. Shows how easily government employees can misuse our financial records.

Belsky, Gary. "Escape From America." *Money,* July 1994, p. 60. An sobering article about how many of America's best and brightest citizens want to leave America for better lives elsewhere.

Bolyard, Nelson. "Wire Taps and Cryptography in Your Future." A talk given to Computer Professionals for Social Responsibility in Palo Alto, California, on May 4, 1994.

Booth, William. "Big Brother is Counting Your Keystrokes." *Science,* October 1987, p. 17. Addresses employer monitoring of employees.

Bulkeley, William M. "Cipher Probe: Popularity Overseas of Encryption Code Has the U.S. Worried." *The Wall Street Journal,* April 28, 1994. Palo Alto, California. An excellent overview of Philip Zimmermann and the PGP controversy.

Carey, John. "Spy vs. Computer Nerd: The Fight Over Data Security." *Business Week,* October 4, 1993, p. 43. Discusses export controls on encryption software.

Chaum, Dr. David. "Achieving Electronic Privacy." *Scientific American,* August 1992, p. 96. Discusses a cryptographic invention known as a 'blind signature' which sets a stage for electronic cash.

CFP '93: *The Third Conference On Computers, Freedom And Privacy.* This annual conference, founded by Jim Warren and Computer Professionals for Social Responsibility, brings together the leading players in the privacy/surveillance debate. The 1993 conference was organized by Bruce Koball of Berkeley, California.

Diffie, Whitfield. "The First Ten Years of Public-Key Cryptography." *Proceedings of the IEEE,* V. 76, n. 5, May 1988, pp. 560-577.

Donlan, Thomas G. "Privacy and Security: Computer Technology Opens Secrets, And Closes Them." *Barron's,* April 25, 1994, page 51. An editorial that promotes RSA as a solution to Internet security.

Electronic Frontier Foundation. "An Analysis of the FBI Digital Telephony Proposal." Washington, D.C.: Electronic Frontier Foundation, September 18, 1992. A report, prepared in coalition with many groups and corporations, about the FBI's proposal that all communications and computers systems be designed to facilitate interception of private messages.

Electronic Frontier Foundation. "The Open Platform: A Proposal by the Electronic Frontier Foundation for a National Telecommunications Infrastructure." Washington, D.C.: Electronic Frontier Foundation, 1992. This document influenced Vice-President Gore's "Information Superhighway" policy.

Figgie, Harry E., Jr. *Bankruptcy 1995: The Coming Collapse of America and How To Stop It.* Foreword by Warren B. Rudman. Boston, Little, Brown & Company, 1992. A sobering look at America's "Buy now and pay later" culture.

Free, John, and Namoi Freundlich and C.P Gilmore. "Bugging." *Popular Science,* August 1987, p. 44. A scary article about tiny listening devices.

Gleason, George. "Encryption, Pragmatic and Principled." *Microtimes,* June 13, 1994, p. 20. Discusses why Gleason's business will use ViaCrypt PGP.

Godwin, Mike. "Privacy From Whom? Computer Chips, Secret Codes and Your Government." *Playboy,* September, 1994, p. 41. Argues against the Clipper Chip.

Kabay, Michel. "ITAR Sticks Users With Unfair Encryption Restrictions." *Network World,* November 8, 1993. The director of education for the National Computer Security Association criticizes export restrictions on encryption software.

Kahn, David. *Kahn On Codes: Secrets of the New Cryptology.* New York: Macmillan Publishing Company, 1983. Gives the reader a far-ranging look at cryptology — from its standard use in warfare to its growing impact on industry.

Kahn, David. *The Code Breakers: The Story Of Secret Writing.* New York: Macmillan Publishing Company, 1968. The unofficial standard reference book on the history of cryptography.

Kantrowitz, Barbara. "Dissent on the Hard Drive." *Newsweek,* June 27, 1994, P.59. Discusses how on-line networks are being used to help free suppressed people and information.

Lewis, Peter H. "Hackers on Internet Posing Security Risks, Experts Say." *New York Times,* July 21, 1994. Front page. Discusses how hackers have gained access to hundreds of government and military computer networks.

Lindgren, David T. "Commercial Satellites Open Skies." *Bulletin of the Atomic Scientists,* April 1988, p. 34. Examines commercial remote-sensing (satellite) systems.

Machiavelli, Niccolo. *The Prince.* Introduction by Christian Gauss. New York: New American Library, 1964. The classical, nitty-gritty book about power. Timeless, the book is as accurate now as when it was written, centuries ago in Italy.

Magid, Lawrence J. *The Little PC Book.* Berkeley, California: Peachpit Press, 1993. An easy-to-read introductory book, which includes the helpful "The DOS Cookbook" and "The Windows Cookbook."

Markoff, John. "An Administration Reversal on Wiretapping Technology." *New York Times,* July 21, 1994, p. C1. Reports on Vice-President Al Gore's willingness to explore industry alternatives to the Clipper Chip.

Markoff, John. "Electronic Privacy Gets a New Lock: But Some See a 'Monster'; Government Will Hold the Key." *San Jose Mercury News,* April 16, 1993, Front page (reprinted from *New York Times).* Explains the Clipper Chip.

Markoff, John. "Flaw Discovered in Federal Plan for Wiretapping." *New York Times.* June 2, 1994, Front page. Discusses how Dr. Matthew Blaze discovered a flaw in the Clipper Chip.

Markoff, John. "U.S. Adopts a Disputed Coding Standard." *New York Times.* May 23, 1994, p. C1. Examines the NSA's proposed digital-signature standard.

Oliver, Charles. "Do We Need a National ID Card? Loss Of Privacy May Offset Any Efficiency Gains." *Investor's Business Daily,* August 12, 1994, Front page. Good overview of the polemic.

Piller, Charles. "Bosses With X-Ray Eyes: Your Employer May Be Using Computers to Keep Tabs on You." *Macworld: Special Report,* July 1993. A perceptive analysis of e-mail and electronic eavesdropping in the workplace.

Piller, Charles. "Privacy in Peril: How Computers Are Making Private Life a Thing of the Past." *Macworld: Special Report,* July 1993. Focuses on managing electronic privacy. Provides a useful model consumer-privacy code.

Quittner, Joshua. "The Merry Pranksters Go To Washington." *WIRED,* June 1994, p. 77. An inside look at the leaders of the Electronic Frontier Foundation.

Rivest, Ron, Adi Shamir, and Leonard Adelman. "A Method for Obtaining Digital Signatures and Public-Key Cryptosystems." *Communications of the ACM,* February 1978, p. 120. The paper that introduced the famous RSA algorithm.

Rosenthal, Ilene. "Export Controls on Mass Market Software with Encryption Capabilities." *CFP '93: The Third Conference on Computers, Freedom and Privacy,* p. 6.25. Rosenthal, the general counsel for the Software Publishers Association, argues that export controls are outdated and threaten American industry.

Rothfeder, Jeffrey. Privacy For Sale: How Computerization Has Made Everyone's Private Life an Open Secret. New York: Simon & Schuster, 1993. An alarming, practical book how who sells information about you and how they do it.

Schneier, Bruce. "The IDEA Encryption Algorithm: An Advanced Block-Cipher Approach to Encryption." *Dr. Dobb's Journal,* December 1993, p. 50. A technical article about the encryption algorithm used in PGP.

Schneier, Bruce. "Untangling Public-Key Cryptography: The Key to Secure Communications." *Dr. Dobb's Journal,* May 1992, page 16. A clearly written, semi-technical overview of public-key crypto.

Schneier, Bruce. *Applied Cryptography: Protocols, Algorithms, and Source Code in C.* New York: John Wiley & Sons., 1994. In this technical book, data-security expert Bruce Schneier details how programmers can use cryptography.

Soviero, Marcelle M. "Lord of the Spies." *Popular Science,* November 1990, p.43. An article about Frank Jones, owner of The Spy Shop.

Stephens, Gene. "High-Tech Crime Fighting: The Threat to Civil Liberties." *The Futurist,* July-August 1990, p. 20. Postulates that new technologies could lead to constant surveillance and forced behavior change.

Sterling, Bruce. *The Hacker Crackdown: Law and Disorder on the Electronic Frontier.* New York: Bantam Books, 1992. An evaluation of high-tech crime in cyberspace.

Stevenson, William. *A Man Called Intrepid.* New York: Harcourt Brace Jovanovich, 1976. A fascinating account of intelligence operations in World War II.

Stewart, Doug. "Spy Tech: Are Your Shoes Listening to You? Is Your Lamp Watching?" *Discover,* March 1988, p. 58. Relates how eavesdropping technology is now in the hands of jealous spouses, nosy neighbors, and prying executives.

Summers, Anthony. *The Secret Life of J. Edgar Hoover.* New York: Pocket Books, 1994. A well-researched look into the former FBI director's twisted double life. Necessary reading for anyone who believes that "law-and-order" regimes reduce corruption.

Taylor, G.W. "Public-Key Encryption and ViaCrypt PGP." *PC News & Reviews,* January 1994, p. 18. Reviews ViaCrypt PGP Version 2.4.

Thomas, Michael M. *Black Money.* New York: Crown Publishers, 1994. A high-tech financial thriller about computers and money-laundering, written by an expert on the financial world.

Wallach, Paul. "Electronic Envelopes? The Uncertainty of Keeping E-Mail Private." *Scientific American,* February 1993, p. 30.

Williams, Robin [with Steve Cummings]. *Jargon: An Informal Dictionary of Computer Terms.* Berkeley, California: Peachpit Press, 1993. An excellent dictionary with a sense of humor.

Wirbel, Loring. "Big Bellcore Team Cracks RSA Code." *Electronic Engineering Times,* May 2, 1994. Discusses Bell Communications Research Inc.'s successful attempt to break a public-key RSA code.

Wrixon, Fred B. *Codes And Ciphers: An A To Z of Covert Communication from the Clay Tablet to the Microdot.* New York, Prentice Hall, 1992. A clearly-written crypto dictionary.

PART SIX

APPENDIX

Pro-Privacy
Cyberspace
Resources

In this Appendix, I highlight three guardians of cyberspace that are 1) Computer experts, 2) Activists, 3) Easy to contact, and 4) Eager to hear from you. In addition I have included the *Privacy Journal* for people who want to know about privacy in a broader context. I urge you to contact these groups. You can learn everything you ever wanted to know about privacy from them. Better yet, you can join forces with these colleagues, improve the quality of your life, and help mold history!

(Note: *The following descriptions of Computer Professionals for Social Responsibility, Electronic Frontier Foundation, Electronic Privacy Information Center, and the Privacy Journal were written by these organizations, not by André Bacard. Each group's write-up has been edited minimally.*)

Computer Professionals for Social Responsibility

P.O. Box 717
Palo Alto, CA 94302

415-322-3778 (voice)
415-322-4748 (fax)
cpsr@cpsr.org (email)

The mission of CPSR is to provide the public and policy makers with realistic assessments of the power, promise, and problems of information technology. As concerned citizens, CPSR members work to direct public attention to critical choices concerning the applications of information technology and how those choices affect society.

Founded in 1981 by a group of computer scientists concerned about the use of computers in nuclear weapons systems, CPSR has grown into a national public-interest alliance of information technology professionals and other people. Currently, CPSR has 22 chapters in the U.S. and contacts with similar groups worldwide.

Every project we undertake is based on five principles:

◆ CPSR fosters and supports public discussion of, and meaningful involvement in, decisions critical to society.

◆ CPSR works to correct misinformation while providing understandable and factual analyses about the impact of societal technology.

◆ CPSR challenges the assumption that technology alone can solve
◆ political and social problems.

◆ CPSR critically examines social and technical issues within the com
puter profession, both nationally and internationally.

◆ CPSR encourages the use of information technology to improve the
quality of life.

CPSR Projects

By sponsoring both national and local projects, CPSR serves as a cata-
lyst for in-depth discussion and effective action in key areas:

◆ The National Information Infrastructure
◆ Civil Liberties and Privacy
◆ Computers in the Workplace
◆ Technology Policy and Human Needs
◆ Reliability and Risk of Computer-Based Systems

In addition, CPSR's chapter-based projects and national working groups
tackle issues ranging from the implementation of Calling Number ID
systems to the development of nanotechnology and virtual reality, from
the use of computers in education to working conditions for computer
professionals, from community networks to computer ethics.

Who Can Join CPSR

CPSR welcomes everyone who uses or is concerned about the role of
information technology in our society.

Membership Benefits

As a member of CPSR, you are joining a nationwide network of concerned people who are committed to bringing a public interest perspective to all aspects of information technology. CPSR's work covers a wide
variety of issues including the proposed National Information
Infrastructure, privacy and freedom of information, the demilitarization
of national technology policy, cryptography, participatory design
approaches to system development, and more.

CPSR has a reputation for being on the forefront of issues pertaining to
the impact of information technology on society, taking action to implement positive examples of the use of information technology such as

local community networks as well as participating in regional and national policy discussions.

♦ Joining with other concerned people to affect policy-making at the local, regional, and national level.

♦ Access to an international network of people who can provide exper tise and well-researched support for progressive positions concerning information technology policy.

♦ Access to on-line information and discussion groups on key topics concerning the socially responsible use of information technology.

♦ The chance to participate in local and national work groups on issues of particular interest to you.

♦ A quarterly newsletter containing in-depth analysis of major issues as well as updates on CPSR activities and action alerts.

♦ Invitations and discounts to CPSR events and publications.

Privacy Notice

The CPSR membership database is never sold, rented, lent, exchanged, or used for anything other than official CPSR activity. CPSR may elect to send members mailings with information from other groups, but the mailings will always originate with CPSR.

CPSR Chapters

Chapters can be found in the following areas: Acadiana, Austin, Berkeley, Boston, Chicago, Denver/Boulder, Los Angeles, Loyola/New Orleans, Madison, Maine, Milwaukee, Minnesota, New Haven, New York, Palo Alto, Philadelphia, Pittsburgh, Portland (Oregon), San Diego, Santa Cruz, Seattle, and Washington, DC.

Internet Access

You can access CPSR's impressive document archive by using this Internet command:

```
gopher gopher.cpsr.org
```

You can also keep abreast of CPSR news on two Usenet news groups:

```
comp.org.cpsr.talk
```

```
comp.org.cpsr.news
```

The Electronic Frontier Foundation

1667 K Street NW, Suite 801
Washington DC 20006 USA

202-861-7700 (voice)
202-861-1258 (fax)
202-861-1225 (BBS - 16.8k ZyXEL)
202-861-1224 (BBS - 14.4k V.32bis)
Internet: ask@eff.org

The Electronic Frontier Foundation (EFF) was founded in July of 1990 to ensure that the principles embodied in the Constitution and the Bill of Rights are protected as new communications technologies emerge.

Since its inception, EFF has worked to shape our nation's communications infrastructure and the policies that govern it in order to maintain and enhance First Amendment, privacy and other democratic values. We believe that our overriding public goal must be the creation of Electronic Democracy, so our work focuses on the establishment of:

◆ New laws that protect citizens' basic Constitutional rights as they use new communications technologies,

◆ A policy of common carriage requirements for all network providers so that all speech, no matter how controversial, will be carried without discrimination,

◆ A National Public Network where voice, data and video services are accessible to all citizens on an equitable and affordable basis, and

◆ A diversity of communities that enable all citizens to have a voice in the information age.

Legal Services

EFF sponsors legal cases where users' online civil liberties have been violated. The Steve Jackson Games case, decided in March of 1993, established privacy protections for electronic mail and publications that are kept online. EFF continues to monitor the online community for legal actions that merit EFF support.

EFF provides a free telephone hotline for members of the online community who have questions regarding their legal rights.

Members of EFF's staff and board speak to law enforcement organizations, state attorney bar associations and university classes on the work that we do and how these groups can get involved.

Civil Liberties

EFF has been working to make sure that common carrier principles are upheld in the information age. Common carrier principles require that network providers carry all speech, regardless of its controversial content. Common carriers must also provide all speakers and information providers with equal, nondiscriminatory access to the network.

Last year, the FBI introduced legislation to require communications technologies to be certified as open to lawful government surveillance before those technologies can be deployed. EFF organized a broad coalition of 39 computer, telephone and public interest groups to oppose this measure.

EFF is working to convince Congress that all measures that support broader public access to information should be enacted into law. For example, the law that establishes citizen access to information, the Freedom of Information Act (FOIA), does not require government agencies to turn over the electronic version of information, which is often the most useful version. EFF supports an Electronic Freedom of Information Act and other legislation to make information more accessible to citizens.

EFF supports both legal and technical means to enhance privacy in communications. EFF, therefore, advocates all measures that ensure the public's right to use the most effective encryption technologies available.

National Network

EFF has been working with policymakers to establish a national network, or network of networks, capable of transporting video images and data, as well as voice. EFF's "Open Platform Proposal" advocates a network that is accessible to all citizens at an affordable price. For the near-term, EFF supports the implementation of ISDN (Integrated Services Digital Network) technology. ISDN makes it possible for the current telephone network to be used to send voice, video and data at a low cost to consumers.

EFF has written a white paper that describes ISDN applications that are currently available for use at home, school, the workplace and beyond.

EFF has been working with policymakers on legislation that encourages individuals and organizations to create tools that make the Internet and the National Research and Education Network (NREN) easier to access and use.

Community Building

EFF, in conjunction with the Consumer Federation of America and the American Civil Liberties Union, coordinates and sponsors the Communications Policy Forum (CPF). CPF enables nonprofit organizations, computer and communications firms, and government policymakers to come together in a nonpartisan setting to discuss communications policy goals and strategies.

In order to foster community and openness, EFF works with local organizations that support online communications issues. In January of 1993, EFF sponsored a summit of groups from around the country to discuss common goals. EFF also participates in an online mailing list for organizations that share our interests.

EFF is a funder and organizer of the annual Computers, Freedom and Privacy conference, where academics, civil libertarians, law enforcement officials and computer users all meet to discuss the privacy implications of communicating online. Each year at the conference, EFF presents its Pioneer Awards to individuals who have made significant contributions to computer communications.

EFF publishes a biweekly electronic newsletter, EFFector Online, that is sent to subscribers at their e-mail addresses and distributed via Usenet's comp.org.eff.news group. EFF also publishes a quarterly hard copy newsletter entitled Networks & Policy.

EFF maintains several communications forums on the Internet. EFF has its own Internet node, eff.org, which houses our ftp and gopher sites, as well as Internet "mailing list" conferences, including eff-talk. EFF also maintains a conference on the Whole Earth 'Lectronic Link (WELL), CompuServe (CIS), and America On Line (AOL), GEnie (GEIS), and elsewhere.

The EFF BBS, started in March 1994, carries a wide selection of the files available on our Internet server.

Internet and USENET:

Forums for Discussion:

If you receive any Usenet newsgroups, your site may carry the news-groups comp.org.eff.news and comp.org.eff.talk. The former is a moderated news group for announcements, newsletters, and other information; the latter is an unmoderated discussion group for talk and debate on EFF and issues relating to the electronic frontier and civil liberties.

For those unable to read the newsgroups, there are redistributions via electronic mail. Send a message containing the commands:

```
HELP

LONGINDEX
```

in the body of your message to listserv@eff.org. Several mailing lists are available, including comp-org-eff-news, comp-org-eff-talk (gated from the previously-mentioned newsgroups), eff-activists (EFF news, plus activist and volunteer planning and discussion), effector-online (EFF newsletter only), the mailing lists for the Computers and Academic Freedom project hosted by EFF, and more. Please note that comp-org-eff-talk can be extremely high-volume at times, so you are advised to use filtering.

Also, Usenet's alt.politics.datahighway (available via email, too) may be of interest. This conference was started by EFF in November of 1993, to provide a forum for discussion of the national (or global) information infrastructure, from deployment plans to civil liberties issues to debunking of hype.

File Archives:

A document library containing all EFF news releases and other publications of interest, including John Perry Barlow's history of EFF - "Crime and Puzzlement," as well as recent and proposed legislation, materials for online activists, archives of electronic publications, records of trials and legal cases, information alerts, and other related documents & papers, is available via anonymous FTP from ftp.eff.org. Send a note to ftphelp@eff.org if you have difficulties or are unable to use FTP.

If you are on the Internet, you can use your host's FTP program to connect to ftp.eff.org (192.88.144.4). Login as "anonymous" and use your e-mail address as the password.

This archive may also be accessed via the Gopher, and World Wide Web (Lynx, Mosaic, Cello, etc.) services, at gopher.eff.org, and http://www.eff.org/, respectively. These utilities present documents and other files in hierarchical, easy-to-navigate menus, allowing you to read online, and save what you want to disk on your own machine.

Outpost - EFF Online (the EFF BBS):

The EFF bulletin board system, Outpost - EFF Online, begun in March 1994, supports 300-14400 bps connections (V.32bis, V.42bis, 8 bits, no parity, 1 stop-bit - 8N1) on it's dial-up lines. The system is available 22 hours per day (3am-5am eastern time reserved for mail transfers and maintenance routines). When fully operational, the board will be available 24 hours per day, will support 4 lines at faster speeds, and will feature online conferences from a variety of networks including FidoNet, Usenet/Internet, and more, as well as the full selection of files available from EFF's FTP archive, EFF membership materials, bulletins on the latest issues affecting civil liberties in cyberspace, and other related files and services. The data phone number for the system is +1 202 861 1224. Outpost's FidoNet address is 1:109/1108. Access to the BBS is free (besides calling costs; at present we do not have a toll-free number.) Other network addresses: WishNet - 19:1202/101; StormNet - 181:193/1; IndraNet - 369:1011/2

The Whole Earth 'Lectronic Link (WELL):

The WELL, based in the San Francisco area, is host to an active EFF conference, as well as many other related conferences of interest to EFF supporters. Telecom access is available through the CompuServe Packet Network. If you have an Internet connection, you can reach the WELL via telnet at well.sf.ca.us; otherwise, dial +1 415 332 6106 (data). The WELL's voice number is +1 415 332 4335. To get to the EFF conference, type "g eff".

CompuServe (CIS):

EFF's forum on CompuServe is also open. GO EFFSIG to join. Many of the files on ftp.eff.org, as well as other items of interest, are mirrored in the EFFSIG Libraries, and a lively debate and chat area exists with more than 15 online message areas. CIS can be reached via telnet at compuserve.com.

America Online (AOL):

EFF has opened up a forum on America Online. Go to keyword EFF to join. Some basic EFF files are available, as well as a large and diverse discussion and debate area. In addition, EFF sponsors occasional interactive discussions in the MCM forum.

GEnie (GEIS):

The Public Forum * Non-Profit Connection RT hosts an EFF forum on GEnie, including a stock of EFF newsletters and info in Library 13, and an EFF discussion area (Category 7, Topic 17). Please support this volunteer effort and add your thoughts to the forum. The Public Forum is keyword PF (or page 545). GEnie's voice sign-up number for new users is 1-800-638-9636; the sign-up code (which will get you some free time online to check out the system) is MHC524.

Byte Information Exchange (BIX):

An EFF forum is available on BIX. The online EFF area is located at topic "eff" in the "security" conference, and BIX can be reached via telnet to x25.bix.com or bix.com. Like our area on GEnie, the BIX forum is a volunteer activist effort - please participate, and help make this a great virtual community of activism and discussion!

Other Services, BBSs, and Networks:

From time to time, EFF-oriented resources may appear on other systems; for instance, Illuminati Online's Metaverse service will feature an EFF "virtual office", while FidoNet locally gates both comp.org.eff.talk and comp.org.eff.news. If you have difficulty finding online material from the listed sources, try shopping around and you may find what you are looking for. All EFF materials are redistributable, and can be found on many BBS systems around the country. System operators interested in carrying our material should contact ask@eff.org, Stanton McCandlish at 1:109/1108, or call 202-347-5400 and ask for Stanton McCandlish.

Why You Should Join the Electronic Frontier Foundation

Every day decisions are being made that will affect your life online. Decisions about what sorts of technology you can use to protect the privacy of your communications. Decisions about what services you will be able to get over the emerging national information infrastructure. Decisions that are made before you even know that there are choices.

The Electronic Frontier Foundation has been working since July 1990 to ensure that the civil liberties guaranteed in the Constitution and the Bill of Rights are applied to new communications technologies. Our members join EFF to make sure that they are informed about the issues and debates that will shape the future of electronic communications. EFF members enjoy the following benefits:

- ◆ Subscription to EFF's quarterly hard copy newsletter Networks & Policy;

- ◆ Subscription to EFF's biweekly electronic newsletter EFFector Online;

- ◆ Online bulletins that will keep you informed about the key legal, legislative and policy developments affecting your online communications;

- ◆ An online response mechanism to make themselves heard on key issues.

EFF is a respected voice for the rights of users of online technologies. EFF feels that the best way to protect your online rights is to be fully informed and to make your opinions heard. EFF members are informed, and are making a difference. Join EFF today!

Electronic Privacy Information Center (EPIC)

666 Pennsylvania Ave., SE, Suite 301
Washington, DC 20003

202-544-9240 (voice)
202-547-5482 (fax)
info@epic.org (email)

The National Information Infrastructure

Our communications world is rapidly changing. The convergence of telephone, television, and computer technology has created a new information "superhighway" referred to as the "National Information Infrastructure" or NII.

The NII has become a priority of the Clinton administration and has long been championed by Vice President Gore. While many aspects of the NII initiative are commendable and worthy of the public interest community's support, the administration's early pronouncements on network privacy raise great concern. For instance, the Information Infrastructure Task Force's "Agenda for Action," issued last year, contained the following passage:

Federal agencies are working with industry to develop new technologies that protect the privacy of citizens, while enabling law enforcement agencies to continue to use court-authorized wiretaps to fight terrorism, drug rings, organized crime, and corruption. Federal agencies are working with industry to develop encryption hardware and software that can be used for this application.

This passage refers to the efforts of the FBI and the National Security Agency (NSA) to dictate the design of the nation's communications networks and to expand their ability to conduct electronic surveillance. Indeed, for almost a decade the intelligence community has sought to control the development of the nation's advanced communications infrastructure, invoking the specter of "terrorism, drug rings, organized crime, and corruption" much as "national security" was invoked during the Cold War.

More recently, the administration has launched two surveillance initiatives that are cause for great concern.

The Clipper Chip

In February of this year, the government announced its adoption of the so-called Clipper Chip, a communications "security" device developed by the National Security Agency (NSA). Clipper and related devices permit law enforcement and intelligence agencies to intercept and "decrypt" private voice and data transmissions. As William Safire wrote in the New York Times,

The "Clipper chip" - aptly named, as it clips the wings of individual liberty - would encode, for Federal perusal whenever a judge rubber-stamped a warrant, everything we say on a phone, everything we write on a computer, every order we give to a shopping network or bank or 800 or 900 number, every electronic note we leave our spouses or dictate to our personal-digital-assistant genies.

In a poll conducted by Time magazine and CNN, 80 percent of the American people opposed this surveillance initiative, and an Internet petition organized by the EPIC staff generated 50,000 electronic messages urging the administration to abandon the Clipper plan. Indeed, the EPIC staff has been in the forefront in opposing the Clipper initiative and educating the public about its ramifications for the information infrastructure.

The FBI's Proposed Wiretap Legislation

In recent testimony on Capitol Hill, FBI Director Louis Freeh called for sweeping new legislation that would require designers of the NII to make the emerging network "wiretap friendly." The FBI plan would mandate that no communications system could be established unless it guaranteed law enforcement the ability to intercept communications. The proposal would also give the FBI an unprecedented ability to collect detailed telephone and "transactional" records. As with the Clipper initiative, public reaction to the FBI proposal has been overwhelmingly negative. The response of the Detroit News was typical:

No one wants criminals to have the upper hand, of course. But democracy fast turns to tyranny when fundamental liberties like privacy are suspended in the name of law enforcement. Americans already concede a great deal of their privacy to Big Brother in the name of crime fighting. ... Privacy, in any real sense of the word, is eroding daily.

Unfortunately, public opposition to these initiatives has not slowed the momentum toward greater surveillance capabilities in the emerging communications infrastructure. The recent proposals are just the latest in a series of FBI and NSA efforts to control our information networks. Although Congress attempted to put the brakes on these activities with the passage of the Computer Security Act in 1987, the intelligence community has marched forward:

◆ A 1989 "Memorandum of Understanding" between the NSA and a civilian agency transferred authority for computer security back to the intelligence community.

◆ A 1989 National Security Directive issued by President Bush further expanded the authority of the NSA and encouraged the Agency to set technical standards for the nation's communications system. The secret directive was made public after EPIC staff forced its disclosure in court.

◆ A 1991 Senate resolution, developed by the FBI, would have urged private companies to develop new network services to facilitate wire surveillance.

◆ An earlier legislative proposal, drafted by the FBI in 1992, would have mandated that all communication equipment in the United States be certified by the Attorney General as capable of wiretap.

It is clear that the surveillance capabilities of the FBI and NSA are now being turned inward toward the citizens of the United States. The late Sen. Frank Church observed in 1975 after conducting a sweeping investigation of intelligence agency abuses, "the danger lies in the ability of NSA to turn its awesome technology against domestic communications." The recent developments have made clear the importance of this warning.

Privacy at Risk

The implications of these recent developments are staggering. If the intelligence and law enforcement agencies are able to dictate the requirements of the nation's communications infrastructure, then the freedom of future users of the nation's information networks are at risk. It is already clear that the many costs of these proposals include:

◆ Diminished privacy technologies that are intended for privacy protec tion, such as cryptography, are deployed with secret "backdoors" that make them less secure.

◆ Government secrecy in the name of "national security" critical docu ments are withheld from public review and principles of open govern ment are suspended.

◆ Government accountability with secrecy comes the loss of public review and the ability to determine whether government claims reflect the true reality. Already, EPIC Freedom of Information litigation has revealed that many of the FBI's dire claims are unfounded.

◆ Routinized surveillance a network designed for surveillance will be used for surveillance. Where once privacy was taken for granted, in the not too distant future monitoring may soon be assumed.

Absent an effective public response, these problems will mount. It is clear that the FBI and the NSA intend to push forward. The question is whether the public will resist these assaults on our fundamental rights.

Time to Act

While the information infrastructure of the future is now in its infancy, the policy decisions that are about to be made will determine the character of our society in the 21st century. The systems now being designed will facilitate our social, political and financial transactions to an extent difficult to imagine today. As the pioneering cryptographer Whitfield Diffie recently told Congress:

At this moment in history, we are transferring our medium of social interaction from the physical to the electronic at a pace limited only by the development of our technology. Many of us spend half the day on the telephone talking to people we may visit in person at most a few times a year and the other half exchanging electronic mail with people we never meet in person.

Communication security has traditionally been seen as an arcane security technology of real concern only to the military and perhaps the banks and oil companies. Viewed in light of the observations above, however, it is revealed as nothing less than the transplantation of fundamental social mechanisms from the world of face to face meetings and pen and ink communication into a world of electronic mail, video conferences, electronic funds transfers, electronic data interchange, and, in the not too distant future, digital money and electronic voting.

The privacy and security of the information infrastructure is one of the most significant civil liberties issues to emerge in decades. The fact that both the FBI and the NSA have made NII surveillance a top priority one source said that the Justice Department informed the Clinton transition team it was their "only" priority should send a clear signal to us all about the importance of this issue.

Unfortunately, few resources have been devoted to examining the issue and working to ensure that basic constitutional values are preserved in the new electronic environment. Even though the EPIC staff has successfully raised many of the potential problems with the various NSA/FBI proposals during the last few years, the absence of a well focused project, specifically dedicated to this problem shows a gaping hole in the public interest community. What is needed is a specific project with expertise in civil liberties, national security, and cryptography to promote oversight, accountability, and public debate about these critical new developments.

What EPIC Will Do

EPIC will undertake in-depth examinations of government efforts to build surveillance capabilities into the emerging information infrastructure. For example, the organization will examine efforts to restrict the widespread use of privacy-enhancing technology, such as cryptography. In furtherance of these reviews, we will continue to make extensive use of the Freedom of Information Act (FOIA) to compel the disclosure of relevant information withheld by the government. Given that much of this information is likely to be concealed behind the shield of classification, an important aspect of EPIC's work will be to examine and challenge the use of "national security" secrecy to withhold information concerning domestic communications systems.

At the conclusion of our reviews, we will produce reports and disseminate widely our findings and recommendations. These report will be an important contribution to the emerging debate on the design and direction of the NII and will provide a counter-balance to the perspective of the law enforcement and intelligence agencies. We are specifically interested in pursuing the following questions:

◆ What are the civil liberties implications of the FBI's and the NSA's activities? What are the potential consequences for the development of the NII?

◆ What should be the proper role of the NSA and the FBI in this area? What does the law require?

◆ Is legislation necessary? Is oversight necessary? What other steps should be taken?

EPIC will conduct ongoing outreach, organize conferences, work with other organizations, and support similar efforts to document the activities of the intelligence agencies in the area of communications. Public education is particularly important as the scope of the National Information Infrastructure expands.

The Administration's NII initiative provides both risks and opportunities. While there is a very real threat that an Orwellian system of mass surveillance might emerge from an otherwise well-intentioned development process, there is also a unique opportunity to ensure that civil liberties and privacy become essential design elements in the data highways of the future.

Sponsoring Organizations

FCG is a Washington-based, non-profit charitable organization established in 1974 to protect civil liberties and constitutional rights. The FCG board of directors includes former government officials, journalists and civil rights advocates.

CPSR is a non-profit membership organization, incorporated in California in 1983. The CPSR National Advisory Board includes distinguished computer scientists, legal scholars, journalists, and public interest advocates. CPSR is based in Palo Alto, California and has 2,500 members and 20 chapters across the United States.

EPIC Advisory Board (in formation)

Hon. John Anderson
Prof. Chris Borgman, UCLA School of Information Science
David Burnham, Transactional Records Access Clearinghouse
Vint Cerf, Internet Society
Dr. Richard Claude, Human Rights Quarterly
Simon Davies, Privacy International
Dr. David Chaum, Digicash

Prof. Oscar Gandy, Annenberg School of Communications

Judy Krug, American Library Association

Prof. Gary Marx, University of Colorado Boulder

Dr. Peter G. Neumann, SRI International

Prof. Eli Noam, Center for Telecommunications and
Information Studies

Michael Pertschuk, Advocacy Institute

Dr. Barbara Simons, USACM

Robert Ellis Smith, Privacy Journal

Dr. Willis Ware, RAND Institute

(affiliations are for identification)

EPIC Staff

Marc Rotenberg is the EPIC Project Director and former head of the
CPSR Washington office. He was counsel to the Senate Judiciary
Committee specializing in technology and the law. He has taught infor-
mation privacy law at Georgetown University Law Center and is cur-
rently a Ford Fellow in International Law. He is a contributing editor to
Government Information Quarterly, the Computer Law and Security
Report, and the Encyclopedia of Computer Science. He is secretary of
Privacy International, an international human rights organization. He is
a graduate of Harvard College and Stanford Law School and a member
of the bar of the United States Supreme Court.

David Sobel is Legal Counsel for EPIC and served as CPSR Legal
Counsel. He was formerly counsel to the National Security Archive.
Since 1982, Mr. Sobel has litigated dozens of Freedom of Information
Act cases. His clients have included ABC News, the U.S. Student
Association, the Fund for Constitutional Government, the Nation
Magazine, Coretta Scott King and former Ambassador Kenneth Rush.
Mr. Sobel is a graduate of the University of Michigan and the University
of Florida Law School, and a member of the bar of the Court of Appeals
for the District of Columbia Circuit and other federal appellate courts.

David Banisar is a Policy Analyst for EPIC. David has organized several
policy conferences on cryptography and privacy, is editor of the
International Privacy Bulletin and continues to research privacy, electronic surveillance and security issues. He also initiates FOIA requests
and coordinates the posting of news to electronic information services.
David is a graduate of the University of Maryland and the Catholic
University Law School in Washington, DC.

The Privacy Journal

P.O. Box 28577
Providence, RI 02908

401-274-7861 (voice)
401-273-4902 (fax)
0005101719@mcimail.com (e-mail)

It Makes Personal Privacy Its Business

Hardly a day goes by that you don't hear some reference to privacy, in one of the many forms the issue arises in the 1990s workplace surveillance, credit-bureau abuses, medical confidentiality, AIDS testing and insurance, Caller ID, telephone monitoring, interception of electronic mail, computer hacking, telemarketing.

It's clear that one of the explosive issues of the 1990s is personal privacy.

The "paper of record" in this field is Privacy Journal, a monthly newsletter that began in 1974 long before many of today's privacy issues had surfaced.

Consequently, Privacy Journal is able to make a guarantee to its readers: to keep them at least 12 months ahead of the daily headlines, three years ahead of consumer demands, and at least five years ahead of new regulations. The reason Privacy Journal has been able to make this guarantee over the past two decades is that the newsletter is edited and published by a real journalist. Robert Ellis Smith is known for digging out government secrets and business practices. Smith is also an attorney, a nationally recognized expert on the legal right to privacy.

Smith is quoted frequently by the national news media. For instance, he appeared on an NBC News special on workplace privacy and was quoted by the New York Times the next week. He's a regular commentator on American Public Radio's consumer-oriented business program, "Marketplace."

Privacy Journal, as the longest established publication in this field, defines the privacy issues broadly. A typical issue of the newsletter will report on the popularity rates of Caller ID phone service throughout the country, on a court case affecting insurance companies' access to AIDS information, on a consumer victimized by credit-card fraud and unable to get his credit report corrected, on a Congressional proposal to regulate monitoring of employees by computer, on the personal-information collection by university fund raisers, on the current administration's record-breaking levels of wiretapping, and on a doctor who spoke to the press about a celebrity's health without consent.

More and more Privacy Journal addresses the privacy concerns of computer-network users and issues arising in the proposed "information highway."

Each month, the newsletter also lists and comments on upcoming conferences and meetings, new publications, recent court cases, and pending legislation in the states and in Congress. "It's as thoughtful and comprehensive as a newsletter can be," says Whole Earth Catalog. "It sounds the alarm about maintaining freedom and privacy in the computer age," says the New York Times. "The paper of record," says U.S. News and World Report.

The Providence, R.I.-based publication is consumer-oriented, but it provides so much essential information in the privacy/technology field that half of its readership are professionals: information-system managers, government officials, legislators, computer professionals, medical-records administrators, journalists, personnel officers, attorneys, lobbyists for major companies, credit managers, law-enforcement officers, and insurance executives.

The other half are individuals interested in protecting their privacy, public-interest groups, and plaintiffs' attorneys.

The monthly newsletter is available on a yearly subscription basis, with a discounted rate for students and others.

Privacy Journal is also the authoritative publishing house for other materials on privacy: an updated reference book of state laws on confidentiality, a legal guide called "The Law of Privacy Explained," a book of real-life invasion-of-privacy "horror stories," a guide to workplace privacy, a directory of professionals in the privacy field, and a report one on uses and abuses of Social Security numbers.

Publisher Robert Ellis Smith says, "We take pride when a reader tells us that she was able to tell a colleague about a press report on these issues: 'I already knew that. I read about it in Privacy Journal.'"

INDEX

L

M